The Abolitionists

Means, Ends, and Motivations

Second edition

Edited and with an introduction by

Hugh Hawkins

Amherst College

D. C. HEATH AND COMPANY

Lexington, Massachusetts Toronto London

Published simultaneously in Canada.

Printed in the United States of America.

International Standard Book Number: 0-669-81992-1

Library of Congress Catalog Card Number: 72-3836

CONTENTS

IV THE TURN TO VIOLENCE

V THE HISTORIANS' SEARCH FOR NEW PERSPECTIVES

Motivations: Personal and Institutional

Racism and the Re-examination of Abolitionists' Ends

VI 1865: THE ABOLITIONISTS CONSIDER WHETHER THEY HAVE ATTAINED THEIR ENDS

INTRODUCTION

At the time of the American Revolution, thoughtful patriots recognized the inconsistency of holding slaves while justifying revolution on grounds of man's inalienable natural right to liberty. By 1804 all the original states north of Maryland and Delaware had taken legal action to end slavery within their borders. In some cases the abolition was immediate, in others gradual. (As late as 1860 the census reported a few slaves in New Jersey.) States in the South, where blacks were more numerous and where the invention of the cotton gin shortly made plantation slavery profitable over wide areas, did not adopt a policy of abolition. But there as in the North, small groups, often led by Quakers, organized to oppose the institution of property in man.

Although some of these state and local antislavery societies dated from revolutionary times, the American Colonization Society, organized in 1817, was the first national society for furthering emancipation. Led by men of social standing in the upper South and aided by the federal government in establishing Liberia, the society proposed to colonize free blacks in Africa and thus to increase voluntary manumissions. But by 1865 the society had transported only a few thousand blacks while the number in the country had grown to over five million.

The 1830s saw a revolt against the gradualist program of this society. New journals and societies made "immediate abolition" their program. The most conspicuous journal, *The Liberator,* was launched in 1831 by William Lloyd Garrison, an impecunious Massachusetts printer recently associated with the colonizationist editor Benjamin Lundy. The largest organization, the American Anti-Slavery Society, was formed in 1833; it had been originally planned by a group of New Yorkers including Arthur and Lewis Tappan, wealthy merchant supporters of revivalist Charles G. Finney. Garrison wrote the society's Declaration of Sentiments and changed his own New England Anti-Slavery Society into its Massachusetts branch.

The reasons for the emergence of a new sort of abolitionism in the 1830s are still very much matters for historical debate. But certain factors were clearly important. Parliament ended slavery in the British West Indies in 1833, and this victory for British antislavery forces followed a shift of their demand from gradual to immediate emancipation. Such evangelical leaders as Finney increasingly emphasized human responsibility in resisting sin, and the application to slavery seemed clear and compelling to some. Meanwhile, disillusionment set in for many who observed the ineffectiveness of colonization and grew suspicious of its rationale, which emphasized the dangers from free blacks as much as the evils of slavery. In a period of vigorous reform activity the drunkard, the prisoner, the lunatic, the debtor, the child, the woman, and the workman were all becoming objects of concern. It would have been strange if amid this ferment the predicament of the slave had been ignored.

There was a decided ambiguity in the term "immediate abolition." Garrison apologized for ever having supported the "pernicious doctrine of gradual abolition" and advocated uncompensated, unconditional, universal emancipation at once; nevertheless, he admitted that slavery would not be "overthrown by a single blow," though "it ought to be." The New York City Anti-Slavery Society, led by the Tappans, also attacked the "delusive dream of gradual abolition" and praised the British doctrine of immediatism, but the society interpreted as immediate such action as was promptly commenced and gradually accomplished. The program of the national society avoided particular plans for abolition, acceptance of the principle being considered the important thing. There were indications, however, that such gradualist procedures as advancing slaves to freedom through stages of peonage or apprenticeship would be acceptable. As far as the public was concerned, such qualifications had little effect. The phrase "immediate abolition" was taken at face value. Indeed, by 1838, deeply impressed by reports of the success of the reform in the

West Indies, leaders of the national society declared their position to be an unqualified immediatism without "the perplexing processes of gradualism."

American reform efforts are notoriously given to internal bickering and the splintering off of dissidents. Immediatists, having broken from the colonizationists, continued to undergo division. A major cause of such splits was the issue of political activity. Even when singly devoted to appeals for moral conversion, abolitionists imagined that political changes would follow the more important "change of heart." During the 1830s, they began to enter the political realm by petitioning Congress to adopt antislavery measures and by questioning candidates of the major parties on their views concerning slavery. Late in the decade some immediatists decided that they should organize a third party explicitly designed to bring about emancipation, but others protested that such a course would only weaken the movement. The Liberty Party was formed in 1839, nominating James G. Birney for President in 1840 and 1844. His vote was small, however, and it grew increasingly hard to limit the Liberty Party strictly to the antislavery issue. By 1848, most politically-minded abolitionists were willing to support the more inclusive Free Soil Party, even though its candidate was Martin Van Buren, an early foe of immediate abolitionists. Opponents of slavery did not escape the dilemma of any moralist involved in democratic politics: only a moderated program promised to attract the votes needed for victory, but what happened to moral conviction if one could compromise on matters of good and evil? William Lloyd Garrison refused to vote or hold office in a nation that tolerated slavery and based itself on coercion, but he did not hesitate to give tactical advice to politically active abolitionists.

In spite of these vicissitudes, there was never so distinct a break between Garrison and other immediatists as there had been between colonizationists and immediatists. It is true that Garrison's tendencies toward religious perfectionism and anarchism set him and his closest followers apart from the majority of immediatists, who engaged in revivalistic preaching services and in political action. But there was a broad area of means which Garrison and almost all other immediatists shared: the appeal to public opinion, the use of an emotional vocabulary, the unremitting exposure of slavery at its worst, and the invocation of "higher law." In a word, the immediatists made agitation their principal method. For this they have been damned and defended from their day to ours.

Beyond agitation lay the possibility of physical assault upon those who held slaves. Nothing seemed further from the intentions of early immediatists. The Declaration of Sentiments of 1833 announced to the world:

> *[Our principles] forbid the doing of evil that good may come, and lead us to reject, and to entreat the oppressed to reject, the use of all carnal weapons for deliverance from bondage; relying solely upon those which are spiritual, and mighty through God. . . . [Our measures] shall be such only as the opposition of moral purity to moral corruption—the destruction of error by the potency of truth—the overthrow of prejudice by the power of love—and the abolition of slavery by the spirit of repentance.*

The Declaration contrasted this renunciation of violence with the means used by the Founding Fathers, who in the American Revolution had been willing "to spill human blood like water, in order to be free." Among the immediatists some came to believe that what was right for the fathers was right for the sons. From an initial position that justified a fugitive slave in resisting recapture, some moved ever further toward belief in a war for liberation. The abolitionist John Brown turned to physical force in the 1850s. Whether he had done right or wrong was a painful but inescapable question for other immediatists. Lewis Tappan, asking Virginia's governor to pardon Brown, repeated the movement's early rejection of "carnal weapons." Garrison declared himself still a "peace man," but to the question "Was John Brown justified in his attempt?" he answered, "Yes, if Washington was in his." Wendell Phillips pronounced John Brown "the impersonation of God's order and God's law, molding a better future, and setting for it an example." In embracing Brown as a martyred hero of their cause, the abolitionists involved themselves deeply in any judgment that is passed on the means he chose.

The issues which involved abolitionists in quarrels among themselves and with their contemporaries have been reflected over the years by historians of the movement. Beginning about 1940, historians attempting to understand this phase of the American past turned for help to the theories of other social sciences. As these theories added complexity to the questions they could ask, and as the civil rights movement of the 1960s exposed the depth of American racism, historians inquired more closely into the relationship between abolitionists and racism. They discovered that in spite of laudable efforts to assist fugitive slaves and end discrimination against blacks in the North, some white abolitionists displayed paternalistic attitudes, even toward their black colleagues in the abolitionist movement, and many resisted social intimacy across racial lines. More important than evidence of racism in abolitionists' behavior, however, is the question of whether or not they recognized the tenacity of American racism and the ease with which it would survive the end of slavery. We are still far from a final answer to that question.

A related issue is the persistence of abolitionists in their undertaking. Some historians charge that abolitionists, taking a perfectionist view of man's capacities, imagined that the slave would rise instantly to full equality once his shackles were struck off. Other scholars have produced evidence of significant recognition by abolitionists of the need to develop economic, political, and educational institutions that could support former slaves in creating a life that was more than slavery in a new guise.

The readings that follow begin with two selections published respectively in 1948 and 1939 by two historians whose interpretations of the abolitionists of a century earlier reveal sharp differences of emphasis. With this background of information and interpretation, the student next encounters a series of documents written by abolitionists between 1831 and 1852, announcing and defending their ends and their methods of seeking them. Some of the issues that faced abolitionists who turned to political action are next considered in two selections, one a recent reinterpretation of Garrisonian abolitionism, the other an editorial written by an abolitionist editor during a presidential election. John Brown is the protagonist in Part IV. Here two historians take opposing stands on violence and the Harpers Ferry Raid, and Brown speaks for himself.

The next section, on new perspectives, includes historians' attempts to make such concepts of the social and behavioral sciences as social status, personality, and institutional development relevant to judgments of the abolitionists, especially their motivations. At least two of these articles reflect the optimism of the civil rights movement of the 1960s, and one reveals the discouragement caused by America's continuing racism. To suggest that historical writing reflects the spirit of its author's own day is by no means to necessarily impugn its validity. These selections demonstrate how rich and varied has been the recent outpouring of historical reconsiderations of abolitionism. If it has been colored by contemporary events, it has also brought us closer to seeing the past truly.

Finally, grounds for reflection on the question of abolitionist persistence are provided in statements which abolitionist leaders themselves made in 1865. These statements came during a lively debate on whether or not the American Anti-Slavery Society had fulfilled its mission. Fully to answer the question of persistence, however, would lead one deeper into Reconstruction history than the limits of this collection allow.

With the help of these primary and secondary sources the student can reach his own evaluation of the abolitionists. Perhaps too he can find ways in which the nature of abolitionism reveals the nature of American society. Although, as the subtitle indicates, this collection provides guidance on the questions of the adequacy of the goals abolitionists set themselves and the sources of their motivations, it is the problem of means that predominates. This problem is particularly apropos for today's radicals and reformers who concern themselves with matters of race. But for any who feel concern over shortcomings in American life, there are insights to be obtained by "rethinking the thoughts" of supporters and critics of abolitionist measures. Does forthright denunciation change those whose social customs are being criticized, or does it rigidify them? Are the risks of moral dilution in political activity compensated by the opportunities for gaining power? When, if ever, is one's own conscience adequate justification for the violation of man-made law? When, if ever, can one condone or practice violence in opposition to a social evil? Such questions were debated over one hundred years ago when immediate abolitionists sought and gained public attention. Their example deserves study by those who must answer such questions today.

Conflict of Opinion

An immediate abolitionist of the 1830s defines her position and defends agitation on the slavery issue:

> If our fundamental principle is right, that no man can rightfully hold his fellow man as *property,* then it follows, of course, that he is bound *immediately* to cease holding him as such. . . . Every slaveholder is bound to cease to do evil *now,* to emancipate his slaves *now. . . .*
>
> "Much evidence," thou sayest, "can be brought to prove that the character and measures of the Abolition Society are not either peaceful or christian in tendency, but that they are in their nature calculated to generate party spirit, denunciation, recrimination, and angry passion." . . . The truth is, the efforts of abolitionists have stirred up the *very same spirit* which the efforts of *all thorough-going* reformers have ever done; we consider it a certain proof that the truths we utter are sharper than any two edged sword, and that they are doing the work of conviction in the hearts of our enemies.
>
> ANGELINA GRIMKÉ

But at the same time a theologian challenges the means of such opponents of slavery:

> It is not by argument that the abolitionists have produced the present unhappy excitement. Argument has not been the characteristic of their publications. Denunciations of slaveholding, as man-stealing, robbery, piracy, and worse than murder; consequent vituperation of slaveholders as knowingly guilty of the worst of crimes; passionate appeals to the feelings of the inhabitants of the northern states; gross exaggeration of the moral and physical condition of the slaves, have formed the staple of their addresses to the public. . . . There is in this conduct such a strange want of adaptation of the means to the end which they profess to have in view, as to stagger the faith of most persons in the sincerity of their professions, who do not consider the extremes to which even good men may be carried, when they allow one subject to take exclusive possession of their minds.*
>
> CHARLES HODGE

By 1852, a leading abolitionist claims that results have justified the approach of immediate abolitionists:

* The statement by Charles Hodge, originally published in 1836, is taken from his *Essays and Reviews* (New York: Robert and Carter Brothers, 1857), pp. 474–475. —Ed.

> To have elaborated for the nation the only plan of redemption, pointed out the only exodus from this "sea of troubles," is much. This we claim to have done in our motto of *Immediate, Unconditional Emancipation on the Soil.* The closer any statesmanlike mind looks into the question, the more favor our plan finds with it.
>
> WENDELL PHILLIPS

One scholar raises doubts about the motives and the methods of abolitionists:

> Perpetual reformers, though resented as meddlers by those they disturbed, have been hailed as pioneers and martyrs who have unselfishly helped to usher in new eras and a better world.
>
> The modern psychologist is somewhat skeptical of such explanations. He talks of youthful experiences, maladjustments, inferiority complexes, and repressed desires. He is not so sure about the sources of the reform impulse or the unselfish character of the reformer. The student of social affairs is likewise less inclined to grant unstinted praise to the fanatic and is not certain about the value of the contribution.
>
> AVERY CRAVEN

However, another suggests why historians may now reach a more favorable judgment:

> Out of their heightened concern with the pressing question of Negro rights, a number of historians, especially the younger ones, have begun to take a new look at the abolitionists, men who in their own day were involved in a similar movement of social change. About both them and ourselves we are asking anew such questions as the proper role of agitation, the underlying motives of both reformers and resistants, and the useful limits of outside interference. From this questioning a general tendency has developed to view the abolitionists in a more favorable light than previously.
>
> MARTIN B. DUBERMAN

One historian sees abolitionists as dedicated to changing the slavery-tolerating consensus of the United States, and forced to do so through revolutionary means rather than by democratic processes because of the intransigence of the slaveholders:

> There is no reason to believe that in the 1850s Northern public opinion, including that of the majority of abolitionists and Garrison himself, would have rejected gradual emancipation procedures on the basis of an antislavery consensus; there is ample evidence that most slave-

> owners would have, for it was not immediate abolition they opposed, but abolition on any terms. The point, then, is not that Garrison created an atmosphere of moral absolutism, but that the choice which the nation faced was objectively between absolutely antagonistic moral systems.
>
> AILEEN S. KRADITOR

Another historian believes that abolitionists' goals were corrupted by racism when they entered the broad antislavery alliance that fought against the South in the Civil War:

> To grant that agitation is "the art of the desirable" is to concede Garrison much. But when Garrison put aside his pacifism and many of his principles to support the Union cause and the Constitution on the ground that "death and hell had seceded," he shifted from agitation to politics, "the art of the possible." Of that art he was wholly innocent. The greatest artist of the possible in his time was now in charge, and Lincoln knew in his bones that unless he fought that war with the support of racists and in the name of white supremacy it would be *his* lost cause and not Jefferson Davis's.
>
> C. VANN WOODWARD

I THE EMERGENCE OF THE ABOLITIONISTS

Charles S. Sydnor

PROLOGUE TO THE END OF SLAVERY

Significantly, one of the best brief accounts of the rise of immediate abolitionism appears in a volume in the series A History of the South. *The rapid spread of plantation slavery through the lower South helped stimulate abolitionist activities and these activities in turn encouraged sectional self-consciousness among Southerners. In the following chapter from* The Development of Southern Sectionalism, 1819–1848, *the late Charles S. Sydnor surveys the varieties of abolitionist strategy and the mounting Southern resentment and fear. A native of Georgia, Sydnor's other writings include* Slavery in Mississippi *and* Gentlemen Freeholders: Political Practices in Washington's Virginia. *Before his death in 1954, he taught for many years at Duke University.*

The issues that troubled the 1820s were nearly all quieted by the end of the nullification controversy. The Missouri Compromise had settled the question of slavery in the territories of the United States. The westward removal of the Indians left little ground for future quarrels between Southern governors and the nation over questions of Indian policy. Jackson's attitude toward internal improvements, particularly his veto of the Maysville Road Bill, brought to a close the series of arguments over the propriety of using federal funds to supply the transportation needs of the nation. Likewise, his veto of the bill to recharter the national bank indicated that it would be fruitless for Congress to attempt to pass another such bill as long as he was President. As for the tariff, the measure that was passed in 1833 set forth a nine-year program, and there was a general agreement on both sides of the fence to respect this settlement. The doctrine of nullification had failed to gain substantial support outside the state of its origin, and there was no reason to think that the nation would soon be disturbed by its resurrection.

With these issues settled, most of them permanently, the rising tide of Southern sectionalism might have been expected to recede after 1833 just as New England sectionalism had ebbed after the War of 1812. But this was not to be. At the very time when the old

From Charles S. Sydnor, *The Development of Southern Sectionalism, 1819–1848,* pp. 222–226, 229–244, 247–248. Volume V of *A History of the South.* Footnotes omitted.

issues were being quieted, the slavery question was entering a new and more disturbing phase.

In the fall of 1829 a pamphlet was discovered in the hands of blacks at Savannah, Georgia, entitled *Walker's Appeal, in Four Articles, together with a Preamble to the Colored Citizens of the World, but in Particular, and Very Expressly to Those of the United States of America.* Its author, David Walker, was a free-born Negro of Wilmington, North Carolina, who had recently moved to Boston and opened a shop for selling old clothes. The *Appeal* was published in Boston in September 1829.

The essential points in the *Appeal* were that American Negroes had been reduced to the *"most wretched, degraded,* and *abject* set of beings that *ever lived* since the world began"; that slaveholders were exceedingly oppressive and cruel; that slaves were capable of attaining freedom by destroying their masters; and that it was their duty as men and as Christians to do so. Walker declared that white men would "take vessel loads of men, women and children, and in cold blood, and through devilishness, throw them into the sea, and murder them in all kinds of ways." He regretted that black men had not fought for their lives. He warned: "Get the blacks started, and if you do not have a gang of tigers and lions to deal with, I am a deceiver . . . let twelve black men get well armed for battle, and they will kill and put to flight fifty whites." He gave the stern counsel: "If you commence, make sure work—do not trifle, for they will not trifle with you—they want us for their slaves, and think nothing of murdering us in order to subject us to that wretched condition—therefore, if there is an *attempt* made by us, kill or be killed."

Within a few months copies of this pamphlet were found in Virginia, North Carolina, South Carolina, and Louisiana as well as additional copies in Georgia. Its discovery caused great excitement, State legislatures—sometimes in secret session—passed laws to keep the slaves from getting possession of writings that might cause unrest or revolution. Georgia and North Carolina, copying the example of South Carolina at the time of the Denmark Vesey insurrection, passed laws to quarantine incoming Negro seamen. Prohibitions were laid, or if already in existence were made more stringent, upon teaching slaves to read and write. North Carolina free Negroes were prohibited from peddling wares outside the counties in which they resided and from leaving the state and returning at will.

Although the discovery of the *Appeal* put the ruling class of the South on the alert and made laws governing black men more severe, little if any hostility was engendered toward the North, for the revolutionary doctrines preached by Walker met with strong Northern disapproval.

Before the excitement aroused by the Walker pamphlet had subsided, the press began to carry reports of a great debate in the British Parliament in August 1830, over the abolition of slavery in the colonies. News that the British were bringing slavery to an end disturbed the planting states; on the other hand, this news stirred American opponents of slavery to more vigorous action and to more radical proposals. One of the individuals who was greatly influenced by the British debate was the twenty-four-year-old William Lloyd Garrison, who was then in Baltimore assisting Benjamin Lundy with the publication of his *Genius of Universal Emancipation.* On the first day of the following year he was in Boston bringing out the first issue of the *Liberator.*

In the second issue, Garrison distinguished between his own program and that advocated in the *Appeal.* "We deprecate," so he wrote, "the spirit and tendency of this Appeal. . . . *We* do not preach rebellion—no, but submission and peace." Although Garrison appealed to conscience rather than to physical force, the violence of his invective, his distortion of facts, and the savagery of his indiscriminate attacks upon all slave-holders seemed more likely to lead to emotional and violent action than to a reasonable and peaceful solution. Furthermore, his demand for immediate action without regard to consequences, his bitter denunciation of all laws that gave a legal basis for slavery, including the Constitution of the United States, and his opposition to the use of political action left scarcely any way of settlement except by physical force. At times, the *Liberator* advocated action in this realm. On July 23, 1831, it published a "Song, Supposed to be Sung by Slaves in Insurrection," urging them to "strike for God and vengeance now." The following month a body of slaves struck in Southampton County, Virginia, under the leadership of Nat Turner.

Turner was born in Southampton County in the year 1800. His

mother was a native African, and she brought him at an early age to believe that he possessed supernatural powers. As he grew to manhood he claimed that he could hear voices directing him, read signs in the heavens, and remember events that had transpired before his birth. By these and other means he gained considerable leadership among his fellow slaves. His influence was strengthened and extended to the neighboring plantations by his being a Baptist preacher. Not much is known as to the motives behind his crime. Inasmuch as he later asserted that his master had treated him well, they cannot be explained on the ground of personal abuse. Neither was it ever proved that he had been influenced by Garrison or by the *Appeal,* although this was suspected because he had been taught to read by his master's son. But it is clear that he had been planning for several years before he finally struck, and according to his account he was pushed onward in his course by voices, visions, and an eclipse of the sun.

A singular blueness in the atmosphere in August 1831 convinced Turner that the time had come. At a secluded spot in the woods he met with four confederates and two neophytes. With a barbecued pig for food and brandy for refreshment and stimulant, they laid plans. One of the new recruits had good reason for hating his owner, but Turner chose the home of his own master, Joseph Travis, as the place to begin. Striking before dawn on Monday, August 22, Turner and his followers slaughtered Travis' family. From then until the following morning they moved from plantation to plantation, killing between fifty and sixty persons without regard to age or sex. Nearly half were children, and more women than men were killed. Bodies were mutilated, and Turner sprinkled his followers with the blood of the dead. As he moved forward, he augmented his force by coercion as well as by persuasion. Estimates of its size have varied all the way from forty to two hundred.

On Tuesday morning the roles of hunter and hunted were reversed when a party of white men overtook, attacked, and scattered the band. Military units were soon scouring the countryside, and self-constituted patrols joined in the hunt. Some of them matched the brutality of Turner, torturing and killing innocent Negroes as well as guilty ones. Fifty-three Negroes were arrested and brought to trial. Of these, twenty-one were acquitted. Among the last was

Turner who had eluded his pursuers more than two months—long after all the others had been killed or captured.

The outbreak in Southampton County turned the thoughts of men in other parts of the South to the danger of similar disasters. The fact that Turner had been taught to read, that he had exercised the influence of a preacher, and that he might have been stirred by the writings of Walker or Garrison suggested that laws be passed to bind the minds and restrict the activities of slaves. Vigorous attempts were made to force free Negroes to leave the South. There were many commentators who believed, however, that the chief need was for better law enforcement rather than for new laws. And there were some, especially in Virginia, who were convinced that the root of the trouble was neither in imperfect legislation nor inadequate enforcement, but in the fact that slavery was injurious to society and was dangerous, and that the danger increased as the ratio of slaves to whites increased. . . .

Northern opinion had little effect upon the genesis or the course of the Virginia slavery debate [of 1831–1832], but while this debate was in progress a movement was developing in the North that was soon to have tremendous influence upon the South. It began as a religious revival in upstate New York in the middle 1820s under the leadership of Charles G. Finney, an eloquent and powerful preacher, who exhorted Christians to *"aim at being useful in the highest degree possible"* by working for temperance, education, and the reformation of society. His phenomenal success rested partly on his power to enlist young men, imbue them with his own fervor, and send them out to carry on the work. His ablest recruit was Theodore Dwight Weld, who by 1830 was the most powerful agent in the West for the American Temperance Society.

Sweeping over the West, Finney's revival reached its crest in the year 1830, with converts being won by the tens and hundreds of thousands; and at the crest Finney invaded New York City. The event was significant, for it brought the powerful religious impulse of the revival movement into close contact with a group of charitable and reformatory societies. Among their objectives were the distribution of Bibles and tracts, the establishment of Sunday schools, the advancement of education, the promotion of Christian missions, the salvation of sailors, and the attainment of temperance, prison reform, and peace among the nations. These organizations were then called benevolent societies, and New York was in some measure the capital of the benevolent empire. Most of the societies held their conventions each May in New York, and that city was the home of a small group of men who furnished the active leadership for most of these national societies. Chief of these men were Arthur and Lewis Tappan, wealthy New York merchants.

The Tappans welcomed Finney. To help him overcome opposition in New York and to assure him moral and financial support, they organized some of their business friends into an Association of Gentlemen. Thus there was formed a powerful alliance of religious fervor, reformatory zeal, organizational experience, and economic power.

This alliance was turned toward the abolition of slavery chiefly by the example and the propaganda of British antislavery forces. The British benevolent societies had been the models and inspiration of most of the American societies; and in 1831, while the question of slavery in the colonies was coming to a crisis in England, the Association of Gentlemen decided to establish an American antislavery society. However, they postponed action until they could take advantage of the high tide of interest which they expected America to feel when Parliament should take its final step against slavery.

When that time came, the gentlemen hesitated; but they were forced to go ahead by Garrison, who was enjoying temporary prestige and power by having been feted and applauded in England as the self-appointed ambassador of American abolitionists. In December, 1833, the American Anti-Slavery Society was organized at Philadelphia. Although Garrison's influence in the society was to be short-lived, his prominence in the meeting that created it invested the young organization with something of his reputation for fanaticism. Besides this unfortunate occurrence, the society did itself great injury by making confused statements of its purpose. It advocated immediate emancipation, but it hastened to explain that this term did not mean what an ordinary man would think it meant; rather it meant immediate emancipation gradually accomplished.

During the first year of its life the society aroused Northern hostility toward abolitionists rather than toward slaveholders, and this hostility was strong enough to subject abolitionists to various forms of physical violence. To overcome these handicaps, the leaders of the society tried to convince the public that Garrison was not the leader or the spokesman of their organization, and they strove without success to silence him. But though 1834 was a year of discouragements, it contained one event that was soon to turn the tide. The theological students at Lane Seminary at Cincinnati, many of whom were converts of Finney, considered the question of abolition in what was called a debate but was in reality more of a protracted revival meeting. Weld, who was one of their number, was mainly responsible for the wholesale transformation of this group of able young men into ardent abolitionists.

The Lane debate caused a great stir. President Lyman Beecher and the trustees sought to repress the abolition activities of the students. Instead, they drove them away to become the nucleus of Oberlin College. In the years 1835 and 1836, thirty of these young men were among the most effective of the missionaries of abolition. With the spirit of zealots and martyrs they endured "harsh words . . . stale eggs, and brick-bats and tar," but they won a hearing. They "precipitated another Great Revival in the nation, a revival in abolition."

Weld was notably courageous and successful. When he entered a new community he usually met with all manner of indignities. While speaking before one audience, he was hit in the face by an egg. Before another, a large stone, hurled through the church window, struck him in the head and stunned him for several minutes. He earned the title of being "the most mobbed man in the United States." But he kept going, usually for many nights in succession; and his calm spirit, his winsome personality, and his fervent eloquence often transformed enemies into abolitionists. By the end of 1835, he had planted the seed widely in Ohio. The next year he worked in Pennsylvania and New York State. Meanwhile, Garrison was keeping up the agitation in New England, antagonizing the clergy and other powerful groups, but winning some converts, notably Wendell Phillips, who respected Garrison for "the austerity of his life and his singleness of purpose." Others, like William Ellery Channing, opposed slavery while remaining aloof from the activities of the American Anti-Slavery Society.

But it was the society which gave form and much of the driving force to the abolition movement. In 1835 it issued a great stream of pamphlets and newspapers, most of which were given away and mailed in bundles to those who might be disposed to distribute them. In June it was planning to "issue gratuitously from 20,000 to 50,000 of some publication or other every week." The mailpouch invasion of the South came to grief in South Carolina. Citizens of Charleston, learning that a considerable quantity of abolition literature was in the post office awaiting distribution, forcibly seized the offensive publications and burned them on the Parade Ground. The New York postmaster, acting on the suggestion of Postmaster General Amos Kendall, announced that he would forward no more antislavery matter to Southern addresses. This event, together with the enactment in most of the Southern States of laws making the circulation of abolition literature a felony, effectively closed the South to the pamphlet campaign of the society.

Even in the North, the results of the pamphlet campaign were discouraging, and in 1836 the society decided to shift its emphasis and resources back to the approach which had earlier proved more effective, namely, the use of zealous agents. Enough new recruits, "men of the most unquenchable enthusiasm and the most obstinate constancy," were carefully trained, and added to "Weld's ardent host" to bring their number up to the New Testament number of seventy. Almost all were theological students or clergymen. A full measure of fervor and devotion was needed, for the abolition doctrine was still detested throughout most of the North. However, a development in Congress in the winter of 1835–1836 began to turn the tide, and the society was quick to take advantage.

In the Congress that assembled in December 1835 there was a sharp increase in the number of petitions praying for the abolition of slavery and of the slave trade in the District of Columbia. At the time, it was well understood that there were probably no more than one Representative and one Senator willing to vote for a change in the status of slavery in the District. Nevertheless, Congressmen who did not favor such legislation continued to present petitions. The explanation for this curious situation lies chiefly in the political situation. Jackson was President, and his party controlled the House. The members of the newly formed Whig party, seeking in every way possible to discredit and obstruct the Democrats, soon struck on the presentation of abolition petitions as an effective instrument to sow dissension between Northern and Southern Democrats and to consume much time that the Democrats needed for carrying out the party's program. Whigs presented more than 95 percent of the petitions that were brought to the House.

Southern Congressmen were stung to the quick by the phrasing of some of the petitions which referred to slavery as "the foul stain of legalized plunder" and to slaveholders as "the villainous enslavers of souls." On December 18, 1835, James H. Hammond of South Carolina exclaimed that: "He could not sit there and see the rights of the southern people assaulted day after day, by the ignorant fanatics from whom these memorials proceed."

In an atmosphere of party conflict complicated by sectional feeling, much of the winter was spent by the Whigs in plaguing the Democrats with abolition petitions, and by the Democrats in trying to find a way to extricate themselves without running counter to the constitutional right of petition. It may be that the problem was insoluble, but both houses of Congress attempted to find a solution. The rule followed in the Senate was less objectionable and aroused less controversy than the rule adopted in the lower house.

On May 25–26, 1836, the House, after acrimonious discussion, resolved that Congress had no authority to interfere with slavery in the states and that it ought not to interfere with slavery in the District of Columbia; that it was important to end agitation on the subject so as to restore tranquillity to the public mind; and that "all petitions, memorials, resolutions, propositions, or papers, relating in any way, or to any extent whatever, to the subject of slavery, or the abolition of slavery, shall, without being either printed or referred, be laid upon the table, and that no further action whatever shall be had thereon. It should be noted that there was little difference between this rule and the previous custom in the House of laying such petitions upon the table after they were presented.

This rule, commonly known as the gag rule, utterly failed to end agitation. Former President John Quincy Adams was now a member of the House of Representatives. He characterized himself as the friend of "universal emancipation," and as the possessor of antislavery views so extreme that "the sturdiest of the abolitionists would have disavowed" them. Adams took up the gauntlet with the solemn declaration: "I hold the resolution to be a direct violation of the constitution of the United States, the rules of this House, and the rights of my constituents."

The question of whether the fateful resolution was in fact unconstitutional has been variously answered by subsequent students. At the time, some abolitionists believed that the logic of the argument permitted them to go no farther than to brand the rule as a "virtual" denial of the right of petition. But constitutional refinements were beyond the understanding of most men. The Northern public, overlooking the party issues at stake, accepted the half-truth that defenders of slavery stood opposed to the right of petition and that slaveholders were willing to subvert the Constitution to maintain their evil institution.

The American Anti-Slavery Society made it its business to keep abolition petitions pouring into Congress. It printed and sent them out by the millions, asking the abolition of the slave trade between the states, the abolition of slavery in the territories, and praying that Arkansas and Florida be denied admission to the Union as slave states. With lists of signatures pasted on, these petitions came back to Congress by the hundreds of thousands. More than 99 percent of the petitions were printed. Between December 1837 and April 1838 enough of them were presented to Congress to fill "a room 20 × 30 × 14 feet, close packed to the ceiling."

The Whigs, who had made such effective use of petitions to sabotage the Democratic administration, came into power in the election of 1840. Throwing consistency to the winds, they enacted gag resolutions more stringent than those against which they had been complaining. Even Adams for the moment forgot the constitutional scruples that had disturbed him, and through him the North; for he remarked that he could "not deny the right of the House to refuse to receive a petition when it is first presented."

Both parties were in some measure now committed to the nonreception of antislavery petitions, and the controversy over the right of petition largely ceased. But during the years it raged, it enabled abolitionists to make Congress their sounding board and to compel even slaveholders to help the cause of abolition. Southern Congressmen, goaded into angry remarks, had fanned the fire that they wanted to extinguish. As one of the abolitionists sagely remarked:

"Slaveholders are prime agitators." The gag rule had put the South in an extremely bad light. And it had enhanced the prestige of the abolitionists. Instead of appearing as pious and meddlesome fanatics, they now appeared as the champions of a great constitutional right.

During the petition controversy, Weld prepared two books that were to have tremendous influence in the abolition crusade. One was designed to show the horrors of slavery; the other, to prove that emancipation would be followed by an agreeable state of affairs. Using material collected by two abolitionists who had been sent to the British West Indies, Weld edited so plausible a study of the satisfactory effects of emancipation that the leaders of the American Anti-Slavery Society abandoned the complex formula of immediate emancipation gradually accomplished and announced that henceforth their goal was immediate abolition. The general public, whether hostile or friendly, had always believed that this was the object of the society.

The other study, entitled *American Slavery as It Is: Testimony of a Thousand Witnesses,* was essentially a case study in the worst features of slavery. Weld, with the help of research assistants, combed thousands of Southern and other newspapers for atrocity stories, and he appealed to abolitionists to supply him with "facts never yet published, facts that would thrill the land with horror." Within four months, 22,000 copies of his powerful indictment of slavery had been sold, and within the first year, nearly 100,000. The influence of *American Slavery as It Is* went far beyond its many readers, for it was an easily accessible store of ammunition for subsequent campaigners. A large part of Charles Dickens' influential chapter on slavery in his *American Notes* was lifted bodily and without any expression of indebtedness from Weld's compilation, and its service to Harriet Beecher Stowe in the preparation of *Uncle Tom's Cabin* was frankly acknowledged.

At the end of the 1830s there occurred an important change in the management and the character of the abolition movement. The American Anti-Slavery Society was torn by quarrels among its leaders, and the Panic of 1837 brought these men and their organization to virtual bankruptcy. State societies revolted against the parent organization, and the women's-rights movement caused distraction and confusion of purpose. But as the New York leadership declined, the empire that it had largely created found a new capital in Washington and a leadership in a small group of Congressmen, assisted by a lobby of their creation.

For a time these Congressmen were prohibited from speaking against slavery by the rule of silence that both parties adopted in the effort to avoid rifts within their ranks. When Thomas Morris, a Democratic Senator from Ohio, challenged this rule and spoke against Calhoun's 1837 resolutions he was refused reelection by the Democratic legislature of his state. Early in 1842, Adams, probably with the approval of the small but well-knit group of abolitionist Representatives, threw down the gauntlet to the Whig party with a bitter and powerful attack upon slavery. A caucus of Southern Whigs decided that he should be censured. Northern Whigs concurred. But when the attempt was made, Adams won a notable victory on the floor though, so it was rumored, at the price of promising to remain silent in the future.

Shortly afterward, the abolitionists commissioned Joshua R. Giddings, an Ohio Whig, to issue another challenge by speaking against slavery. He did so and was censured. Thereupon he resigned his seat, appealed to his constituency, and was reelected by a large majority. Back in Congress, he resumed his attack upon slavery, and the Whig leaders knew that they could not stop him; for in the fight in Ohio over his reelection, the forces of abolition had proved stronger than the power of the Whig organization. The day had dawned when the Whig party could not forbid discussion of this issue even though its discussion was likely to rend the party into Southern and Northern factions. Abolitionists could now look to Congressmen to give them leadership and to speak and vote for their cause.

This great turning point is a convenient moment for reviewing certain developments in the antislavery movement during the previous decade. In sheer numbers, its growth was phenomenal. Its respectability and influence had likewise increased. Instead of being scorned and stoned in Northern villages, abolitionists now had a great following among respectable folk, and they had vigorous leaders in Congress.

In respect to their goal, the abolitionists were singularly consistent throughout the years. Although they had abandoned the idea of gradualism, they never swerved from their essential goal of extinguishing slavery throughout the United States at the earliest possible date. Neither had they ever assumed responsibility for suggesting how to cushion the shock of emancipation or how to deal with the problems that would follow it. On the other hand, their strategy was somewhat codified. At first the abolitionists appealed both to Southerners and Northerners; but when the South barricaded itself against printed appeals and condemnations, the program of the abolitionists became primarily an attempt to convince Northerners, who neither owned slaves nor possessed the legal power to abolish slavery, that slavery was terrible and ought to be ended. An occasional abolitionist was worried by the impractical character of their approach. One of them implored Weld to supply him with "a plain common Sense view of . . . *how* emancipation and abolition are to be brought about by the correction of public sentiment at the North. . . . Can you not furnish . . . some *facts* pertinent to . . . the *effectiveness* of Northern abolition on the South?" But most of the antislavery men, like the majority of the other reformers of their day, showed less zeal for reforming sinners than for persuading the righteous to denounce sinners.

In the early days of the movement there were debates among abolitionists as to whether slavery was an evil or a sin; but the doctrine soon gained general acceptance among them that human bondage was contrary to the will of God. From this decision there flowed several important consequences. The slavery debate was turned into Biblical channels, with both sides in the controversy searching the Scriptures for proof that their views were in accordance with the revealed will of God. A second consequence was the condemnation of the slaveowner as a sinner; and while such a man as Finney thought the sinner ought to be reproved in a spirit of love and humility, the doctrine of the sinfulness of slavery led to a censorious attitude toward the slaveholder.

The doctrine that slavery was a sin was a natural outgrowth of the religious origin of the abolition movement. It was also natural that as the religious impulse diminished, as it did in time, the fight against slavery should lose some of its lofty, spiritual tone. Francis Wayland, president of Brown University and a strong opponent of slavery, agreed with "the late lamented Dr. [William E.] Channing, in the opinion that the tone of the abolitionists at the north has been frequently, I fear I must say generally, 'fierce, bitter, and abusive.'" It was, thought Wayland, "very different from the spirit of Christ." Finney, watching the course of events, was much disturbed, fearing lest abolition without a foundation of sincere and genuine Christianity would bring the nation "fast into a civil war."

But Weld was not fearful. At times he seemed to long for the appearance of "a storm blast with God in the midst." If slaveholders had refused to heed his warnings and reproofs, which he was sure were the warnings and reproofs of God, was it not inevitable and proper for them to be destroyed by insurrection and war? Some twenty years earlier John Quincy Adams had looked upon disunion and civil war as sublime and glorious if for the purpose of ending slavery, and there is much to indicate that his mind was still filled with these thoughts during his great fight for the right of petition in Congress.

In spite of all that has been written about the abolition crusade, no one can tell with certainty how much it accelerated the ending of slavery in America, whether civil war could have been avoided without it, or whether in the long run it made the problem of race more or less acute. To take a broader sweep, no one can prove beyond question that the South, or the nation, or the Negro's status in America was made better or worse by the activities of the abolitionists. But on less important points, some of which bear upon these larger questions, something can be said about the effects of the abolition movement.

As for the slave, his lot was not much changed; certainly it was not improved. A thoughtful Scotch minister, who was no friend of slavery, came to the opinion after extended travel in America in 1844 that

> *Nowhere does the condition of the colored people appear worse than in the slave States which border the free States. . . . Whatever may be the ultimate advantages, the immediate effect of the agitation for emancipation, and all the anxious, uncertain, suspicious, and angry feelings it engenders, is unfavorable to the improvement either of master or slave, making one more suspicious, and the other the more deeply to feel his chain.*

The free Negro population of the South also suffered. In Maryland and Virginia, where the number had been increasing more rapidly than the number of slaves until there were more than 100,000 free Negroes in 1830, the rate of increase was thereafter sharply cut. In Louisiana and Mississippi there was an absolute decrease between 1840 and 1850.

Travelers in the South began to find that they were objects of suspicion. The Reverend George Lewis was asked soon after he arrived at Savannah in the year 1844: "Are you come to be a spy here?" Before entering Virginia in 1837 a British naturalist, Charles B. B. Daubeny, took the precaution of disposing of some antislavery writings that had been in his traveling bag. The experiences of the prominent English Quaker, Joseph J. Gurney, illustrate the behavior and the treatment of the abolitionist in the South. In Virginia he freely stated his "views respecting the oppressed negro population" to Governor David Campbell. Although Gurney felt that he was kindly received, he recorded that Campbell "bitterly complained of what he called the violence of the Northern abolitionists" and asserted "that their proceedings had operated, in Virginia, as an effectual bar to the progress of emancipation." In Charleston he asked Mayor Henry L. Pinckney to convene some of the principal persons of the city to hear his story of the favorable workings of freedom in the West Indies, but Pinckney thought it would be imprudent. On the other hand, Gurney was given free access to whatever he wished to inspect, including the jail, the Negro prison, and a plantation on Edisto Island. He left the city with the opinion that "we had certainly been received with much more kindness and polite attention, than we had ventured to expect."

Slave traders in the neighborhood of Washington must have become accustomed to sight-seers and to persons collecting data on the evils of slavery, and they seem to have shown them about with an easy tolerance. Planters occasionally submitted their estates to examination even at the risk of having to listen to private lectures on the evils of slavery or of having their visitors seek to create unrest among the slaves.

But it was not the occasional visitor who disturbed the Southerner so much as the incessant attack in Northern press and pulpit and upon the floor of Congress. Despite the religious impulse behind the barrage of advice, warning and denunciation, the slaveholder failed to see therein much evidence of the Christian virtues of truth, humility, and love. He was impressed, rather, by the holier-than-thou spirit of his mentors, a spirit which seemed to imply that Northern consciences were more enlightened than any to be found in the South.

Undoubtedly, the slaveholder did not give the abolitionists a fair hearing. His traditions, his economic interests, and his way of life all fought against his considering slavery in a detached, objective fashion; and his dealings with the North for some years past had destroyed any faith he may have had in Northern disinterestedness and fair dealing. As he looked to the region that was now inviting him to perform a costly and revolutionary act, he remembered that the opposition of this region to the extension of slavery in 1819 had been blended with a plan to increase New England's political power. As he recounted the contests in subsequent years over protective tariffs, over the expenditure of federal funds for roads and canals, and over other issues, he could recall little but self-interest, and at times a very ruthless self-interest, in the words and votes of Northern Congressmen.

Perhaps slaveholders should have distinguished between such men as Weld and Finney, who fought slavery because they considered it morally wrong, and Northern politicians, who voted for measures that would enhance Northern prosperity even at the expense of the South. But slaveholders failed to make that distinction; and after 1840, when the abolition movement entered politics with the formation of a bloc of antislavery Congressmen, the distinction largely ceased to exist.

As Southern opinion hardened toward abolitionists, Southern criticism of slavery waned. By the year 1837 there was not an antislavery society in all the South. "In the general indignation," excited by abolitionists, wrote George Tucker of Virginia in 1843, "the arguments in favor of negro emancipation, once open and urgent, have been completely silenced, and its advocates among the slaveholders, who have not changed their sentiments, find it prudent to conceal them." The careers of politicians were scrutinized to discover whether they were safe on this point. James McDowell, Jr., an antislavery spokesman during the Virginia debate over slavery, had his record flung against him when the legislature was considering him for the governorship in 1840; and although one of his friends assured the legislature that McDowell was hostile to Northern abolitionists, he failed of election at this time.

The effect of abolitionism on Southern opinion is illustrated by the official statements of two Mississippi governors. In 1828, Gerard C. Brandon declared that slavery was "an evil at best" because it was harmful to the poor white man, it widened the gulf between rich and poor, and it kept the state from attracting a numerous white population and from enjoying the influence and power that such a population would bring. Eight years later John A. Quitman, after reviewing and condemning the rise of the abolition movement, stated before the legislature: "It is enough, that we, the people of Mississippi, professing to be actuated by as high regard for the precepts of religion and morality, as the citizens of other states, and claiming to be more competent judges of our own substantial interests, have chosen to adopt into our political system, and still choose to retain, the institution of domestic slavery."

This was the sort of calm but determined statement proper in official messages, but it does not reflect the surging emotion aroused in the South. Southern hotheads threatened to lynch abolitionists if they came south of the Potomac River and offered rewards of thousands of dollars to anyone who would put them in reach of Southern vengeance. A Mississippi newspaper declared that the quarrel over slavery had reached such a point that it would "not be settled by negotiation, but by the *sword,*—by balls and the *Bayonet. We can do without the North.*"

Although the abolition movement was followed by a decline of antislavery sentiment in the South, it must be remembered that in all the long years before that movement began no part of the South had made substantial progress toward ending slavery. The free and full discussion in Virginia in 1832 was promising, but the decision was in the negative. The trends are not clear enough to warrant prophecy as to what the South would have done about slavery had it not been disturbed by the abolitionists, but it is at least certain that before the crusade began Southern liberalism had not ended slavery in any state.

The Southern defense of slavery antedated the organization of the American Anti-Slavery Society. Shortly after the discovery of the Denmark Vesey plot at Charleston, Richard Furman, president of the Baptist State Convention, published a Scriptural defense of slavery together with a plea for better religious care of slaves. Dew and Leigh defended slavery against the attacks made upon it in the Virginia debate. Under the scourging of the abolition attacks, these defenses were much expanded and new arguments were evolved. To offset the harshly distorted descriptions of abolitionists, Southern champions depicted slavery as a kindly and altogether beneficial institution. They turned the pages of history, they dissected human cadavers, and they diligently searched the Bible for arguments to prove that the Negro was made for slavery and that slavery served a useful purpose in society.

The intellectual defense of slavery failed to convert the North—it failed as completely as the abolitionists had failed to convince the South that slavery was sinful. One is tempted to believe that the appeal to reason was in this instance worse than a failure, for instead of bringing the problem nearer to solution, it served merely to convince each contestant of its own righteousness and of its opponent's wickedness, and to stir emotions for an ultimate contest in which reason would play little part. . . .

Even though the constitutional right of the individual state to retain slavery were respected, slavery would be mortally wounded if slaves could not be sold from state to state, if slavery were abolished in the territories and in the District of Columbia, if no new slave states were admitted, and if the powers delegated to the national government—such as the power to tax and to distribute mail—were directed toward injuring slavery.

FIGURE 1. The Boston Anti-Abolitionist Mob of October 21, 1835, with its Victim, William Lloyd Garrison, at Center. *(Historical Pictures Service, Chicago)*

Dwight L. Dumond

THE ABOLITION INDICTMENT OF SLAVERY

In the 1930s the publications of Dwight L. Dumond and Gilbert H. Barnes reshaped the history of abolitionism. These two Midwestern scholars emphasized the significance of their region and of evangelical religion in the rise of immediate abolitionism. They also deflated earlier views of William Lloyd Garrison's importance in the movement. The following portion of Dumond's Antislavery Origins of the Civil War in the United States, *typical of this revised view, gives an intimate account of the activities in Ohio and Kentucky of Theodore D. Weld and James G. Birney. At the time he gave the lectures from which the following passages come, Dumond had edited Southern editorials on secession, the letters of Birney, and (with Barnes) the letters of Weld, Angelina Grimké Weld, and Sarah Grimké. In 1961 he published his monumental* Antislavery: The Crusade for Freedom in America. *The fruit of many years' research, the book revealed an even stronger sympathy for abolitionism than the lectures here represented. Dumond teaches at the University of Michigan.*

On September 15, 1834, James G. Birney and Theodore D. Weld met at a farmhouse twenty miles north of Georgetown, Kentucky. They had come on horseback, one from Danville, the other from Cincinnati, exercising care to prevent recognition and to preserve the utmost secrecy in their deliberations. Two years before Weld had been entertained at Birney's home in Huntsville, Alabama. Now, he feared to be seen with Birney in Kentucky lest his presence should add to the already heavy burden of opposition Birney was seeking to overcome. This was a day of confirmation. Both men had passed from hope to skepticism and then to outright disbelief in the efficacy of colonization. They had published their convictions; had pledged anew their faith in abolition; and had met again to plan the course of future action. Neither man yet knew the full measure of sacrifice it would entail, nor is it likely either cared.

Birney had always lived in solid comfort, if not in luxury. His father was a wealthy trader and rope manufacturer of Louisville. His

Reprinted from *Antislavery Origins of the Civil War in the United States* by Dwight L. Dumond (pp. 21–48, 88–92) by permission of the University of Michigan Press.

relatives, his friends, and his professional associates all were members of the Southern aristocracy. He himself had been a slaveholding planter and prominent attorney in Huntsville. He had served in Alabama's first constitutional convention and had been intimately connected with the founding of its university. Had he remained in Alabama and loyal to his class, he would undoubtedly have risen to high position in public service. He was a man of indomitable courage and unyielding conviction, a devoted husband and father, an old-school Presbyterian, and a Whig of the landed-gentry vintage. Irish by birth, a humanitarian by instinct, a lawyer by training, he recognized no institutional authority of church, political party, or social caste to modify or to restrain one's individual responsibility to the celestial fire of conscience.

Weld was born in Connecticut and reared in western New York, the son of a conservative, small-town pastor. His formal education was meager, his learning prodigious, his powers of reasoning superb. While yet a young man he went about the western country lecturing upon manual laborism, the science of mnemonics, temperance and moral reform—an itinerant Socrates, with unkempt hair and beard and the simplest attire, caring only for personal cleanliness and the souls of men. He wrote of himself as "an untamed spirit, wild as the winds," stern, contemptuous of opposition, and "proud as Lucifer," "too proud to be *ambitious,* too proud to seek applause, too proud to tolerate it when lavished on me . . . too proud to *betray* emotions, too proud ever for an instant to loose my self possession whatever the peril, too proud ever to move a hair for personal interest, too proud ever to defend my character when assailed or my motives when impeached, too proud ever to *wince* even when the hot iron enters my soul and passes through it." Gifted with rare powers of analysis and persuasion, a natural leader of men, he radiated his influence into every sphere of social reform. He was, in fact, the nerve center of the antislavery movement until the schism of 1840.

We do not know the precise date at which either man began to look askance at slavery, but it was early enough for them to have discussed the subject at length when Weld visited Huntsville in the spring of 1832. Birney's interest arose from personal knowledge of the sordid aspects of the institution, concern for the future of his young sons, an intense patriotism that saw in slavery a cancerous growth within the body politic, and the common fear that Negro concentration would overwhelm the lower South. It was sufficiently well known for the Colonization Society to offer him the general agency for the southwestern states on June 12, 1832. Weld was the protégé of Charles Stuart, who financed his education, interested him in the slavery question, and was the one living man to whom he bared his heart and made obeisance; but their early association was as members of Charles Grandison Finney's band of revivalists, and Weld's fame as an orator was established before Stuart himself turned to the question of slavery. Weld's trip in 1832 was in behalf of Oneida Institute and manual laborism particularly, and of a prospective theological seminary incidentally. As early as March 1830 Stuart had been writing to interest Weld in slavery; Weld joined with Tappan, Jocelyn, Goodell, and others in a discussion of the subject in 1831; and he turned aside on his journey in 1831–1832 to indoctrinate the faculty at Western Reserve College, including Beriah Green, Elizur Wright, and President George Storrs; but in what? In opposition to slavery, of course, though certainly not in hostility to colonization and an endorsement of immediate emancipation of slaves to be retained and elevated among their former masters, because he wrote to Birney in September 1832 from Cincinnati:

> *When I look at the great slave question, trace its innumerable and illimitable bearings upon the weal of the world, every year augmenting its difficulties, its dangers, its woe and its guilt, my heart aches with hope deffered* [sic], *mocks all prescriptions and refuses to be comforted. I am ripe in the conviction that if the Colonization Society does not dissipate the horror of darkness which overhangs the southern country, we are undone. Light breaks* in from no other quarter.

Birney, in the interim, had abandoned his legal practice and for one year strove mightily to convert the Southwest to the cause of colonization. Like Weld, he was opposed to slavery, but an immediate emancipationist could hardly have written:

> *If the abolitionist be really desirous of benefiting his fellowmen, and of advancing the cause of human happiness . . . we would invite him to visit those parts of the* South, *where there is, already, a large proportion of the free colored class. If he be diligent, judicious and dispassionate, we risk nothing in saying, that he will be convinced of the superior wisdom of*

> *trying every other plan, bearing upon its face the least appearance of feasibility, before experiment be made of his favorite* Abolition.

The point I wish to make is that, to say a man was opposed to slavery means very little except that he was not a devotee of the positive-good argument. There was a vast difference between anti-slavery and abolition. The tests of abolitionism were: (1) willingness by those who owned no slaves to bring about a state of emancipation by compulsion; (2) refusal to countenance expatriation; and (3) insistence upon according to the emancipated slaves all the privileges and civil liberties of free men. Neither Weld nor Birney was an abolitionist in the summer of 1832, though they were to play the stellar roles in the great human drama of the next decade.

The two years between these conferences—July 1832, and September 1834—was a preparatory period for the complete acceptance of abolition doctrine, a period in which they were convinced: (1) that colonization was impracticable; that its moving impulse was race prejudice; that it was strengthening rather than weakening the institution of slavery; that it was economically unsound and morally wrong; (2) that slaveholders would never voluntarily enter upon a program even of gradual emancipation; and (3) that the display of intolerance which greeted the mildest discussion of the subject lifted the controversy from the realm of specific reform in a particular section and presaged another episode in the ageless struggle for human rights. Would that the historian might somehow recover the emotions which surge through men's hearts and alter civilizations! It was only a short decade from the day that Birney turned his attention to colonization until he was nominated for the presidency by the Liberty Party, but it was a decade replete with as choice a repertoire of human drama as the nation has ever produced.

Birney's work as agent for the Colonization Society need not detain us long. Its tangible results were negligible: the organization of a few scattered auxiliary societies, the launching of a small parcel of emigrants on the steamer *Ajax* from New Orleans, the publication of a series of fifteen essays on the subject, the delivery of many lectures to mere handfuls of listeners. He discovered a total lack of interest in the subject on the part of both Negroes and whites. Few came to hear him lecture. Newspapers were reluctant to publish his expositions, and only the first seven were reprinted in the official organ of the parent society. Friends implored him to abandon a hopeless cause. Finally, he admitted failure, resigned his agency, severed old friendships, and in September 1833, sought the hoped-for congenial atmosphere of Danville, Kentucky, scene of his childhood days. On December 11, 1833, he expressed the opinion in a letter to R. R. Gurley, general secretary of the American Colonization Society, that slavery was "altogether un-Christian"; that it would ruin the country unless speedily abolished; and that it was futile to expect its elimination through colonization. Gurley replied to Birney with an an amazingly prophetic letter, saying in part:

> *I deeply regret that there should exist so much apathy, indeed may I not say error of opinion, on the subject of slavery at the South. . . . My own opinion is, that the South must, if its own dearest interests are to be preserved, if the Union is to last, act with vastly more zeal and energy on this subject than has yet been manifested. . . . I hope all this may be done. But I have many fears it will not be effectually done. . . . If it be once understood that the South designs to* perpetuate *Slavery, the whole North will be speedily organized into Anti-Slavery Societies, and the whole land will be flooded with antislavery publications.*

Almost at the time these letters were written—early December 1833—a number of gentlemen near Danville formed the Kentucky Society for the Gradual Relief of the State from Slavery, pledging themselves to emancipate all slaves born thereafter when they reached the age of twenty-five years. The Address of the Society signed by John Green, but almost certainly written by Birney, contains some surprisingly advanced doctrine. Of slavery it said: "The sentence of condemnation has been passed upon it by the *Civilized World;* and we venture the opinion that no respectable person will be found in our State, to arraign the decision." The introduction of slavery and its continuance were denounced as "violations of the law of nature," but the latter was the greater wrong because of our "enjoying the full blaze of that light which our own revolution and other similar events have thrown upon the principles of civil and religious liberty—by us who hold up our institutions as patterns from which the statesmen and patriots of other nations are invited to copy, and who boast our country to be the freest on the Globe, and an asylum for the oppressed of every other."

The fundamental principle of the association was stated to be:

That domestic slavery, as it exists under the laws and constitution of this state—perpetual and absolute,—is a great moral and political evil; and that its continuance cannot be justified, before God, the world, or our own consciences, any longer than is necessary to bring it to a termination, less injurious to the parties, than slavery itself.

Repudiating general emancipation without previous preparation as a "wild experiment—endangering the peace and security of the whites, and the very existence of the colored race," it presented the society's program as "*immediate* preparation for *future* emancipation," justifying it on the ground "that *adequate preparation* for that kind of future gradual emancipation, which will operate beneficially to both the master and slave, can be successfully *commenced* in no other way, than by deciding *first, that slavery shall cease to exist—absolutely, unconditionally, and irrevocably.* When that is settled, then, and not till then, *the whole community* [of whites] *will feel a common interest, in making the best possible preparation for the event.*"

On December 4 there was organized at Philadelphia the American Anti-Slavery Society, whose doctrine was immediate emancipation, defined as gradual emancipation immediately begun. Professor Gilbert H. Barnes has interpreted this straitened use of the term as an effort to bring British precedent to the movement's support and as realization by its sponsors of the difficulty of applying imperial methods in a country whose general government was one of distinctly limited and delegated powers. Without denying the validity of that interpretation, may I venture to assert that the eastern men were probably no further advanced in their opinions than the Kentuckians, though less gifted with clarity of expression. I have never seen a more crystal-clear statement of what the antislavery leaders of the next ten years were trying to accomplish than the Kentucky statement of the indispensable prerequisite of any program: the decision "*first, that slavery shall cease to exist—absolutely, unconditionally, and irrevocably.*"

Before leaving Alabama Birney had abandoned hope for the redemption of the lower South and all his life felt that that region eventually would be overwhelmed by Negroes and abandoned by the whites. He urged Gurley to concentrate all efforts on Kentucky, Virginia, and Maryland, holding that the slave power would collapse and the Union be saved if these states could be induced to get rid of their slaves. He labored indefatigably during the winter of 1833–34 to win his own state to a program of gradual emancipation, lecturing at Frankfort, Louisville, and Lexington with Judge John Green and President John Young of Centre College. Many others, including Professor James Buchanan, President Luke Munsell of the Danville Deaf and Dumb Asylum, the Reverend David Nelson of the Danville Presbyterian Church, and Dr. David Bell, lent their moral support and personal influence. The effort was unavailing, though little organized opposition was encountered, and Birney took the final step of repudiating both colonization and gradualism. Meanwhile events of far-reaching import had occurred at Cincinnati. The students of Lane Seminary, gathered from all parts of the country, were making history under the guiding genius of Weld.

Cincinnati contained more than one-third of the seventy-five hundred Negroes in the state of Ohio, many of whom were emancipated slaves who had been or were then paying for themselves or for their friends or relatives still in bondage. No other place in the United States offered a better opportunity to test the ability of the Negro to make advancement if given the opportunity. Into this mass of humanity these students had thrown themselves without restraint and had established Sabbath schools, day and evening schools, a lyceum where they lectured four evenings a week on grammar, geography, arithmetic, natural philosophy, and so forth. They mingled freely with the Negro population, relieving distress and cultivating intellectual and moral progress, and incidentally furnishing an excuse for the revival of mob violence. They organized a college lyceum and discussed at length the question of slavery in all its aspects, with particular emphasis upon colonization and emancipation. Colonization was repudiated as unworthy of the support and patronage of Christians, and immediate emancipation was endorsed. There then ensued the first and one of the greatest contests for academic freedom in the history of the country.

The students had given a practical demonstration in refutation of the prevailing belief that Negroes were inherently incapable of advancement and destined by nature to a position of inferiority. They had pooled their intimate knowledge of slavery gained by long residence in the slave states, had reasoned and rationalized as became gentlemen trained in the school of the Great Revival, and had concluded that slavery was a sin great enough to justify their undivided attention.

Thirty members of this theological class were over twenty-six years of age, fourteen were over twenty-eight, and nine were between thirty and thirty-five. All were college graduates, most of them having received degrees from eight to seventeen years previously. Six were married men. One was a practicing physician, and twelve had been public lecturers of prominence. They had come to Lane Seminary perfectly cognizant of the strategic location of the institution. J. L. Tracy, a former schoolmate of Weld at Oneida Institute, then teaching at Lexington, Kentucky, had written to Weld, November 24, 1831: "You are well aware of the fact that this western country is soon to be a mighty giant that shall wield not only the destinies of our own country but of the world. 'Tis yet a babe. Why not then come and take it in the feebleness of its infancy and give a right direction to its powers, that when it grows up to its full stature we may bless God that it has such an influence?" The students themselves declared: "The Valley was our expected field; and we assembled here, that we might the more accurately learn its character, catch the spirit of its gigantic enterprise, grow up in its genius, appreciate its peculiar wants, and be thus qualified by practical skill, no less than by theological erudition, to wield the weapons of truth."

Here in Cincinnati, the most strategic location in the United States, was a new theological seminary with as fine a body of young men as any school in the country, as proved by testimony of their president and by their later accomplishments, and with the possibility of becoming the center of the intellectual and cultural life of the entire valley. Yet all but two or three of the faculty and trustees were so blinded by race prejudice, so devoted to the cause of colonization, so sensitive to popular clamor, and so destitute of knowledge about the true purpose of the educational process as to proscribe the right of free discussion. The students were commanded to discontinue their anti-slavery society and prohibited from holding meetings and from discussing the subject even at the dinner table. A committee was vested with discretionary power of dismissal. Almost the entire student body requested honorable dismissal. The faculty granted it, but thereafter threw every possible obstacle in the way of the work they were seeking to accomplish. Filled with the glorious vigor of youth, the fervor of religious conviction, and the enthusiasm of the crusader in a worthy cause, the rebels redoubled their efforts among the Negro population, pursued their studies independently, and, finally, went to Oberlin College, where Asa Mahan served as president and Finney came to head theology. But, leaving, they hurled defiance at the faculty in words that stand out as one of the greatest prophecies of the century:

> *Sirs, you have mistaken alike the cause, the age and the men, if you think to intimidate by threats, or to silence by clamor, or shame by sneers, or put down by authority, or discourage by opposition, or appal by danger, those who have put their hands to this work. . . . Slavery, with its robbery of body and soul from birth to death, its exactions of toil unrecompensed, its sunderings of kindred, its frantic orgies of lust, its intellect levelled with dust, its baptisms of blood, and its legacy of damning horrors to the eternity of the spirit—Slavery, in this land of liberty and light . . . its days are numbered and well-nigh finished. . . . The nation is shaking off its slumbers to sleep no more.*

Meanwhile, Birney, within four months of the date of launching the Kentucky Society for the Gradual Relief of the State from Slavery, became convinced, as he says, that slavery was sinful, although only a hairsplitting divine could explain how a man who had spoken of slavery as unchristian, morally wrong, and a greater evil than original enslavement needed to be convinced that slavery was a sin. What is probably more nearly the truth was Birney's conviction that only through an appeal to the conscience of the slaveholder by preaching the sin of slavery could anything be gained. Early in May 1834, before the students dispersed for vacation, and previous to the faculty action proscribing academic freedom, Birney wrote his famous "Letter on Colonization, Addressed to the Rev. Thornton J. Mills, Corresponding Secretary of the Kentucky Colonization Society," and followed it shortly with his "Letter to the Ministers and Elders on the Sin of Holding Slaves, and the Duty of Immediate Emancipation." The first was published in the Lexington *Intelligencer,* the second in the Cincinnati *Journal,* and thousands of copies were mailed by the students to ministers and prominent laymen in the Mississippi Valley.

They were promptly reprinted in the New York *Evangelist* and the *Emancipator,* and as separate pamphlets by the American Anti-Slavery Society.

Birney and Weld were in constant communication during the summer months (1834). Birney decided to abandon everything else and to devote his life to antislavery work. Arrangements were made for his support by the national society, and it was agreed that he remain in Kentucky, organize a state antislavery society, and establish an antislavery newspaper. He was to labor with the Presbyterian synod of the state to secure antislavery resolutions. Weld was to circle through Ohio and Pennsylvania to Pittsburgh and attend the general assembly there, make arrangements for the organization of an Ohio antislavery society, secure subscriptions to Birney's paper, and return by way of Marietta and Steubenville. The conference near Georgetown in September put the finishing touches to these plans.

During the winter months the Lane rebels trekked to Oberlin, and Weld blazed a trail of abolitionism across Ohio and Pennsylvania. Birney quietly went about his task in Kentucky, organizing the state antislavery society at Danville on March 18, 1835, with James Buchanan as president and Luke Munsell as secretary, publishing a prospectus of his proposed paper—the *Philanthropist*—and making arrangements for printing at the office of the *Olive Branch* in Danville. Then the storm broke.

Thirty-three gentlemen of standing addressed to Birney, on July 12, 1835, a sharp remonstrance against the publication of his paper. Deprecating the failure of the legislature to have laws against such incendiary publications passed—whether from the feeling that none so base could be found in Kentucky society or from the belief that the Negroes were too illiterate to cause concern, or from a desire to preserve the freedom of the press—they requested that Birney forbear until legislation could be secured which would prevent his publication and thus obviate the necessity of resort to mob violence. Birney's reply was a denial of legislative power to interfere with the constitutional guarantee of freedom of the press; a defense of the value of discussion concerning matters of great moment to the people; an assertion that discussion had already begun, would continue, and would be dangerous to the peace of society only if forced underground, concealed, and surreptitiously carried on; and a warning that silence in the slave states would increase discussion in the free states.

Both communications were published in the *Olive Branch,* and the slaveholders, firm in their position that "no *American Slaveholding Community* has found itself able to bear" the experiment of free discussion, called a public meeting at the Baptist Church on July 25. James Barbour, president of the Branch Bank of Kentucky and treasurer of Centre College, presided. The Reverend J. K. Burch, moderator of the Presbyterian synod of Kentucky, was a principal speaker. The meeting, probably of five hundred, left no doubt of its determination to resort to mob violence if necessary to prevent publication of the *Philanthropist,* and passed a series of resolutions denouncing it as a scheme "wild, visionary, impracticable, unpolitical, and contrary to the spirit of our laws, and at war with the spirit of our Constitution." Four days later a mob assembled to destroy the press, but dispersed when its former owner, a member of their own party, took possession of the establishment.

That day marked the end of the organized antislavery movement in Kentucky. Within a month Birney moved his family to Cincinnati. The Reverend David Nelson published a blistering farewell sermon to his congregation and moved to Marion College, Missouri, but was forced to seek safety for himself and family at Carlinville, Illinois. Professor Buchanan accepted a professorship at Oberlin, remained a term, and then also went to Carlinville. Here they joined with the Reverend Robert Holman, Birney's old friend of Huntsville, Alabama, Elijah Lovejoy, and Edward Beecher in founding the Illinois Anti-Slavery Society. Luke Munsell moved to Indianapolis, assisted in organizing the Indiana State Anti-Slavery Society, and became its first president. Of the little coterie only President Young remained, in his heart an abolitionist, openly supporting gradualism, secretly keeping up his contact with Birney.

As for the Lane rebels, it would be difficult to overestimate the influence of these two years. They served as agents of the American Anti-Slavery Society in 1836, abolitionized Ohio, and then formed the nucleus of the famous "Seventy." Henry B. Stanton was financial

---

FIGURE 2. Fighting the Mob in Indiana. (*Historical Pictures Service, Chicago*)

and corresponding secretary of the American Anti-Slavery Society, an active member of the Free Soil Party, and editor of the New York *Sun.* Asa Mahan became successively president of Oberlin College, Cleveland University, and Adrian College. James A. Thome taught for many years at Oberlin, wrote, with Horace Kimball, the powerful tract *Emancipation in the West Indies,* and served influential pastorates in Cleveland and at Mount Vernon. Philemon Bliss entered Congress from Elyria, Ohio, became chief justice of Dakota Territory and dean of the Law School of the University of Missouri. George Whipple became professor of mathematics at Oberlin, secretary of the American Missionary Association, and a participant in the Freedman's Aid. Augustus Wattles spent a fortune and the best years of his life teaching free Negroes to become economically self-sufficient, and edited the *Herald of Freedom* in Kansas during that territory's troublous years. Marius Robinson founded and edited until 1861 the *Anti-Slavery Bugle* at Salem, Ohio, and then became president of the Ohio Mutual Fire Insurance Company. Hiram Wilson directed for many years the work of rehabilitation of fugitive slaves in Canada. Hiram Foote, Edward Weed, Calvin Waterbury, John W. Alvord, William T. Allen, and others held prominent pastorates in the West after the agency phase of the movement had been supplanted by political agitation. Professor Calvin Stowe, who "came right" on the question within a few months after the Lane debate, married Harriet Beecher, moved to far-off Andover, and from the recollections of these stirring days came *Uncle Tom's Cabin.*

Judged only by the training of these early apostles of freedom, the events of the two years at Danville and Cincinnati would merit the attention of historians. More important still, they gave character and direction to the movement, making it a powerful religious crusade in the direction of moral reform. It was theological students in a theological seminary, drawing their inspiration largely from the Great Revival, who sat in judgment on the institution of slavery. Weld and Stanton selected the "Seventy" and rarely departed from type in the selection of agents. From first to last churches were the forums, preachers the most consistent and powerful advocates, and the sin of slavery the cardinal thesis of the new social philosophy. The religious character of the antislavery meetings, the Christian piety, meekness, and humility of the pioneer abolition lecturers, the religious fanaticism which soon enshrouded the entire movement, the particular instructions of the central committee to agents in the field to "insist principally on the *sin of slavery,* because our main hope is in the consciences of men, and it requires little logic to prove that it is always safe to do right," and the intimate notes from one to another, every line of which is a prayer in itself, leave no doubt as to the true character of the first phases of the movement. Birney's emphasis upon the incompatibility of slavery and the fundamental philosophy on which the nation was established blossomed eventually, through his leadership, as the principle upon which Northern sectionalism sought to administer the government.

Finally, the exile of Birney, the very soul of dignity, integrity, and Christian virtue, from his native state and the proscription of academic freedom at Lane Seminary established precedents and enthroned a principle: the slaveholders' interests were paramount and their fiat was law. Birney's perspective was never clearer than when he wrote to Gerrit Smith:

> *It is as much as all the patriotism in our country can do, to keep alive the spirit of liberty in the* free states. *The contest is becoming—has become—one, not alone of freedom for the* black, *but of freedom for the* white. *It has now become absolutely necessary, that slavery should cease in order that freedom may be preserved to any portion of our land. The antagonist principles of liberty and slavery have been roused into action and one or the other must be victorious. There will be no cessation of the strife until Slavery shall be exterminated or liberty destroyed.*

No other reform movement is quite like the antislavery crusade, because it was based upon an appeal to the consciences of men; yet the sinners were almost wholly insulated from the preachment, and the anxious seat was crowded with saints, so that the historian is tempted to agree with Pascal, that "There are but two classes of men, the righteous, who think themselves to be sinners, and the sinners, who think themselves righteous." One *expects* to find the contemporary literature of the great controversy strongly biased, but race prejudice still lives, and the writings of trained historians, also, have such an overtone of moralizing or apology as to leave the impression their wishes determined what they should accept as truth. Fortunately, we do not need to agree on the precise nature of American Negro slavery. Historians have too long focused their attention upon that controversial point, to the neglect of more important things. One can no more describe the life of the slave than describe a typical plantation. There was too much diversity, and the human element entered in too largely to permit even a highly centralized picture. To attempt it is to become lost in a labyrinth of qualifications. Abolitionists omitted the qualifications and strengthened their case accordingly, but weakened it in the light of historical research.

One may find in abolition literature, not here and there but in dreary succession, charges of vilest depravity: miscegenation between owners, owners' sons, and overseers—whom Birney called the "feculum" of society—and the female slaves, with all the accompanying tragedies of mixed blood, sale of children by their fathers, pollution of men's souls and degradation of the home; slave breeding, ranging from the encouragement of promiscuity and inducements for continuous bearing of children, to compulsory submission to service by Negroes and whites of fine physique and degenerate character; separation of families, of husbands and wives, brothers and sisters, and children of tender age from mothers, either from financial stringency, liquidation of estates, or downright disregard of human feelings; virtual freedom to comely young females willing to prostitute themselves and share their earnings, mutilation of bodies, in anger, in search of punishment equal to the nature of the offense, or in satisfaction of sadistic impulses; branding, shackling, placing in stocks, burdening with iron collars, chains, and so forth, to prevent running away; criminal neglect of the injured, the seriously ill, the incurably diseased for the sake of economy; and the merciless hunting down of fugitives with bloodhounds and guns, with the levity and zest of the possum hunt.

The weakness of this sort of propaganda lay in the necessity (1) for a constant increase in the enormity of the offense charged; (2) for variation, since attention was more easily arrested by the novelty of the guilt than by its degree; and (3) for unimpeachable supporting evidence to satisfy the skeptic. Some of the pornographic calendar is so stereotyped in form as to bear the impress of legend. Some of it was hearsay, undoubtedly magnified in the telling. The more repulsive incidents were of uncommon occurrence and were no more authentic criteria by which to judge the institution as a whole than was Jefferson Davis' experiment in self-government for his slaves.

It was the sort of stuff that warms the heart of the true propagandist and fascinates the sanctimonious pietist as well as the irreligious miscreant. But such aspects of slavery as miscegenation, separation of families, cruel punishments, and barbarous treatment of fugitives cannot be minimized either by one who seeks a true picture of slavery or by one who seeks the causes of the Civil War. Historians have no justification for ignoring abolition literature in their work on slavery. The great bulk of this part of it was written by high-minded men and women who were either born and reared in the South or had lived there many years. One would hardly expect to find mention of these sordid aspects of the institution in plantation records, in private diaries or letters, or in treatises written in defense of slavery. The fact that Southerners who did write about them were living at the time in states where there was no slavery does not detract from, but rather increases, the probability of their accuracy. Supported, as they were, by certain other indisputable facts we shall shortly refer to, they would have given all but the most obdurate champions of slavery cause for serious reflection; but the generality of Southerners had not the slightest conception of abolition arguments or of the principles for which they were contending.

The restlessness of slaveholders over colonization activities crystallized into a militant defense of slavery as antislavery agitation increased in the North—a defense which denied freedom of speech and of the press, excluded abolition literature from the mails, and drove everyone suspected of heresy out of the South, and hence closed the public forums to all antislavery doctrine. At the same time the fulminations of those abolitionists who allowed their opposition to slavery to lead them along the psychopathic trail to a hatred of slaveholders and who took special delight in foul invective and ribald abuse of everyone connected with the institution were copied into the Southern newspapers as a warning of the impending Northern plague. Perhaps it was inevitable that men who hated slavery should hate slaveholders. Perhaps it is just to lump the sinner with the sin. That is a matter of opinion. In any case it was not conducive to calm reflection or sympathetic understanding or a peaceable solution of the question. Year after year the Southerners went on enduring these charges of moral turpitude, with their holier-than-thou implications, nursing their wrath, and finding consolation in self-justification.

This catalogue of specific wrongs was also a part of the more general indictment of slavery as a sin. The antislavery movement was a powerful religious crusade, and religion played a far more important part in American life then than it does today. The Bible was presented as irrefutable proof that Jesus taught a doctrine of universal brotherhood; that man was created in the image of God; and that slavery reduced him to a piece of merchandise to be bought and sold in the market place. Said Theodore Weld, when the American Anti-Slavery Society was organized: "God has committed to every moral agent the privilege, the right and the responsibility of personal ownership. This is God's plan. Slavery annihilates it, and surrenders to avarice, passion and lust, all that makes life a blessing. It crushes the body, tramples into the dust the upward tendencies of the intellect, breaks the heart and kills the soul." Said the Central Executive Committee: "Every man who has put on the armor of Jesus Christ is under the paramount pledge to do all in his power for the salvation of the souls for which He died. How can you, my brother, do more than by *now* espousing the cause of those for whose souls there are *no men* to care." Slavery was denounced as a sin, "always, everywhere and only sin," *aside* from the evils of its administration. Abolitionists demanded that slaveholders be excluded from the pulpits of Northern churches and from the privileges of the sacraments, and those Southerners who finally championed the cause of secession lingered long on this aspect of the cause for action. Said the distinguished John S. Preston of South Carolina before the Virginia Convention:

> *This diversity at this moment is appearing not in forms of denominational polemics, but in shapes as bloody and terrible as religion has ever assumed since Christ came to earth. Its representative, the Church, has bared her arm for the conflict—her sword is already flashing in the glare of the torch of fanaticism—and the history of the world tells us that when that sword cleaves asunder, no human surgery can heal the wound. There is not one Christian slaveholder here, no matter how near he may be to his meek and lowly master, who does not feel in his heart that from the point of that sword is now dripping the last drop of sympathy which bound him to his brethren at the North. With demoniac rage they have set the Lamb of God between their seed and our seed.*

In support of their charge that these violations of the standards of contemporary civilization were far more prevalent than Southerners were willing to admit, were inherent in slavery, and were indicative of the general moral tone of the institution, abolitionists presented a line of argument which was not easily contradicted. Slaves were property. They were bought and sold. The purchase price alone determined who might be a slaveholder. Society set no standards of intelligence, character, or integrity for slaveholding. There were no public or private agencies charged with responsibility for the slave's welfare. Human nature being what it is or, better still, what it then was, what security was there for the individual slave against abuse of arbitrary power? Said Weld: "Arbitrary power is to the mind what alcohol is to the body; it intoxicates. It is perhaps the strongest human passion; and the more absolute the power, the stronger the desire for it; and the more it is desired, the more its exercise is enjoyed. . . . The fact that a person intensely desires power over others, *without restraint,* shows the absolute necessity of restraint." This condition was greatly aggravated by the fact that slaves were subject not only to the will of their owner, but to the authority of every white person with whom they came in contact off the owner's property, and to the slightest whim of the owner's family, even of children too immature to have disciplined themselves; and by the further fact that, in spite of abject servility and personal desire to suppress emotions, evidences of resentment must have been a common occurrence. "The idea of *property* having a will," said Weld, "and that too in opposition to the will of its *owner,* and counteracting it, is a stimulant of terrible power to the most relentless human passions." In support of his logic he brought together in *American Slavery As It Is* what he chose to call the "testimony of a thousand witnesses," the most devastating arraignment of slavery ever published. Hundreds of thousands of copies of the pamphlet were distributed, and its influence was incalculable. There was no effective reply to it, nor could there have been.

Not only did abolitionists examine slavery in the light of the Scriptures and of the moral standards prevailing in contemporary civilization; they also pronounced it contrary to the fundamental principles of the American way of life because it plundered the slaves of their inalienable rights as men: ownership of their own bodies: freedom of choice, as to use of time and to occupation; the rights of marriage, family life, and paternal authority; the right to worship according to conscience; the right to cultivate their minds, utilize their peculiar talents and influence their fellow men; the right to protect themselves, their homes, and their families against violence; the right to the protection of the law. These were things which, especially in those days of rugged individualism, made a powerful impression upon the average American.

The lack of legal protection for the slave constituted the greatest single indictment against the slaveholding states. The slave owner had no restraint but his own will over the type and amount of labor assigned to the slave. He might hire him out to other men; he might permit him to labor on his own account and claim his wages; he might inflict any kind or degree of punishment without fear of redress; he might assign absolute authority over the slave to any agent. He might sell the slave at will. The slave was both a chattel and real estate and liable to be sold in satisfaction of debts. He could not testify in court in any case involving a white man. If he raised his hand against a white man in any circumstances whatsoever, the penalty was death. He had no recourse against intolerable conditions but perilous flight. He could own no property, make no contracts, receive no education, claim no religious instruction. Whatever legislation had been passed with respect to slaves was purely for protection of property rights and the security of the institution. One may find, only rarely, feeble recognition by legislatures and courts of slaves as human beings. This was slavery's most vulnerable spot and was so considered by the abolitionists.

The practical application of the law, said the apologists for slavery, was far less rigorous than the provisions of the law, which was simply ignoring the point at issue. When they spoke of the slave codes as being unenforced except at rare intervals when mass hysteria followed attempted insurrections, a particularly brutal murder, or the apprehension of a suspected incendiary, they were speaking of laws passed for the protection of society, that is, laws forbidding slaves to assemble without the presence of a white person; forbidding slaves to leave their owners' premises without a written permit; forbidding slaves to preach or masters to teach them to read; and requiring the regular patrol of all public highways. The important point is that that great body of law, both common and statute, and the courts, the instrument of its operation, to which men have looked since time immemorial for the administration of justice and for the protection of their most elementary human rights simply did not exist for three million slaves. Privileges they might have and no doubt did enjoy in generous measure from indulgent masters, but they had no more semblance of rights than the beasts of the field.

More difficult to evaluate with respect to its place in the Northern educational program was the abolition argument concerning the effect of slavery upon the two races and upon the South from the viewpoint of general culture and economy. This was in the nature of a rebuttal to the positive-good argument, the development of which preceded the abolition crusade of the thirties. The positive-good dogma embraced four theses: (1) that slave labor was essential to the development and continued prosperity of the southern country; (2) that the Negro race was inferior and destined by nature to a subordinate position; (3) that slavery had lifted a savage people from barbarism to Christian civilization; and (4) that the white race had not degenerated as a consequence, but, on the contrary, had developed a unique and high degree of culture. Ancillary to these there were, of course, a number of supporting theses. Divine sanction was invoked for the institution with the Bible as evidence. Historical precedent of the existence of slavery in every age was cited. Culture, it was said, could thrive only if the few enjoyed leisure from exploitation of the many, and black slavery threw wide the door of opportunity to all white men by substituting race exploitation for class exploitation. Southern bond slavery was compared to Northern wage slavery to prove that the black slave shared more abundantly in the necessaries of life than the Northern wage earner.

Much of the abolitionists' reply to the Southern claims of cultural superiority and the defense of slavery as a humane and civilizing institution is to be found in the general indictments of slavery as a sin and as incompatible with the standards of contemporary civilization. They did not hesitate, however, to meet the argument on specific points, twitting the slaveholders about their lack of a common school system, their resort to murder under the *code duello* for the satisfaction of every fancied wrong, their compulsory diversion of all mixed blood back into the black race to hide the shame of their immorality, and their propensity for gambling and hard drinking. They ridiculed the idea that a system which made the happiness of a defenseless people "the sport of every whim, and the prey of every passion that may . . . infest the master's bosom" could possibly develop a profound sense of responsibility in the slaveholder, holding that the "daily practice of forcibly robbing others and habitually living on the plunder can not but beget in the mind the *habit* of regarding the interests and happiness of those whom it robs, as of no sort of consequence in comparison with its own." As for the slave, his very dependence impaired his manliness and independence of character, crushed his soul, and destroyed his ability to distinguish right from wrong. It cultivated immorality, placed a premium upon deception, and made lying and stealing acts of self-preservation.

The Bible argument waxed long and furiously, with perhaps a slight advantage to the abolitionists. Over the long view it appears to have been a rather fruitless discussion, without much influence one way or the other. Slavery's role in history was assessed as a liability rather than as a contribution to the glory and stability of Rome. It was condemned as an impediment to a balanced economy in the South, absorbing the capital necessary to industrial enterprise, denying the entrepreneur the public cooperation essential to the development of manufacturing, destroying the fertility of the soil through forced and incompetent labor, driving the nonslaveholder to the free states or ever farther back upon the margin of a bare subsistence level, turning the stream of foreign immigration elsewhere, and creating a contempt for manual labor on the part of the whites, the fruits of which were indolence on the one hand and arrogant snobbery on the other.

Finally, slavery was condemned as a menace to the peace and safety of the nation. Concentration of Negroes in the Black Belt entered into every phase of the slavery question. From the earliest days the champions of slavery had admitted the necessity of maintaining a proper ratio between the two races. The subject arose in connection with colonization. Southern pamphleteers conceded the desirability of diffusion as an aid to the alleviation of the system's harsher features. Fear of insurrection increased as the center of the slave population moved steadily toward the Southwest. It was advanced in defense of the prohibition against teaching slaves to read, permitting them to assemble without the presence of whites, and so forth. It played an important part in the discussion over the expansion of slave territory and in the Confederate Constitutional Convention with respect to the nonseceding states in 1861.

Abolitionists took particular delight, it would seem, in playing upon this fear of the South by exposing it as a national weakness, calling attention to the vulnerability of the southern coast to attack, chiding the South for dependence upon the great strength of the nation to protect from outside interference and from internal combustion an institution it insisted upon regarding as its own domestic concern, lashing out with bitter invective against the slavocracy for involving the whole nation in a war of conquest, and bringing all the pressure at their command against the state department's representations to Great Britain in the *Creole* and other cases.

The particular emphasis placed upon each of these several indictments depended upon the time, the occasion, and the person discussing the subject. It is essential to remember that the antislavery movement was almost completely unorganized until the founding of the American Anti-Slavery Society in December 1833. There were the New York City Manumission Society, organized by John Jay and Alexander Hamilton in 1785; the Pennsylvania Abolition Society, organized by Benjamin Franklin in 1789; and scattered local societies in North Carolina, Tennessee, and southern Ohio; but the organized movement for the entire abolition of slavery in the United States began in the early thirties. From 1833 to 1840 it was under the direction of a powerful executive committee of the American Anti-Slavery Society, located in New York City. After 1839 there were two national organizations: the American Anti-Slavery Society, under the control of William Lloyd Garrison at Boston, and the American and Foreign Anti-Slavery Society, under the control of Lewis Tappan in New York City. During the first period work was carried on largely through local and traveling agents and was predominantly religious, with churches the forums, the sin of slavery the theme, and the organization of state and local auxiliary societies and the founding of antislavery newspapers an important function of the agents. After 1840 neither of the national organizations exercised much influence or control over the movement; but, so far as they did, the American and Foreign Anti-Slavery Society was the functional continuation of the original American Anti-Slavery Society, distinctly religious and friendly to the churches and promoting the old policy of seeking the abolition of slavery by moral suasion. The real work of maintaining agencies and newspapers and depositories for antislavery literature, however, was carried on by the powerful state societies. The function of giving direction to the movement and defining its objectives was now under the control of a small group of politically minded abolitionists, and state societies shortly became almost identical with state antislavery political parties. The American Anti-Slavery Society under Garrison at Boston—the old society name without the substance—was distinctly antichurch, antipolitical, and strongly flavored with peace, no-human-government, and woman's rights. . . .

Men like Theodore Weld and Julius LeMoyne were not convinced that political action was "*essential* as a means to the great end in view." They looked upon it as only another distracting issue such as woman's rights, no-human-government, and peace—collateral questions which would "divide, distract, embarrass and alienate the abolition body, and . . . divert their attention and efforts from the first and grand object." This was particularly true, said Le Moyne, because, "except for the *single object* of our association, no body of men who are associated, are composed of such various and almost incongruous materials—men of all religions and no religion—of all politics and shades of policy—of all habits of thought and prejudices of education and locality—which our country furnishes example." To this reason for opposition they added the fear of revealing the paucity of their numbers, the impropriety of undertaking to promote a religious enterprise by means of an essentially different character, and the possibility of the movement falling under the control of politicians and vote-getting expediency supplanting principle to the end of an abandonment of high antislavery ground. . . .

Most antislavery men, among the rank and file, were opposed to independent political action in the beginning, largely of course, because they were good Whigs or good Democrats. Political creeds were an inheritance and a habit, soul-deadening and death-defying. However much men might deprecate the proslavery bent of their party leaders and party platforms, or be willing to annoy them with embarrassing questions relative to slavery, they were not willing to take any action which might lead to the dissolution of their party or to withhold a vote which might enable the opposition to win. Slavery was an important issue, one capable of sorely disturbing the conscience and freighted with dire consequences to the national security, but so were other things—banking, for instance, or the tariff, or internal improvement, or the disposition of the public lands—and men were not willing to forego registering a vote on such questions, even though they appreciated the importance of a powerful protest vote against slavery domination of the old line parties.

To all such staunch party men Birney wrote:

> *The security of life—of liberty—of civil and religious privileges—of the rights of conscience—of the right to use our own faculties for the promotion of our own happiness—of free locomotion,—all these, together with the defense of the barriers and outposts thrown around them by the laws, constitute the highest concerns of the government. These, for the last six years, we have seen invaded one after another—the administration aiding in the onset—till the* feeling of security *for any of them has well nigh expired. A censorship of the mail is usurped by the deputy postmasters throughout more than half of the country, and approved by the administration under which it takes place. The pillage of the Post Office is perpetrated in one of our principal cities, and its contents made a bonfire of in the public square;—no one is brought in question for the outrage. Free speech and debate on the most important subject that now agitates the country, is rendered impossible in our national legislature; the* right *of the people to petition Congress for a redress of grievances is formally abolished by their own servants! And shall we sit down and dispute about the currency, about a subtreasury or no-sub-treasury, a bank or no-bank, while such outrages on constitutional and essential* rights *are enacting before our eyes?*

Many of those who first supported independent political action were convinced of its efficacy as a method of rendering slavery odious and of forcing one or the other of the old parties to adopt a firmer stand against slavery. So far as Myron Holley, James G. Birney, Alvan Stewart, Joshua Leavitt, William Goodell, and others were concerned, however, it represented a settled conviction that the attempt to maintain a harmonious union between sections with such diametrically opposite principles was impossible, and that the time had come for those who believed in the republican principles and habits of the Northern states to make a militant stroke for control of the federal government and thereby gain complete ascendency over the slave power. It was the first step in the formation of two great sectional parties which were to contend for control of the government in 1860, and men knew it to be so. Said Weld: "Nothing short of miracles, constant miracles, and such as the world has never seen can keep at bay the two great antagonist forces. . . . They must drive against each other, till *one* of them goes to the bottom. *Events,* the master of men, have for years been silently but without a moment's pause, settling the basis of two great parties, the nucleus of one slavery, of the other freedom. . . ."

II THE ABOLITIONISTS' DEFENSE OF THEIR MEANS AND ENDS

William Lloyd Garrison

TO THE PUBLIC

The following statement of aims by William Lloyd Garrison (1805–1879) in the first issue of his journal, The Liberator, *is one of the most quoted documents in American history. Small though its circulation was, the launching of this journal on its thirty-five-year career symbolized and in a measure caused the emergence of immediate abolitionism as a powerful reform impulse. Besides the famous Garrisonian rhetoric, this editorial reveals how early abolitionists were forced to debate the question of means.*

In the month of August, I issued proposals for publishing *The Liberator* in Washington City; but the enterprise, though hailed in different sections of the country, was palsied by public indifference. Since that time, the removal of the *Genius of Universal Emancipation* to the seat of government has rendered less imperious the establishment of a similar periodical in that quarter.

During my recent tour for the purpose of exciting the minds of the people by a series of discourses on the subject of slavery, every place that I visited gave fresh evidence of the fact, that a greater revolution in public sentiment was to be effected in the free states—*and particularly in New England*—than at the South. I found contempt more bitter, opposition more active, detraction more relentless, prejudice more stubborn, and apathy more frozen, than among slaveowners themselves. Of course, there were individual exceptions to the contrary. This state of things afflicted, but did not dishearten me. I determined, at every hazard, to lift up the standard of emancipation in the eyes of the nation, *within sight of Bunker Hill and in the birthplace of liberty.* That standard is now unfurled; and long may it float, unhurt by the spoliations of time or the missiles of a desperate foe—yea, till every chain be broken, and every bondman set free! Let Southern oppressors tremble—let their secret abettors tremble—let their Northern apologists tremble—let all the enemies of the persecuted blacks tremble.

I deem the publication of my original prospectus unnecessary, as

From Wendell Phillips Garrison and Francis Jackson Garrison, *William Lloyd Garrison, 1805–1879: The Story of His Life Told by His Children* (New York: The Century Company, 1885), Vol. I, pp. 224–226.

it has obtained a wide circulation. The principles therein inculcated will be steadily pursued in this paper, excepting that I shall not array myself as the political partisan of any man. In defending the great cause of human rights, I wish to derive the assistance of all religions and of all parties.

Assenting to the "self-evident truth" maintained in the American Declaration of Independence, "that all men are created equal, and endowed by their Creator with certain inalienable rights—among which are life, liberty and the pursuit of happiness," I shall strenuously contend for the immediate enfranchisement of our slave population. In Park-Street Church, on the Fourth of July, 1829, in an address on slavery, I unreflectingly assented to the popular but pernicious doctrine of *gradual* abolition. I seize this opportunity to make a full and unequivocal recantation, and thus publicly to ask pardon of my God, of my country, and of my brethren the poor slaves, for having uttered a sentiment so full of timidity, injustice, and absurdity. A similar recantation, from my pen, was published in the *Genius of Universal Emancipation* at Baltimore, in September, 1829. My conscience is now satisfied.

I am aware that many object to the severity of my language; but is there not cause for severity? I *will be* as harsh as truth, and as uncompromising as justice. On this subject, I do not wish to think, or speak, or write, with moderation. No! no! Tell a man whose house is on fire to give a moderate alarm; tell him to moderately rescue his wife from the hands of the ravisher; tell the mother to gradually extricate her babe from the fire into which it has fallen;—but urge me not to use moderation in a cause like the present. I am in earnest —I will not equivocate—I will not excuse—I will not retreat a single inch—*and I will be heard.* The apathy of the people is enough to make every statue leap from its pedestal, and to hasten the resurrection of the dead.

It is pretended, that I am retarding the cause of emancipation by the coarseness of my invective and the precipitancy of my measures. *The charge is not true.* On this question my influence,—humble as it is,—is felt at this moment to a considerable extent, and shall be felt in coming years—not perniciously, but beneficially—not as a curse, but as a blessing; and posterity will bear testimony that I was right. I desire to thank God, that he enables me to disregard "the fear of man which bringeth a snare," and to speak his truth in its simplicity and power. And here I close with this fresh dedication:

Oppression! I have seen thee, face to face,
And met thy cruel eye and cloudy brow;
But thy soul-withering glance I fear not now—
For dread to prouder feelings doth give place
Of deep abhorrence! Scorning the disgrace
Of slavish knees that at thy footstool bow,
I also kneel—but with far other vow
Do hail thee and thy herd of hirelings base:—
I swear, while life-blood warms my throbbing veins,
Still to oppose and thwart, with heart and hand,
Thy brutalizing sway—till Afric's chains
Are burst, and Freedom rules the rescued land,—
Trampling Oppression and his iron rod:
Such is the vow I take—*so help me God!*

William Lloyd Garrison
Boston, January 1, 1831

American Anti-Slavery Society

DECLARATION OF SENTIMENTS OF THE AMERICAN ANTI-SLAVERY SOCIETY

Inspired by Parliament's emancipation of slaves in the British Empire and increasingly disillusioned with the program of the American Colonization Society, a group of immediate abolitionists met in Philadelphia late in 1833 to establish the American Anti-Slavery Society. Among those forming the new organization were evangelical Protestants from New York, Philadelphia Quakers, and free Americans of African ancestry. Garrison, just back from a triumphal tour of Great Britain, led a New England contingent. He was the author of the society's "Declaration of Sentiments," adopted December 4, 1833.

The Convention, assembled in the City of Philadelphia to organize a National Anti-Slavery Society, promptly seize the opportunity to promulgate the following *Declaration of Sentiments,* as cherished by

From *The Liberator* 3 (December 14, 1833): 198.

them in relation to the enslavement of one-sixth portion of the American people.

More than fifty-seven years have elapsed since a band of patriots convened in this place, to devise measures for the deliverance of this country from a foreign yoke. The corner-stone upon which they founded the *Temple of Freedom* was broadly this—"that all men are created equal; that they are endowed by their Creator with certain inalienable rights; that among these are life, LIBERTY, and the pursuit of happiness." At the sound of their trumpet-call, three millions of people rose up as from the sleep of death, and rushed to the strife of blood; deeming it more glorious to die instantly as freemen, than desirable to live one hour as slaves.—They were few in number—poor in resources; but the honest conviction that *Truth, Justice,* and *Right* were on their side, made them invincible.

We have met together for the achievement of an enterprise, without which, that of our fathers is incomplete, and which, for its magnitude, solemnity, and probable results upon the destiny of the world, as far transcends theirs, as moral truth does physical force.

In purity of motive, in earnestness of zeal, in decision of purpose, in intrepidity of action, in steadfastness of faith, in sincerity of spirit, we would not be inferior to them.

Their principles led them to wage war against their oppressors, and to spill human blood like water, in order to be free. *Ours* forbid the doing of evil that good may come, and lead us to reject, and to entreat the oppressed to reject, the use of all carnal weapons for deliverance from bondage—relying solely upon those which are spiritual, and mighty through God to the pulling down of strongholds.

Their measures were physical resistance—the marshalling in arms —the hostile array—the mortal encounter. *Ours* shall be such only as the opposition of moral purity to moral corruption—the destruction of error by the potency of truth—the overthrow of prejudice by the power of love—and the abolition of slavery by the spirit of repentance.

Their grievances, great as they were, were trifling in comparison with the wrongs and sufferings of those for whom we plead. Our fathers were never slaves—never bought and sold like cattle—never shut out from the light of knowledge and religion—never subjected to the lash of brutal taskmasters.

But those, for whose emancipation we are striving,—constituting at the present time at least one-sixth part of our countrymen,—are recognized by the laws, and treated by their fellow beings, as marketable commodities—as goods and chattels—as brute beasts;—are plundered daily of the fruits of their toil without redress;—really enjoy no constitutional nor legal protection from licentious and murderous outrages upon their persons;—are ruthlessly torn asunder—the tender babe from the arms of its frantic mother—the heart-broken wife from her weeping husband—at the caprice or pleasure of irresponsible tyrants;—and, for the crime of having a dark complexion, suffer the pangs of hunger, the infliction of stripes, and the ignominy of brutal servitude. They are kept in heathenish darkness by laws expressly enacted to make their instruction a criminal offense.

These are the prominent circumstances in the condition of more than TWO MILLIONS of our people, the proof of which may be found in thousands of indisputable facts, and in the laws of the slaveholding States.

Hence we maintain—

That in view of the civil and religious privileges of this nation, the guilt of its oppression is unequalled by any other on the face of the earth;—and, therefore,

That it is bound to repent instantly, to undo the heavy burden, to break every yoke, and to let the oppressed go free.

We further maintain—

That no man has a right to enslave or imbrute his brother—to hold or acknowledge him, for one moment, as a piece of merchandise—to keep back his hire by fraud—or to brutalize his mind by denying him the means of intellectual, social and moral improvement.

The right to enjoy liberty is inalienable. To invade it, is to usurp the prerogative of Jehovah. Every man has a right to his own body—to the products of his own labor—to the protection of law—and to the common advantages of society. It is piracy to buy or steal a native African, and subject him to servitude. Surely the sin is as great to enslave an *American* as an *African.*

Therefore we believe and affirm—

That there is no difference, *in principle,* between the African slave trade and American slavery;

That every American citizen, who retains a human being in involuntary bondage, is [according to Scripture] a *man-stealer;*

That the slaves ought instantly to be set free, and brought under the protection of law;

That if they had lived from the time of Pharaoh down to the present period, and had been entailed through successive generations, their right to be free could never have been alienated, but their claims would have constantly risen in solemnity;

That all those laws which are now in force, admitting the right of slavery, are therefore before God utterly null and void; being an audacious usurpation of the Divine prerogative, a daring infringement on the law of nature, a base overthrow of the very foundations of the social compact, a complete extinction of all the relations, endearments and obligations of mankind, and a presumptuous transgression of all the holy commandments—and that therefore they ought to be instantly abrogated.

We further believe and affirm—

That all persons of color who possess the qualifications which are demanded of others, ought to be admitted forthwith to the enjoyment of the same privileges, and the exercise of the same prerogatives, as others; and that the paths of preferment, of wealth, and of intelligence, shall be opened as widely to them as to persons of a white complexion.

We maintain that no compensation should be given to the planters emancipating their slaves—

Because it would be a surrender of the great fundamental principle that man cannot hold property in man;

Because *Slavery is a crime, and therefore it is not an article to be sold;*

Because the holders of slaves are not the just proprietors of what they claim;—freeing the slaves is not depriving them of property, but restoring it to the right owner;—it is not wronging the master, but righting the slave—restoring him to himself;

Because immediate and general emancipation would only destroy nominal, not real property: it would not amputate a limb or break a bone of the slaves, but by infusing motives into their breasts, would make them doubly valuable to the masters as free laborers; and

Because if compensation is to be given at all, it should be given to the outraged and guiltless slaves, and not to those who have plundered and abused them.

We regard, as delusive, cruel and dangerous, any scheme of expatriation which pretends to aid, either directly or indirectly, in the emancipation of the slaves, or to be a substitute for the immediate and total abolition of slavery.

We fully and unanimously recognize the sovereignty of each State, to legislate exclusively on the subject of the slavery which is tolerated within its limits. We concede that Congress, *under the present national compact,* has no right to interfere with any of the slave States, in relation to this momentous subject.

But we maintain that Congress has a right, and is solemnly bound, to suppress the domestic slave trade between the several States, and to abolish slavery in those portions of our territory which the Constitution has placed under its exclusive jurisdiction.

We also maintain that there are, at the present time, the highest obligations resting upon the people of the free States, to remove slavery by moral and political action, as prescribed in the Constitution of the United States. They are now living under a pledge of their tremendous physical force to fasten the galling fetters of tyranny upon the limbs of millions in the southern States;—they are liable to be called at any moment to suppress a general insurrection of the slaves;—they authorize the slave owner to vote for three-fifths of his slaves as property, and thus enable him to perpetuate his oppression;—they support a standing army at the south for its protection;—and they seize the slave who has escaped into their territories, and send him back to be tortured by an enraged master or a brutal driver.

This relation to slavery is criminal and full of danger: *it must be broken up.*

These are our views and principles—these, our designs and measures. With entire confidence in the overruling justice of God, we plant ourselves upon the Declaration of our Independence, and upon the truths of Divine Revelation, as upon the *everlasting rock.*

We shall organize Anti-Slavery Societies, if possible, in every city, town and village of our land.

We shall send forth Agents to lift up the voice of remonstrance, of warning, of entreaty and rebuke.

We shall circulate, unsparingly and extensively, antislavery tracts and periodicals.

We shall enlist the *pulpit* and the *press* in the cause of the suffering and the dumb.

We shall aim at a purification of the churches from all participation in the guilt of slavery.

We shall encourage the labor of freemen over that of the slaves, by giving a preference to their productions;—and

We shall spare no exertions nor means to bring the whole nation to speedy repentance.

Our trust for victory is solely in GOD. *We* may be personally defeated, but our principles never. *Truth, Justice,* and *Humanity,* must and will gloriously triumph. Already a host is coming up to the help of the Lord against the mighty, and the prospect before us is full of encouragement.

Submitting this DECLARATION to the candid examination of the people of this country, and of the friends of liberty all over the world, we hereby affix our signatures to it;—pledging ourselves that, under the guidance and by the help of Almighty God, we will do all that in us lies, consistently with this Declaration of our principles, to overthrow the most execrable system of slavery that has ever been witnessed upon earth—to deliver our land from its deadliest curse—to wipe out the foulest stain which rests upon our national escutcheon—and to secure to the colored population of the United States all the rights and privileges which belong to them as men and as Americans—come what may to our persons, our interests, or our reputations—whether we live to witness the triumph of justice, liberty and humanity, or perish untimely as martyrs in this great, benevolent and holy cause.

Angelina Grimké

LETTERS TO CATHERINE E. BEECHER

Born into an aristocratic slaveholding family in Charleston, South Carolina, Angelina Grimké (1805–1879) and her sister Sarah grew dissatisfied with the practice of slavery and the formalism of the Episcopal church. They moved north, became Quakers, and in time obtained their share of the family slaves and freed them. Angelina in 1836 published an antislavery pamphlet, Appeal to the Christian Women of the South, *and was promptly denounced in her native city. At a time when such public activity by women was considered immodest, even indecent, the sisters gave lectures on the need for abolition. The following open letters answered criticisms published by Catherine Beecher, daughter of Lyman Beecher, leading New School Presbyterian minister and president of Lane Seminary, and sister of the not-yet-famous Harriet Beecher Stowe. Miss Beecher's objections to Angelina's abolitionist activities are clear from the answering arguments. In 1838 Angelina married the man who had abolitionized Lane Seminary, Theodore Weld.*

Letter I. Fundamental Principle of Abolitionists

Brookline, Mass. 6 month, 12th, 1837.

My Dear Friend: Thy book has appeared just at a time, when, from the nature of my engagements, it will be impossible for me to give it that attention which so weighty a subject demands. Incessantly occupied in prosecuting a mission, the responsibilities of which task all my powers, I can reply to it only by desultory letters, thrown from my pen as I travel from place to place. I prefer this mode to that of taking as long a time to answer it, as thou didst to determine upon the best method by which to counteract the effect of my testimony at the north—which, as the preface of thy book informs me, was thy main design.

Thou thinkest I have not been "sufficiently informed in regard to the feelings and opinions of Christian females at the North" on the subject of slavery; for that in fact they hold the same *principles* with Abolitionists, although they condemn their measures. Wilt thou permit

From Angelina E. Grimké, *Letters to Catherine E. Beecher, in Reply to an Essay on Slavery and Abolitionism, Addressed to A. E. Grimké* (Boston: Isaac Knapp, 1838), pp. 3–4, 6–13, 29–32, 34, 51–57, 94–99.

me to receive their principles from thy pen? Thus instructed, however misinformed I may heretofore have been, I can hardly fail of attaining to accurate knowledge. Let us examine them, to see how far they correspond with the principles held by Abolitionists.

The great fundamental principle of Abolitionists is, that man cannot rightfully hold his fellow man as property. Therefore, we affirm, that *every slaveholder is a man-stealer.* We do so, for the following reasons: to steal a man is to rob him of himself. It matters not whether this be done in Guinea, or Carolina; a man is a *man,* and *as* a man he has *inalienable* rights, among which is the right to personal *liberty.* Now if every man has an *inalienable* right to personal liberty, it follows, that he cannot rightfully be reduced to slavery. But I find in these United States, 2,250,000 men, women and children, robbed of that to which they have an *inalienable* right. How comes this to pass? Where millions are plundered, are there no *plunderers?* If, then, the slaves have been robbed of their liberty, *who* has robbed them? Not the man who stole their forefathers from Africa, but he who now holds them in bondage; no matter *how* they came into his possession, whether he inherited them, or bought them, or seized them at their birth on his own plantation. The only difference I can see between the original man-stealer, who caught the African in his native country, and the American slaveholder, is, that the former committed *one* act of robbery, while the other perpetrates the same crime *continually.*

. . . These are Abolition sentiments on the subject of slaveholding; and although our principles are universally held by our opposers at the North, yet I am told on the 44th page of thy book, that "the word man-stealer has one peculiar signification, and is no more synonymous with slaveholder than it is with sheep-stealer." I must acknowledge, thou has only confirmed my opinion of the difference which I had believed to exist between Abolitionists and their opponents. As well might Saul have declared, that he held similar views with Stephen, when he stood by and kept the raiment of those who slew him.

I know that a broad line of distinction is drawn between our principles and our measures, by those who are anxious to "avoid the appearance of evil"—very desirous of retaining the fair character of enemies to slavery. Now, our *measures* are simply the carrying out

---

FIGURE 3. Angelina Grimké. (*Historical Pictures Service, Chicago*)

of our *principles;* and we find, that just in proportion as individuals embrace our principles, in spirit and in truth, they cease to cavil at our measures. Gerrit Smith is a striking illustration of this. Who cavilled more at Anti-Slavery *measures,* and who more ready now to acknowledge his former blindness? Real Abolitionists know full well, that the slave never has been, and never can be, a whit the better for mere abstractions, floating in the *head* of any man; and they also know, that *principles, fixed in the heart,* are things of another sort. The former have never done any good in the world, because they possess no vitality, and therefore cannot bring forth *the fruits* of holy, untiring effort; but the latter live in the lives of their possessors, and breathe in their words. And I am free to express my belief, that *all* who really and heartily approve our *principles,* will also approve our *measures;* and that, too, just as certainly as a good tree will bring forth good fruit.

But there is another peculiarity in the views of Abolitionists. We hold that the North is guilty of the crime of slaveholding—we assert that it is a *national* sin: on the contrary, in thy book, I find the following acknowledgement:—"*Most* persons in the non-slaveholding States, have considered the matter of southern slavery as one in which they were no more called to interfere, than in the abolition of the press-gang system in England, or the tithe-system in Ireland." Now I cannot see how the same principles can produce such entirely different opinions. "Can a good tree bring forth corrupt fruit?" This I deny, and cannot admit what thou art anxious to prove, viz. that "Public opinion may have been *wrong* on this point, and yet *right* on all those great *principles* of rectitude and justice relating to slavery." If Abolition principles are generally adopted at the North, how comes it to pass, that there is no abolition action here, except what is put forth by a few despised fanatics, as they are called? Is there any living faith without works? Can the sap circulate vigorously, and yet neither blossoms put forth nor fruit appear?

Again, I am told on the 7th page, that all Northern Christians believe it is a sin to hold a man in slavery for *"mere purposes of gain"*; as if this was the *whole* abolition principle on this subject. I can assure thee that Abolitionists do not stop here. Our principle is, that *no circumstances can ever justify* a man in holding his fellow man as *property;* it matters not what *motive* he may give for such a monstrous violation of the laws of God. The claim to him as *property* is an annihilation of his right to himself, which is the foundation upon which all his other rights are built. It is high-handed robbery of Jehovah; for He has declared, "All souls are *mine*." For myself, I believe there are hundreds of thousands at the South, who do *not* hold their slaves, by any means, as much "for purposes of gain," as they do from *the lust of power:* this is the passion that reigns triumphant there, and those who do not know this, have much yet to learn. Where, then, is the similarity in our views?

I forbear for the present, and subscribe myself,
Thine, but not in the bonds of gospel Abolitionism,

A. E. Grimké

Letter II. Immediate Emancipation

Brookline, Mass. 6th month, 17th, 1837

Dear Friend: Where didst thou get thy statement of what Abolitionists mean by immediate emancipation? I assure thee, it is a novelty. I never heard any abolitionist say that slaveholders "were physically unable to emancipate their slaves, and of course are not bound to do it," because in some States there are laws which forbid emancipation. This is truly what our opponents affirm; but *we* say that all the laws which sustain the system of slavery are unjust and oppressive—contrary to the fundamental principles of morality, and, therefore, null and void.

We hold, that all the slaveholding laws violate the fundamental principles of the Constitution of the United States. In the preamble of that instrument, the great objects for which it was framed are declared to be "to establish justice, to promote the *general* welfare, and to secure the blessings of *liberty* to us and to our posterity." The slave laws are flagrant violations of these fundamental principles. Slavery subverts justice, promotes the welfare of the *few* to the manifest injury of the many, and robs thousands of the *posterity* of our forefathers of the blessings of liberty. This cannot be denied, for Paxton, a Virginia slaveholder, says, "the *best* blood in Virginia flows in the veins of slaves!" Yes, even the blood of a Jefferson. And every southerner knows, that it is a common thing for the *posterity of our forefathers* to be sold on the vendue tables of the South. *The pos-*

terity of our fathers are advertised in American papers as runaway slaves. Such advertisements often contain expressions like these: "has sometimes passed himself off as a *white* man,"—"has been mistaken for a *white* man,"—"*quite white,* has *straight* hair, and would not readily be taken for a slave," and so forth.

Now, thou wilt perceive, that, so far from thinking that a slaveholder is bound by the *immoral* and *unconstitutional* laws of the Southern States, *we* hold that he is solemnly bound as a man, as an American, to *break* them, and that *immediately* and openly; as much so, as Daniel was to pray, or Peter and John to preach—or every conscientious Quaker to refuse to pay a militia fine, or to train, or to fight. *We* promulgate no such time-serving doctrine as that set forth by thee. When *we* talk of immediate emancipation, we speak that we do mean, and the slaveholders understand us, if thou dost not.

Here, then, is another point in which we are entirely at variance, though the *principles* of abolitionism are "generally adopted by our opposers." What shall I say to these things, but that I am glad thou hast afforded me an opportunity of explaining to thee what *our principles* really are? for I apprehend that *thou* "hast not been sufficiently informed in regard to the feelings and opinions" of abolitionists.

It matters not to me what meaning "Dictionaries or standard writers" may give to immediate emancipation. My Dictionary is the Bible; my standard authors, prophets and apostles. When Jehovah commanded Pharaoh to "let the people go," he meant that they should be *immediately emancipated.* I read his meaning in the judgments which terribly rebuked Pharaoh's repeated and obstinate refusal to "let the people go." I read it in the *universal* emancipation of near 3,000,000 of Israelites in *one awful night.* When the prophet Isaiah commanded the Jews "to loose the bands of wickedness, to undo the heavy burdens, and to let the oppressed go free, and that ye break every yoke," he taught no gradual or partial emancipation, but *immediate, universal emancipation. . . .*

If our fundamental principle is right, that no man can rightfully hold his fellow man as *property,* then it follows, of course, that he is bound *immediately* to cease holding him as such, and that, too, in *violation of the immoral and unconstitutional laws* which have been framed for the express purpose of "turning aside the needy from judgment, and to take away the right from the poor of the people, that widows may be their prey, and that they may rob the fatherless." Every slaveholder is bound to cease to do evil *now,* to emancipate his slaves *now.*

Dost thou ask what I mean by emancipation? I will explain myself in a few words. 1. It is "to reject with indignation, the wild and guilty phantasy, that man can hold *property* in man." 2. To pay the laborer his hire, for he is worthy of it. 3. No longer to deny him the right of marriage, but to "let every man have his own wife, and let every woman have her own husband," as saith the apostle. 4. To let parents have their own children, for they are the gift of the Lord to *them,* and no one else has any right to them. 5. No longer to withhold the advantages of education and the privilege of reading the Bible. 6. To put the slave under the protection of equitable laws.

Now, why should not *all* this be done immediately? Which of these things is to be done next year, and which the year after? and so on. *Our* immediate emancipation means, doing justice and loving mercy *to-day*—and this is what we call upon every slaveholder to do.

I have seen too much of slavery to be a gradualist. I dare not, in view of such a system, tell the slaveholder, that "he is physically unable to emancipate his slaves." I say *he is able* to let the oppressed go free, and that such heaven-daring atrocities ought to *cease now,* henceforth and forever. Oh, my very soul is grieved to find a northern woman thus "sewing pillows under all armholes," framing and fitting soft excuses for the slaveholder's conscience, whilst with the same pen she is *professing* to regard slavery as a sin. "An open enemy is better than such a secret friend."

Hoping that thou mayest soon be emancipated from such inconsistency, I remain until then,

Thine *out* of the bonds of Christian Abolitionism,

A. E. Grimké

Letter V. Christian Character of Abolitionism

Newburyport, 7th month, 8th, 1837

Dear Friend: As an Abolitionist, I thank thee for the portrait thou hast drawn of the character of those with whom I am associated. They deserve all thou hast said in their favor; and I will now endeavor to vindicate those "men of pure morals, of great honesty of purpose, of real benevolence and piety," from some objections thou hast urged against their measures.

"Much evidence," thou sayest, "can be brought to prove that the character and measures of the Abolition Society are not either peaceful or christian in tendency, but that they are in their nature calculated to generate party spirit, denunciation, recrimination, and angry passion." Now I solemnly ask thee, whether the character and measures of our holy Redeemer did not produce exactly the same effects? Why did the Jews lead him to the brow of the hill, that they might cast him down headlong; why did they go about to kill him; why did they seek to lay hands on him, if the tendency of his measures was so very *pacific?* Listen, too, to his own declaration: "I came not to send peace on earth, but a sword"; the effects of which, he expressly said, would be to set the mother against her daughter, and the daughter-in-law against her mother-in-law. The rebukes which he uttered against sin were eminently calculated to produce "recrimination and angry passions," in all who were determined to *cleave* to their sins; and they did produce them even against "him who did no sin, neither was guile found in his mouth." He was called a winebibber, and a glutton, and Beelzebub, and was accused of casting out devils by the prince of the devils. Why, then, protest against our measures as *unchristian,* because they do not smooth the pillow of the poor sinner, and lull his conscience into fatal security? The truth is, the efforts of abolitionists have stirred up the *very same spirit* which the efforts of *all thoroughgoing* reformers have ever done; we consider it a certain proof that the truths we utter are sharper than any two edged sword, and that they are doing the work of conviction in the hearts of our enemies. If it be not so, I have greatly mistaken the character of Christianity. I consider it pre-eminently aggressive; it waits not to be assaulted, but moves on in all the majesty of Truth to *attack* the strongholds of the kingdom of darkness, carries the war into the enemy's camp, and throws its fiery darts into the midst of its embattled hosts. Thou seemest to think, on the contrary, that Christianity is just such a weak, dependent, puerile creature as thou hast described woman to be. In my opinion, thou hast robbed both the one and the other of all their true dignity and glory. Thy descriptions may suit the prevailing christianity of this age, and the general character of woman; and if so, we have great cause for shame and confusion of face.

I feel sorry that thy unkind insinuations against the christian character of Wm. Lloyd Garrison have rendered it necessary for me to speak of him individually, because what I shall feel bound to say of him may, to some like thyself, appear like flattery; but I must do what justice seems so clearly to call for at my hands. Thou sayest that "though he professes a belief in the christian religion, he is an avowed opponent of most of its institutions." I presume thou art here alluding to his views of the ordinances of baptism and the Lord's supper, and the Sabbath. Permit me to remind thee, that in *all* these opinions, he coincides entirely with the Society of Friends, whose views of the Sabbath never were so ably vindicated as by his pen: and the insinuations of hypocrisy which thou hast thrown out against him, may with just as much truth be cast upon *them.* The Quakers think that these are not *christian* institutions, but thou hast assumed it without any proof at all. Thou sayest farther, "The character and spirit of *this man* have for years been exhibited in the Liberator." I have taken that paper for two years, and therefore understand its character, and am compelled to acknowledge, that harsh and severe as is the language often used, I have never seen any expressions which *truth* did not warrant. The abominations of slavery *cannot* be otherwise described. I think Dr. Channing exactly portrayed the character of brother Garrison's writings when he said, "That deep feeling of evils, which is *necessary* to *effectual* conflict with them, which marks *God's most powerful messengers to mankind, cannot* breathe itself in soft and tender accents. The deeply moved soul *will* speak strongly, and *ought* to speak strongly, so as to move and shake nations." It is well for the slave, and well for this country, that such a man was sent to sound the tocsin of alarm before slavery had completed its work of moral death in this "hypocritical nation." Garrison began that discussion of the subject of slavery, which J. Q. Adams declared in his oration, delivered in this town on the 4th inst. "to be the only safety-valve by which the high pressure boiler of slavery could be prevented from a most fatal explosion in this country"; and as a Southerner, I feel truly grateful for all his efforts to redeem not the slave only, but the *slaveholder,* from the polluting influences of such a system of crime.

In his character as a man and a Christian, I have the highest confidence. The assertion thou makest, "that there is to be found in that paper, or *any thing else, any* evidence of his possessing the peculiar traits of Wilberforce, (benignity, gentleness and kind heartedness, I suppose thou meanest,) not even his warmest admirers will maintain," is altogether new to me; and I for one feel ready to declare, that I have never met in any one a more lovely exhibition of these traits of character. . . .

In much haste, I remain thy friend,

A. E. Grimké

Letter VIII. Vindication of Abolitionists

Groton, Mass., 6th month, 1837

Dear Friend: . . . As to Cincinnati having been chosen as the city in which the Philanthropist should be published after the retreat of its editor from Kentucky, thou hast not been "sufficiently informed," for James G. Birney pursued exactly the course which *thou* hast marked out as the most prudent and least offensive. He edited his paper at New Richmond, in Ohio, for nearly three months before he went to Cincinnati, and did not go there until the excitement appeared to have subsided.

And so, thou thinkest that abolitionists are accountable for the outrages which have been committed against them; they are the tempters, and are held responsible by God, as well as the tempted. Wilt thou tell me, who was responsible for the mob which went with swords and staves to take an innocent man before the tribunals of Annas and Pilate, some 1800 years ago? And who was responsible for the uproar at Ephesus, the insurrection at Athens, and the tumults at Lystra and Iconium? Were I a mobocrat, I should want no better excuse than thou hast furnished for such outrages. Wonderful indeed, if, in free America, her citizens cannot *choose* where they will erect their literary institutions and presses, to advocate the self-evident truths of our Declaration of Independence! And still more wonderful, that a New England woman should, *after years of reflection,* deliberately write a book to condemn the advocates of liberty, and plead excuses for a relentless prejudice against her colored brethren and sisters, and for the persecutors of those, who, according to the opinion of a *Southern* member of Congress, are prosecuting "the *only plan* that can ever overthrow slavery at the South." I am glad, *for thy own sake,* that thou hast exculpated abolitionists from the charge of the "deliberate intention of fomenting illegal acts of violence." Would it not have been still better, if thou hadst spared the remarks which rendered such an explanation necessary?

I find that thou wilt not allow of the comparison often drawn between the effects of christianity on the hearts of those who obstinately rejected it, and those of abolitionism on the hearts of people of the present day. Thou sayest, "Christianity is a system of *persuasion,* tending by kind and gentle influences to make men *willing* to leave their sins." Dost thou suppose the Pharisees and Sadducees deemed it was very *kind* and *gentle* in its influences, when our holy Redeemer called them "a generation of vipers," or when He preached that sermon "full of harshness, uncharitableness, rebuke and denunciation," recorded in the xxiii. chapter of Matthew? . . .

Our view of the doctrine of expediency, thou art pleased to pronounce "wrong and very pernicious in its tendency." Expediency is emphatically the doctrine by which the children of this world are wont to guide their steps, whilst the rejection of it as a rule of action exactly accords with the divine injunction, to "walk by faith, *not* by sight." Thy doctrine that "the wisdom and rectitude of a given course depend entirely on the *probabilities of success,*" is not the doctrine of the Bible. According to this principle, how absurd was the conduct of Moses! What probability of success was there that he could move the heart of Pharaoh? None at all; and thus did *he* reason when he said, "Who am *I,* that I should go unto Pharaoh?" And again, "Behold, they will not believe *me,* nor harken unto my voice." The *success* of Moses's mission in persuading the king of Egypt to "let the people go," was not involved in the duty of obedience to the divine command. Neither was the success of Isaiah, Jeremiah, and others of the prophets who were singularly *unsuccessful* in their mission to the Jews. All who see the path of duty plain before them, are bound to walk in that path, end where it may. They then can realize the meaning of the Apostle, when he exhorts Christians to cast all their burden on the Lord, with the promise that He would sustain them. This is walking by *faith,* not by sight. In the work in which abolitionists are engaged, they are compelled to "walk by faith"; they feel called upon to preach the truth in season and out of season, to lift up their voices like a trumpet, to show the people their transgressions and the house of Jacob their sins. The *success* of this mission, *they* have no more to do with, than had Moses and Aaron, Jeremiah or Isaiah, with that of theirs. Whether the South will be saved by Anti-Slavery efforts, is not a question for us to settle—and in some of our hearts, the *hope of its salvation has utterly gone out.* All nations have been punished for oppression, and why should ours escape? Our light, and high professions, and the age in which we live, convict us not only of enormous oppression, but of the vilest hypocrisy. It may be that the rejection of the truth which we are now pouring in upon the South, may be the final filling up of their iniquities, just previous to the bursting of God's exterminating thunders over the Sodoms and Gomorrahs, the Admahs and Zeboims of America. The *result* of our labors is hidden from our eyes; whether the preaching of Anti-Slavery truth is to be a savor of life unto life, or of death unto death to this nation, we know not; and we have no more to do with it, than had the Apostle Paul, when he preached Christ to the people of his day.

If American Slavery goes down in blood, it will but verify the declarations of those who uphold it. A committee of the North Carolina Legislature acknowledged this to an English Friend ten years ago. Jefferson more than once uttered his gloomy forebodings; and the Legislators of Virginia, in 1832, declared that if the opportunity of escape, through the means of emancipation, were rejected, "though they might *save themselves,* they would rear their posterity to the business of the dagger and the torch." I have myself known several families to leave the South, solely from a fear of insurrection; and this twelve and fourteen years ago, long before any Anti-Slavery efforts were made in this country. And yet, I presume, *if* through the cold-hearted apathy and obstinate opposition of the North, the South should become strengthened in her desperate determination to hold on to her outraged victims, until they are goaded to despair, and if the Lord in his wrath pours out the vials of his vengeance upon the slave States, why then, Abolitionists will have to bear all the blame. Thou hast drawn a frightful picture of the final issue of Anti-Slavery efforts, as thou are pleased to call it; but none of these things move me, for with just as much truth mayest thou point to the land of Egypt, blackened by God's avenging fires, and exclaim, "Behold the issue of Moses's mission." Nay, verily! See in that smoking, and blood-drenched house of bondage, and consequences of oppression, disobedience, and an obstinate rejection of truth, and light, and love. What had Moses to do with those judgment plagues, except to lift his rod? And if the South soon finds her winding sheet in garments rolled in blood, it will *not* be because of what the North has told her, but because, like impenitent Egypt, she hardened her heart against it, whilst the voices of some of her own children were crying in agony, "O! that thou hadst known, even thou, in this thy day, the things which belong to thy peace; but now they are hid from thine eyes."

Thy friend,

A. E. Grimké

Letter X. "The Tendency of the Age towards Emancipation" Produced by Abolition Doctrines

. . . Thou seemest to think that the North has *no right* to rebuke the South, and assumest the ground that Abolitionists are the enemies of the South. We say, we have the right, and mean to exercise it. I believe that every northern Legislature has a right, and ought to use the right, to send a solemn remonstrance to every southern Legislature on the subject of slavery. Just as much right as the South has to send up a remonstrance against our free presses, free pens, and free tongues. Let the North follow her example; but, instead of asking her to enslave her subjects, entreat her to *free* them. The South may pretend *now,* that we have no right to interfere, because it suits her convenience to say so; but a few years ago (1820), we find that our Vice President, R. M. Johnson, in his speech on the Missouri question, was amazed at the "cold insensibility, the eternal apathy towards the slaves in the District of Columbia," which was exhibited by *northern* men though they had ocular demonstrations of slavery. *Then* the South wondered *we did not interfere with slavery*—and *now* she says we have no right to interfere.

I find, on the 57th p. a false assertion with regard to Abolitionists. After showing the folly of our rejecting the worldly doctrine of expediency, so excellent in thy view, thou then sayest that we say, the reason why we do not go to the South is, that we should be murdered. Now, if there are any halfhearted Abolitionists, who are thus recreant to the high and holy principle of "Duty is ours, and events are God's," then I must leave such to explain their own inconsistences; but that this is the reason assigned by the Society, as a body, I never have seen nor believed. So far from it, that I have invariably heard those who understood the principles of the Anti-Slavery Society best, *deny* that it was a duty to go to the South, *not* because they would be killed, but because the *North was guilty,* and therefore ought to be labored with *first.* They took exactly the same view of the subject, which was taken by the southern friend of mine to whom I have already alluded. "Until northern women, (said she,) do their duty on the subject of slavery, *southern* women cannot be expected to do theirs." I therefore utterly deny this charge. Such may be the opinion of a few, but it is not and cannot be proved to be a principle of action in the Anti-Slavery Society. The fact is, we need no excuse for not going to the South, so long as the North is as deeply involved in the guilt of slavery as she is, and as blind to her duty.

One word with regard to these remarks: "Before the Abolition movements commenced, both northern and southern men expressed their views freely at the South." This, also, I deny, because, as a southerner, *I know* that *I* never could express my views freely on the abominations of slavery, without exciting anger, even in professors of religion. It is true, "the *dangers, evils* and *mischiefs* of slavery" could be, and were discussed at the South and the North. Yes, we might talk as much as we pleased about *these,* as long as we viewed slavery as a *misfortune* to the *slaveholder,* and talked of "the dangers, evils and mischiefs of slavery" to *him,* and pitied *him* for having had such a "sad inheritance entailed upon him." But could any man or woman ever "express their views freely" on the SIN of slavery at the South? I say, never! Could they express their views freely as to the dangers, mischiefs and evils of slavery to the *poor suffering slave?* No, never! It was only whilst the *slaveholder* was regarded as *an unfortunate sufferer,* and sympathized with *as such,* that he was willing to talk, and be talked to, on this "delicate subject." Hence we find, that as soon as *he* is addressed as a *guilty oppressor,* why then he is in a phrensy of passion. As soon as we set before him the dangers, and evils, and mischiefs of slavery to *the down-trodden victims of his oppression,* O then! the slaveholder storms and raves like a maniac. Now look at this view of the subject: as a southerner, I know it is the only correct one.

With regard to the discussion of "the subject of slavery, in the legislative halls of the South," if thou hast read these debates, thou certainly must know that they did not touch on the SIN of slavery at all; they were wholly confined to "the dangers, evils and mischiefs of slavery" to the *unfortunate slaveholder.* What did the discussion in the Virginia legislature result in? In the *rejection of every* plan of emancipation, and in the passage of an act which they believed would give additional permanency to the institution, whilst it divested it of its dangers, by removing the free people of color to Liberia; for which purpose they voted $20,000, but took very good care to provide, "that no slave to be thereafter emancipated should have the benefit of the appropriation," so fearful were they, lest masters might avail themselves of this scheme of expatriation to manumit their slaves. The Maryland scheme is altogether based on the principle of banishment and oppression. The colored people were to be "got rid of," for the benefit of their lordly oppressors—*not* set free from the noble principles of justice and mercy to *them.* If Abolitionists have put a stop to all *such* discussions of slavery, I, for one, do most heartily rejoice at it. The fact is, the South is enraged, because we have exposed her horrible hypocrisy to the world. We have torn off the mask, and brought to light the hidden things of darkness.

Thy Friend,

A. E. Grimké

Wendell Phillips

PHILOSOPHY OF THE ABOLITION MOVEMENT

Aroused when he heard the attorney general of Massachusetts expressing satisfaction at the death of Elijah Lovejoy, Wendell Phillips (1811–1884) thereupon launched a career of vitriolic oratory against slavery and those willing to tolerate it. His course deeply offended most of his fellow Boston patricians. Phillips was loyal to William Lloyd Garrison in the internal divisions of the abolitionist movement, but he did not agree with all Garrisonian positions, notably not with nonresistance. When Garrison urged dissolution of the American Anti-Slavery Society in 1865, Phillips became its president and continued to agitate on behalf of Negroes. He entered many other reform movements during the post-Civil War years. The following extracts from one of Phillips's many addresses to Boston abolitionists present a summary and justification of the course followed by advocates of immediatism. The speech has the tone of one vindicated, since by 1852 antislavery measures were widely embraced by political and religious leaders who had scorned them in the 1830s.

In 1831, Mr. Garrison commenced a paper advocating the doctrine of immediate emancipation. He had against him the thirty thousand churches and all the clergy of the country,—its wealth, its commerce, its press. In 1831, what was the state of things? There was the most entire ignorance and apathy on the slave question. If men knew of the existence of slavery, it was only as a part of picturesque Virginia life. No one preached, no one talked, no one wrote about it. No whisper of it stirred the surface of the political sea. The Church heard of it occasionally, when some colonization agent asked [for] funds to send the blacks to Africa. Old school-books tainted with some antislavery selections had passed out of use, and new ones were compiled to suit the times. Soon as any dissent from the prevailing faith appeared, every one set himself to crush it. The pulpits preached at it; the press denounced it; mobs tore down houses, threw presses into the fire and the stream, and shot the editors; religious conventions tried to smother it; parties arrayed themselves against it. Daniel Webster boasted in the Senate, that he had never introduced

From Wendell Phillips, *Speeches, Lectures, and Letters* (Boston: Lee and Shepard, 1894), pp. 148–153.

the subject of slavery to that body, and never would. Mr. Clay, in 1839, makes a speech for the Presidency, in which he says, that to discuss the subject of slavery is moral treason, and that no man has a right to introduce the subject into Congress. Mr. Benton, in 1844, laid down his platform, and he not only denies the right, but asserts that he never has and never will discuss the subject. Yet Mr. Clay, from 1839 down to his death, hardly made a remarkable speech of any kind, except on slavery. Mr. Webster, having indulged now and then in a little easy rhetoric, as at Niblo's and elsewhere, opens his mouth in 1840, generously contributing his aid to both sides, and stops talking about it only when death closes his lips. Mr. Benton's six or eight speeches in the United States Senate have all been on the subject of slavery in the Southwestern section of the country, and form the basis of whatever claim he has to the character of a statesman, and he owes his seat in the next Congress somewhat, perhaps, to antislavery pretensions! The Whig and Democratic parties pledged themselves just as emphatically against the antislavery discussion,—against agitation and free speech. These men said: "It sha'n't be talked about, it won't be talked about!" These are *your statesmen!*—men who understand the present, that is, and mold the future! The man who understands his own time, and whose genius molds the future to his views, he is a statesman, is he not? These men devoted themselves to banks, to the tariff, to internal improvements, to constitutional and financial questions. They said to slavery:

> *Back! no entrance here! We pledge ourselves against you. And then there came up a humble printer-boy, who whipped them into the traces, and made them talk, like Hotspur's starling, nothing* but *slavery. He scattered all these gigantic shadows,—tariff, bank, constitutional questions, financial questions,—and slavery, like the colossal head in Walpole's romance, came up and filled the whole political horizon! [Enthusiastic applause.] Yet you must remember he is not a statesman; he is a "fanatic." He has no discipline . . . ; he does not understand the "discipline that is essential to victory"!*

This man did not understand his own time,—he did not know what the future was to be,—he was not able to shape it,—he had no "prudence,"—he had no "foresight"! Daniel Webster says, "I have never introduced this subject, and never will,"—and died brokenhearted because he had not been able to talk enough about it. Benton says, "I will never speak of slavery," and lives to break with his party on this issue! Mr. Clay says it is "moral treason" to introduce the subject into Congress, and lives to see Congress turned into an antislavery debating-society, to suit the purpose of one "too powerful individual"!

These were statesmen, mark you! Two of them have gone to their graves covered with eulogy; and our national stock of eloquence is all insufficient to describe how profound and far-reaching was the sagacity of Daniel Webster! Remember who it was that said, in 1831, "I am in earnest,—I will not equivocate,—I will not excuse,—I will not retreat a single inch,—*and I will be heard!*" [Repeated cheers.] That speaker has lived twenty-two years, and the complaint of twenty-three millions of people is, "Shall we never hear of anything but slavery?" [Cheers.] I heard Dr. Kirk, of Boston, say in his own pulpit, when he returned from London,—where he had been as a representative to the "Evangelical Alliance,"—"I went up to London, and they asked me what I thought of the question of immediate emancipation. They examined us all. Is an American never to travel anywhere in the world but men will throw this troublesome question in his face?" Well, it is all *his* fault [pointing to Mr. Garrison]. [Enthusiastic cheers.]

Now, when we come to talk of statesmanship, of sagacity in choosing time and measures, of endeavor, by proper means, to right the public mind, of keen insight into the present and potent sway over the future, it seems to me that the Abolitionists, who have taken —whether for good or for ill, whether to their discredit or to their praise—this country by the four corners, and shaken it until you can hear nothing but slavery, whether you travel in railroad or steamboat, whether you enter the hall of legislation or read the columns of a newspaper,—it seems to me that such men may point to the present aspect of the nation, to their originally avowed purpose, to the pledges and efforts of all your great men against them, and then let you determine to which side the credit of sagacity and statesmanship belongs. Napoleon busied himself, at St. Helena, in showing how Wellington ought not to have conquered at Waterloo. The world has never got time to listen to the explanation. Sufficient for it that the Allies entered Paris. In like manner, it seems hardly the province of a defeated Church and State to deny the skill of measures by which they have been conquered.

It may sound strange to some, this claim for Mr. Garrison of a profound statesmanship. Men have heard him styled a mere fanatic so long, that they are incompetent to judge him fairly. "The phrases men are accustomed," says Goethe, "to repeat incessantly, end by becoming convictions, and ossify the organs of intelligence." I cannot accept you, therefore, as my jury. I appeal from Festus to Caesar; from the prejudice of our streets to the common sense of the world, and to your children.

Every thoughtful and unprejudiced mind must see that such an evil as slavery will yield only to the most radical treatment. If you consider the work we have to do, you will not think us needlessly aggressive, or that we dig down unnecessarily deep in laying the foundations of our enterprise. A money power of two thousand millions of dollars, as the prices of slaves now range, held by a small body of able and desperate men; that body raised into a political aristocracy by special constitutional provisions; cotton, the product of slave labor, forming the basis of our whole foreign commerce, and the commercial class thus subsidized; the press bought up, the pulpit reduced to vassalage, the heart of the common people chilled by a bitter prejudice against the black race; our leading men bribed, by ambition, either to silence or open hostility;—in such a land, on what shall an Abolitionist rely? On a few cold prayers, mere lip-service, and never from the heart? On a church resolution, hidden often in its records, and meant only as a decent cover for servility in daily practice? On political parties, with their superficial influence at best, and seeking ordinarily only to use existing prejudices to the best advantage? Slavery has deeper root here than any aristocratic institution has in Europe; and politics is but the common pulse-beat, of which revolution is the fever-spasm. Yet we have seen European aristocracy survive storms which seemed to reach down to the primal strata of European life. Shall we, then, trust to mere politics, where even revolution has failed? How shall the stream rise above its fountain? Where shall our church organizations or parties get strength to attack their great parent and molder, the Slave Power? Shall the thing formed say to him that formed it, Why hast thou made me thus? The old jest of one who tried to lift himself in his own basket, is but a tame picture of the man who imagines that, by working solely through existing sects and parties, he can destroy slavery. Mechanics say nothing but an earthquake strong enough to move all Egypt, can bring down the Pyramids.

Experience has confirmed these views. The Abolitionists who have acted on them have a "short method" with all unbelievers. They have but to point to their own success, in contrast with every other man's failure. To waken the nation to its real state, and chain it to the consideration of this one duty, is half the work. So much we have done. Slavery has been made the question of this generation. To startle the South to madness, so that every step she takes, in her blindness, is one step more toward ruin, is much. This we have done. Witness Texas and the Fugitive Slave Law. To have elaborated for the nation the only plan of redemption, pointed out the only exodus from this "sea of troubles," is much. This we claim to have done in our motto of *immediate, unconditional emancipation on the soil.* The closer any statesmanlike mind looks into the question, the more favor our plan finds with it. The Christian asks fairly of the infidel, "If this religion be not from God, how do you explain its triumph, and the history of the first three centuries?" Our question is similar. If our agitation has not been wisely planned and conducted, explain for us the history of the last twenty years! Experience is a safe light to walk by, and he is not a rash man who expects success in future from the same means which have secured it in times past.

III THE TURN TO POLITICS

Aileen S. Kraditor

POLITICAL ACTION

In contrast to Dwight Dumond, Aileen S. Kraditor has reasserted the centrality of William Lloyd Garrison in the antislavery movement. In contrast to Garrison's most recent biographers, she defends his tolerance, suggesting that Garrison did not seek to impose his radical social and religious views on other abolitionists. This selection discusses the conflict over abolitionist involvement in politics, which was among the causes that split the American Anti-Slavery Society in 1840. Garrison remained as president of the old organization. Some of his opponents went into the new American and Foreign Anti-Slavery Society, some into the Liberty Party (founded in 1839), and some into both. Garrison and his followers were more willing to discuss political tactics and questions of expediency than historians have usually recognized. The Garrisonians remained committed, however, to a revolutionary reconstituting of American society. Professor Kraditor has undertaken a series of studies of American reform. Besides her book on abolitionists, she has published two volumes on American feminism.

The failure to distinguish between Garrison's opinions as a nonresistant and the tactics he thought the abolitionist movement (as a coalition of adherents of many philosophies) ought to pursue has led to an understandable confusion among historians who discuss his views on political tactics. Noting his repudiation of all forceful government and, after 1842, his denunciation of the United States Constitution, they have dismissed his advocacy of certain types of political action as evidence of muddy thinking and have paid too little attention to the theory underlying that advocacy.

The starting point for his discussion of political action was his conception of the abolitionist movement as a broad coalition. Just as he would not exclude from the AASS any abolitionist whose philosophy differed from his, so he could, without prescribing modes of action, theorize about the sort of political tactics proper for an abolitionist who shared little with him but the principles of the society's constitution—the sinfulness of slavery and the duty of immediate emancipation. Given the average abolitionist's acceptance of the United States government and the propriety of voting, what types of political action, Garrison might ask, were consistent with that abolitionist's principles? Second, which among those tactics was the most effective way of fighting slavery in the political field?

Garrison's answers to the first question coincided with those of the majority of political abolitionists. That is, the abolitionist could with propriety adopt the "scattering" policy, meaning he could cast a write-in vote for an individual not on the ballot, to demonstrate his dissatisfaction with all the regular nominees; in a thoroughly abolitionized district, these scattering votes could, he thought, represent enough strength to force concessions from the regular parties at the next election. The same effect could be produced by temporary nominations by abolitionists. Or, the abolitionist could work actively as part of a pressure group to force a major party to take acceptable positions and nominate antislavery candidates on the local level, while he would of course refuse to vote for its presidential candidates as long as they were acceptable to the party's Southern wing. Eventually, many abolitionized local parties might force a change in the party's national character. The scattering policy could be combined with this second mode of action. Still another possibility was for the abolitionist to join with others to organize a third party. Garrison and most of his group never condemned the Liberty party as wrong in principle. They condemned it when they answered the second question, that concerning the effectiveness of each of the tactics that were in principle acceptable.

> *We admit [wrote Garrison] that the* mode *of political action, to be pursued by abolitionists, is not strictly a question of principle, but rather one of sound expediency. We have never opposed the formation of a third party as a measure inherently wrong, but have always contended that the abolitionists have as clear and indisputable right to band themselves together politically for the attainment of their great object, as those of their fellow-citizens who call themselves whigs or democrats. . . . But every reflecting mind may easily perceive, that to disregard the dictates of sound expediency may often prove as injurious to an enterprise as to violate principle. It is solely on this ground that we oppose what is called the "liberty party." We believe it is highly inexpedient, and therefore not the best mode to advance the antislavery cause.*

Since Garrison the nonresistant opposed all parties on principle so long as the government was based on force, he could not prefer one party to another or condemn one more than another on any but expedient grounds. It would also follow that to the abolitionist who was not a nonresistant there could, he believed, be no principled objection to a third party.

The disagreements on political tactics between the radicals and Libertymen, then, hinged, in Garrison's opinion, on the question of expediency, not principle. They agreed that the two parties were corrupt and the servants of the slave power, but they proposed different ways of reforming them. According to the radicals, the parties were corrupt because the people were. Only a reformed public opinion could reform the parties in any meaningful, lasting way. Who, they asked, would join the third party? Committed abolitionists. Would they be more useful there or in their old parties? If their task was to convert the masses of voters, they would be more effective if they remained where those masses were.[1] In an abolitionized district both parties would have to make concessions to keep their own abolitionist members from defecting, and a third party, by withdrawing those members from both major parties, would permit them to continue to ignore the interests of the slave. But if abolitionists adopted the scattering policy and demonstrated their refusal to vote for unacceptable candidates and their willingness to cross party lines to vote for abolitionists despite differences on other issues that separated the parties, they could constitute a real balance of power between them. A third party would be a less effective instrument for influencing public opinion than agitation by the AASS and by abolitionists voting as individuals. And once public opinion had been converted, the major parties would, for the sake of votes, reflect the change in their platforms and nominations, and a third party would be unnecessary. This argument was urged whether the third party was of the one-idea or broad-platform type.

The fullest exposition of the Garrisonian theory is in an imaginary

[1] This may seem inconsistent with the come-outer principle defended by Garrisonians (especially Maria Weston Chapman), who stressed the educational value of bearing witness to an ideal by ostentatiously withdrawing from institutions that trampled on it. Again it should be pointed out that these tactical suggestions were intended to apply only to those abolitionists who did not subscribe to nonresistance, come-outerism, and other aspects of Garrison's radical creed, those who believed in working within the framework of the United States government.

dialogue, by Lydia Maria Child, between A and B. In response to A's inquiry about the position of the AASS on political action, B explains:

> *[It] stands on precisely the same principles that it did the first year of its formation. Its object was to change public opinion on the subject of slavery, by the persevering utterance of truth. This change they expected would show itself in a thousand different forms:—such as conflict and separation in churches; new arrangements in colleges and schools; new customs in stages and cars; and new modifications of policy in the political parties of the day. The business of antislavery was, and is, to purify the* fountain, *whence all these streams flow; if it turns aside to take charge of any* one *of the streams, however important, it is obvious enough that the whole work must retrograde; for, if the fountain be not kept pure, no one of the streams will flow with clear water. But just so sure as the fountain is taken proper care of, the character of all the streams* must *be influenced thereby. We might form ourselves into a railroad society, to furnish cars with the same conveniences for all complexions; but we feel that we are doing a far more effectual work, so as to change popular opinion, that there will be no* need *of a separate train of cars. We might expend all our funds and energies in establishing abolition colleges; but we feel sure that we have the power in our hands to abolitionize* all *colleges.*

In answer to a later question, B contends that before the Liberty party was organized, both parties in Massachusetts were afraid of abolitionists and hence willing to grant their requests; this is no longer so. A: "But those legislators were not genuine abolitionists, or they would not have refused concessions once the pressure was removed."

> *B: Those men, let me tell you, did the work of sound antislavery; and in doing it, got imbued more or less with antislavery sentiment, in spite of themselves. The machinery of a third political party may send into Congress, or the halls of state legislation, a few individuals, who are antislavery to the back-bone. But could one Alvan Stewart do as much for our cause in Congress, as twenty of Joshua R. Giddings? Fifty men, who have a strong motive for obliging the abolitionists, could surely do more for our cause, in such a position, than merely two or three radical abolitionists. I too want to see all our legislators antislavery; but when that time comes, there will most obviously be no need of a distinct abolition party; and in order to bring about that time, we must diligently exert moral influence to sway* all *parties. . . .*

And why, continues B, assume that the Liberty party will be comprised of more disinterested men? Many are joining it who never were abolitionists. In one county, Democrats join temporarily, to defeat a Whig; in another county, Whigs join to defeat a Democrat. Are these recruits more reliable than major-party legislators who are willing to give abolitionists what they ask? Many Libertymen are sincere abolitionists, but "by the natural laws of attraction, their party will draw around them the selfish and the ambitious." If party machinery is so mischievous, asks A, how can you work with Whigs and Democrats? B: "By adhering closely to moral influence, we work *through* both parties, but not *with* them. They do our work; we do not *theirs.* We are simply the atmosphere that makes the quicksilver rise or fall."

Later A remarks that the South dreads antislavery at the ballot box more than anywhere else, and B replies:

> *I never doubted that political action would be a powerful engine for the overthrow of slavery.—The only question between you and the American Society seems to be, whether the speediest and most extensive political effect would be produced by the* old *scheme of holding the balance between the two parties; or the* new *scheme of forming a distinct party. I apprehend what the slaveholders would like least of all things, would be to see* both *the great political parties consider it for their interest to nominate abolitionists; and this* would *be the case if antislavery voters would only be consistent and firm.*

A: "But they will not be consistent and firm; under the old plan they always turned aside to vote for a Harrison or a Van Buren. B:

> *If that is so, will the Liberty party keep them from doing so? Will a two-thirds abolitionized Democrat, who has joined to defeat a Whig, vote Liberty when his ballot is needed by his own party? An antislavery member of an old party will be more reliable if his party interests coincide with his abolitionism and if his work as an abolitionist will mean an increase in the number of antislavery votes for his own party. But you remove that stimulus when you organize a separate party: you force him to give up his party position on all issues besides slavery. And the success of such a third party would be its undoing, for if it gains enough power to influence legislation in a state, one Libertyman will be protariff and another antitariff, and they will be swallowed by their former parties again.*

A suggests that perhaps these lawmakers will be willing to sacrifice those other considerations for the sake of antislavery. In that case, B replies, their constituents will complain that their other interests are neglected and will vote the legislators out of office. And so we have come back to moral influence as the legitimate work of an abolitionist. But, asks A, can we not exert moral influence and work for the Liberty party at the same time? B: "In practice, things have not worked out that way; Libertymen now talk scornfully of moral influence." A: "But now that the Liberty party exists, should we not vote for its candidates?" B: "That is the bait that has hooked half their numbers. . . . *Moral* influence dies under *party* action."

The radicals decried what they believed was the tendency of some to exaggerate the significance of legal enactments; when William Goodell, for example, argued that slavery was the creature of law and that its abolition was "nothing more nor less than the repeal of these slave laws," they replied that slavery was "the creature of avarice and love of domination" and was "only *sanctified* and regulated" by law. Wrote Rogers of New Hampshire:

> *The best and utmost that political movements—the constitutions, enactments, and decisions could effect for the slave, is to translate him into that anomaly in a* christian republic, *called a "free nigger." New Hampshire has thus transmuted him by the magic force of its politics. What is the liberty of a New Hampshire emancipated colored man? It barely qualifies him to pass muster as a candidate for the mercy of the Colonization Society. . . . New York has abolished slavery by* law; *yet it is as much as a colored man's life is worth to live in her cities. . . . Slavery has been* legally *abolished in half the states of the Union, and the best they can do for the fugitive slave is to give him race ground to Canada before the Southern bloodhounds and for the freed man of color is to let in upon him the gray hounds of colonization.*

Garrison and those who thought like him insisted that to abolish the law would be useless without transformation of the spirit that the law reflected.

The advocates of a third party, wrote Oliver Johnson, have betrayed a degree of impatience with the progress of the cause. They should note that in England the abolitionists continued to hold the balance of power without organizing their own party, until they won. It may be replied, he continued, that the parties in the United States are more subservient to the slave power than they were in England. True, he conceded, but that merely proves that the people here are more corrupted by slavery than were the English; and will a third party counteract that corruption and purify their hearts?

> *All attempts to abolish slavery by legislation before the people of the country are converted to antislavery principles must of necessity be unsuccessful. A political party is not needed as a means of converting the people, and when they are converted, such a party will of course be unnecessary. When we say that efforts to abolish slavery by legislation must for the present be necessarily unsuccessful, we do not mean to intimate that such efforts should not constantly and vigorously be made; but only that the want of success should be attributed to the right cause, and not lead to the adoption of a measure which is at best of doubtful utility.*

The Libertymen mistook "the right cause" when they contended that the major parties were incorrigibly proslavery and from that contention deduced the need for a third party. The fundamental principles of both parties, said the Garrisonians, were laudable. The Democratic creed preached liberty, reform, and equal rights; the Whig creed, stability, supremacy of law, and security of property; between them the rights of the people and the interests of property were championed. If not for the slave power, temporarily dominating and perverting both, abolitionists who accepted the legitimacy of the government could adhere to one or the other without violating their antislavery principles. Abolitionist agitation, then, must aim to bring both parties back to their own principles, to make the leaders of both act consistently with their own professions. Expecting less from organized political action than did the Libertymen, Garrison could not see a political party, regardless of what it called itself, as the insurance of an office-holder's fidelity to the cause. That role he assigned to unorganized (but infinitely more coercive) public opinion.

Running through all the tactical thinking of Garrison and his followers is an emphasis on what today would be called "building a constituency." Their political theory may be seen as a part of their general theory of agitation, a corollary of which was their conception of the AASS itself as no more than a propaganda center, from which abolitionists with a wide variety of philosophies and affiliations would go, armed with agitational weapons to use in whatever parties, churches, or other organizations they chose to belong to. Without public opinion on its side, the movement could accomplish nothing; with public opinion, it could transform all organizations dependent on public opinion into tactical weapons for the cause.

Garrison did not see political action as a way of achieving his goals by parliamentary means. Those goals were far too radical—far too subversive of the fundamental arrangements of American society—to be realized by the vote of a few hundred men, including slaveholders and their allies, in the Capitol in Washington, even if a majority of them had been willing to so vote, which was inconceivable. It would, therefore, be an oversimplification to say that he refused to engage in political action because such action would represent participation in a government whose legitimacy he, as a nonresistant, denied, although this purely abstract formulation was sufficient for the "ultraists" whose spokesman he was. But what of the principles that should, in Garrison's opinion, guide the tactics of those abolitionists who did not repudiate the coercive United States government? One gets the impression from his writings on the subject that he at least sensed the practical danger that other radicals throughout American history have sometimes encountered: that *ad hoc* alliances for partial ends may under certain circumstances strengthen the hegemony of the enemy by legitimizing the institutions, and the ideological justifications of those institutions, by means of which the enemy exercises his hegemony. The radical who recognizes this danger (or who at least senses it, as I think Garrison did) may form such alliances, but on his own terms, with explicit safeguards against his participation being used to foster illusions that political action is more than a temporary tactic for very limited purposes; he will, that is, make it clear that he is using the political machinery and that it is not using him. It is in the light of Garrison's partial insight into this principle that we should interpret his insistence, as against the Libertymen, that the major parties were redeemable; they were redeemable not as parties but as the politically organized constituencies among which nonradical abolitionists could agitate for abolition. . . .

Discussing Garrison's denunciation of both candidates in the 1836 presidential election, John L. Thomas remarks:

> *Faced with a decision that involved choosing the lesser of two evils—a cardinal rule in democratic politics—Garrison refused to take the step which he believed an abandonment of principle. In thus committing his followers to a boycott of elections he was in effect challenging the democratic process.*[2]

I believe a more pertinent comment on Garrison's policy is to be found in George Santayana's *Character and Opinion in the United States,* in a passage that does not refer specifically to the abolitionists. "The practice of English liberty" (which in this context means the same thing as Thomas's "democratic process") "presupposes," writes Santayana,

> *two things: that all concerned are fundamentally unanimous, and that each has a plastic nature which he is willing to modify. If fundamental unanimity is lacking and all are not making in the same general direction, there can be no honest cooperation, no satisfying compromise. . . . To put things to a vote, and to accept unreservedly the decision of the majority, are points essential to the English system; but they would be absurd if fundamental agreement were not presupposed. Every decision that the majority could conceivably arrive at must leave it still possible for the minority to live and prosper, even if not exactly in the way they wished. . . . In a hearty and sound democracy all questions at issue must be minor matters; fundamentals must have been silently agreed upon and taken for granted when the democracy arose. To leave a decision to the majority is like leaving it to chance—a fatal procedure unless one is willing to have it either way.*[3]

When Garrison proclaimed the choice between two proslavery candidates and parties in 1836 a choice between evils, he was challenging not the democratic process but the fundamental consensus within which that particular democratic process took place. His many statements, quoted elsewhere in this book, on the differences between the Whig and Democratic parties on issues other than

[2] *The Liberator: William Lloyd Garrison*, pp. 220–221. Cf. Barrington Moore, Jr., *Social Origins of Dictatorship and Democracy:* "In the circumstances of midnineteenth-century American society, any peaceful solution, any victory of moderation, good sense, and democratic process, would have had to be a reactionary solution" (pp. 131–132), and "An attitude, a frame of mind, without a realistic analysis and program is not enough to make democracy work even if a majority share this outlook. Consensus by itself means little; it depends what the consensus is about" (p. 139).

[3] New York, 1920, pp. 205–206.

slavery, demonstrate that he would have been willing to function within a democratic process that had silently agreed upon antislavery and nonresistance fundamentals.

When the fundamentals are agreed upon, a choice made within the democratic process is not between the lesser and the greater evils (both bad), but between the lesser and the greater goods (both acceptable), with the successive choices, in the eyes of the reformer, leading the society step by step closer to an ideal approximation of the fundamental principles silently agreed upon at the start. But what of the radical, as opposed to the reformer—the radical to whom the fundamentals silently agreed upon are qualitatively evil and to whom a quantitative advance toward realization of those principles is at best irrelevant and at worst a betrayal of his cause? The fundamentals, Santayana points out, are never put to a vote, because the opposing sides are not "willing to have it either way." In the antebellum United States slavery was one of those fundamentals, and in fact slavery was not abolished by the democratic process, for by the middle of the century it could never have been put to a vote. When antislavery was, in Elkins's word, "democratized" in a major part of the country, revolution became inevitable—"revolution," that is, in the literal sense of a change in the fundamentals, and not necessarily in the sense of a violent overthrow—for the fundamentals were no longer silently agreed upon, and a new consensus had to come into existence.

Thomas contends that Garrison "more than any other American of his time . . . was responsible for the atmosphere of moral absolutism which caused the Civil War and freed the slave."[4] If Garrison helped to destroy the antebellum consensus (which remains to be proved by a study of the abolitionist movement's impact on public opinion), it was not because he helped to make Northern public opinion reject compromise and gradual abolition but because he helped to make Northern public opinion actively antislavery. There is no reason to believe that in the 1850s Northern public opinion, including that of the majority of abolitionists and Garrison himself, would have rejected gradual emancipation procedures on the basis of an antislavery consensus; there is ample evidence that most

[4] Thomas, *The Liberator: William Lloyd Garrison*, p. 4.

slaveowners would have, for it was not immediate abolition they opposed, but abolition on any terms. The point, then, is not that Garrison created an atmosphere of moral absolutism, but that the choice which the nation faced was objectively between absolutely antagonistic moral systems. And Garrison's real choice was not between democratic and undemocratic, or fanatical and reasonable, agitation; it was between antislavery agitation and silence.

Frederick Douglass

OUR POSITION IN THE PRESENT PRESIDENTIAL CANVASS

Born a slave in Maryland, Frederick Douglass taught himself to read and write and escaped to freedom in 1838 at the age of twenty-one. Drawn to the abolitionist movement by his passionate opposition to the system that had enslaved him, he gained prominence through his remarkable oratorical abilities and his autobiography, published in 1845. He lived for a time in Great Britain, but returned to America in 1847 and founded an antislavery newspaper in Rochester, New York. By editing a periodical, he hoped to demonstrate that "the Negro was too much of a man to be a chattel."

As a close follower of Garrison, Douglass had agreed that no abolitionist should vote or hold office, that the Constitution was proslavery, and disunion justified. But Rochester was the leading center of Liberty Party activity, and there Douglass gradually came to believe that the Constitution, correctly interpreted, was antislavery and that abolitionists should enter politics. His new positions brought on a vituperative feud with old friends in the American Anti-Slavery Society, especially Garrison himself (though Douglass remained a member of the society). Douglass's instinct for political tactics led him to justify certain compromises and the practice of forming political coalitions. In the editorial of 1852 that follows, he upholds the "Free Democracy" (the Free Soil Party under a new name). He continued his support of John P. Hale, the Free Soil candidate for President, even though one faction of the Liberty Party nominated a candidate on a stronger antislavery platform. Later, Douglass was to support an even broader coalition, the Republican Party.

Frederick Douglass' Paper, September 10, 1852, as reprinted in Philip S. Foner, *The Life and Writings of Frederick Douglass*, II (New York, 1950), pp. 211–219.

We shall, perhaps, surprise some and grieve others when we declare now, our fixed purpose to support with whatever power we possess, John P. Hale for President and George W. Julian for Vice-President of the United States—the candidates unanimously nominated by the "Free Democratic" party at Pittsburgh. We promise to the free Democracy the aid of our pen, voice and vote, and that if their candidates are not elected it will be from no fault of ours. This pledge, however, is given with the distinct understanding, that, should these gentlemen in accepting their nomination write letters of a compromising character, we shall drop them and take up such as are already in the field, by the action of a small division of the Liberty Party.

That this course of ours will be condemned in some quarters, and by some persons with whom we have of late acted, we have no doubt. Valuing the good opinion of these friends, and happy to find ourselves at agreement with them, we beg to state with some distinctness, and at length the reasons for thus taking our stand with the "Free Democracy." Convinced ourselves of the wisdom of this policy, we find it easy to believe that others can be so convinced.

In dealing with this subject we cannot address ourselves to any such as have made up their minds to vote for either General Scott, or for *General* Pierce. These gentlemen are out of the controversy for the present. We address ourselves to voting abolitionists, those who hold themselves bound to carry their moral convictions into the government, and to do all they can to establish "an every-way-righteous civil government." *"We speak unto wise men; judge ye what we say."*

1. *Slavery* is, beyond all comparison, the first and greatest evil in this country. It not only rests with crushing weight on the troubled bosoms of the helpless millions, whose claims to sympathy and relief alone are quite overwhelming; but it involves the whole country in a common guilt and shame, and stands directly in the way of all righteous progress, making true liberty impossible. It pollutes and must pollute while it continues, press, pulpit, and people, and render them unfit and unwilling to attend to moral considerations in connection with their political duties and responsibilities. In proof of this position, argument is needless. The evidence is as broad as the

---

FIGURE 4. Frederick Douglass. (*Historical Pictures Service, Chicago*)

country, and extends through every part of it. We have but to open our eyes to see it, and our ears to hear it. The lesson taught by this, is, that slavery is the first great evil to be removed, and liberty the first great good to be attained by the American people.

2. It is not less the voice of reason and nature, than it is the voice of the sacred scriptures, that freedom is a fundamental condition of accountability and the foundation of all manly virtue. Moses was charged by the Almighty to tell Pharaoh to let the Hebrews go free, as the first condition to religious obedience. *"Let my people go free, that they may serve me."* Such is the voice of God, and such is the deduction of reason. It was not said, let my people *serve me,* that they may go *free;* but emancipation was demanded as the first condition needful to render service to God. We commend this consideration to our Bible-reading and Bible-voting friends, feeling that it may help to relieve them on a point upon which they entertain scruples against casting a merely anti-slavery vote.

3. *To guard against misunderstanding.*—While we hold that slavery is emphatically the *first* great evil which concerns the people of this country, and that liberty is the first great interest to be secured and preserved, we would not be understood as being indifferent to other interests. No evil should go unopposed, and no good should go unsought. This is our meaning, there is a natural order of things, and in this order the abolition of slavery in this country stands first, and is for the time being sufficiently important to be the first object of political action.

4. It will be objected that this theory limits a man's political duties, and destroys the significance of a vote. "I want my vote," says one, "to represent fully all my moral convictions of what should be politically done"; and a vote that does less than this is a compromising vote, doing but part of what it ought to do, and leaving undone a part of that which it ought to do. The fallacy here is in the assumption that what is *morally* right is, at all times, equally politically possible. One man may see nineteen applications of the principles of justice, another twenty; but, on the principle stated above, the man of the twenty would be bound to separate from him of the nineteen, altho' in the nineteen points they are perfectly agreed. Again, the absurdity of the objection is seen in the fact, that the principle would make party action, or combined effort impossible, by requiring complete identity of opinion, and failing to recognize

(as it does) those differences which result from location, education, habits of thought, temperament, and mental development, it leaves no ground for a minority to stand upon.

To differ with them is to be divided, not merely in opinion, but in action. We heard one of this class say that he would vote for the candidates of the Liberty Party, or that he would not vote at all. Before he would vote for John P. Hale, he would stay away from the polls. Now, what would be thought of a man who should see a thousand men drowning, and should quietly fold his hands on the shore, declaring, that inasmuch as he could not save *all,* he would not save any?—Further, he might say, "If I save that man yonder, who is battling with the waves for life, may not that perishing woman, with her babe in her arms, justly feel herself neglected, and pierce my soul with her reproachful glance?" This reasoning would be quite as much entitled to respect as his, who would not vote to attain one or more great political blessings, or to move one or more great political wrongs, because such a vote would not accomplish all that he might desire to have accomplished by his vote. Yet this is, as we understand it, the very ground taken by those of the Liberty Party at Canastota, last week, who left the party because they were outvoted, and nominated candidates for themselves.

5. Having shown thus briefly, and we think conclusively, the unsoundness of that philosophy of political party action, adopted by our friends at Canastota, for whom, by the way, we entertain sentiments of high respect and warm affection, they may very well call upon us to indicate a rule or principle of political party action, which is free from all valid objection. Very well. It is evident that all reforms have their beginning with ideas, and that for a time they have to rely solely on the tongue and pen for progress, until they gain a sufficient number of adherents to make themselves felt at the ballot-box. The idea of "Free Trade," "Direct Taxes," "Land-Reform," "Right of Suffrage," "Women's Rights," together with "opposition to Capital Punishment," to "secret societies," and "intervention," may all, in certain circumstances, receive due attention, while yet remaining within the region of ideas, and about which there may be a difference of opinion, and yet those who differ may very properly unite *in political action* for some one great and good end. We ask no man to lose sight of any of his aims and objects. We only ask that they may be allowed to serve out their natural probation. Our rule of political

action is this: the voter ought to see to it that his vote shall secure the highest good possible, at the same time that it does no harm.

6. According to this rule, we may vote in many instances with perfect propriety; for men, who, in regard to many things, entertain ideas totally different from ours. We can vote for a man who affirms, and will carry out one important truth, even though he should be totally blind in respect to others that we might deem important, provided, of course, he does not require us to deny any part of the truth which we hold; or, in other words, we can affirm his truths just so far and so long as he does not require us to negative ours. It seems to us, there can be no valid objection against this rule of action, or the philosophy by which it is sustained, especially when it is remembered that, often the very best way of promoting one cause, is by promoting the triumph of another.—Draw out the old tooth and give place to the new one. One thing at a time, or, at least, only so many as at the time being, strongly commend themselves as proper to be done. Abolish slavery; remove this stupendous system of iniquity, under whose death-like shade moral feeling is deadened, and intellect languishes, and you have done a double good. You have helped forward a thousand good causes, by promoting the triumph of one. We repeat, do all the good you can, and do no harm.

7. It may be said that these arguments do not apply to the case under consideration; that they lose their force, in the fact that the Free Democracy cannot do more in the struggle for the Presidency than bear its own testimony in favor of certain rights, and against certain wrongs; and that, therefore, *"the Liberty Party"* really stands upon an equal footing with the Free Democracy. Indeed, it may possibly be contended that, based on broader principles, and animated by higher aspirations, "the Liberty Party" holds decided advantage over *"the Free Democracy."* We admit the pertinency of this objection, and it deserves to be met. We assume what we believe to be true, that in point of fundamental principles, *"the Liberty Party"* and *"the Free Democracy"* occupy common ground; the difference between them, on the subject of slavery, is exceedingly slight. Verbal, rather than real. It is plain, therefore, that reasons for preferring the one to the other, must be sought in something aside from the moral superiority of the one over the other. The advantage of *"the Free Democracy"* over *"the Liberty Party,"* is to be found in the superiority

of its circumstances. It has the power to unite a very influential minority on a sound principle of universal application. It can give to the good cause the energy derived from complete organization, and animate and encourage, by the power of sympathy.—It can give us the wisdom of two heads instead of one; and the might of a multitude instead of a few. "United we stand, divided we fall," will apply to the case in hand; and should only be forgotten when the object for which we are united is worth less than the good to be obtained by separation. We repeat, assuming that there is, really, no moral difference between the two organizations on the question of slavery, we are led by a fair view of the advantages of a united army against slavery, to rally under one standard in the coming election.

8. But if this be sound argument, it may be asked, why may we not abandon "the Free Democracy," and go over to the Whig party, and General Scott? The reason is obvious, neither the Whig party nor General Scott aim at the regeneration, or reformation of the American Government. Both stand pledged against all reformation; both are quite content with things as they are; both are wedded to the slave power, and neither purposes to do anything to blot out the foul disgrace and scandal of slavery, or for the repeal of that most shocking of all human enactments, the fugitive slave act. They cherish slavery as a blessing, and stand by it as its special friends and guardians.

The Democratic party is equally unworthy, equally to be shunned and deserted with the Whig party. They stand on one common footing of wickedness, their only struggle is for place and power. Without ringing the changes here, it is enough to say that the cases supposed have no likeness, and that therefore the argument based upon the premises has no force or application. The whole matter is settled, by the fact that the Free Democracy is a party of progress and reform, while the other parties are anti-progress, anti-reform, and are such from the very nature of their organizations.

9. It is feared by some, that *"the Free Democratic Party"* will by-and-by retrograde, and finally sell out to one or the other of the great political parties. It would be idle not to admit such a thing to be possible; but the probabilities are strongly against such a supposition. *"The Free Democratic Party"* has disencumbered itself of the causes which have dragged down both the old parties to their

present depth of degradation, and has grasped with decisive energy the principles which are at the bottom of all political progress, to wit, "Justice, Liberty, and Humanity." It asks no support of those who would corrupt it, and gathers its friends from the shrine of truth and freedom. But what if in an evil hour that party should fall, as others have done before, there is still a God in Israel. The remedy is at hand. Abandon it and build another house. Out of the wisdom gained by experience, organize a better party. Fealty to party has no claims against fidelity to truth.

10. It is objected to *"the Free Democracy,"* that it does not deny the possibility of legalizing slavery; but is this so? We understand *"the Free Democracy"* to admit, what it would be folly to deny, that *"property in man"* can be asserted and maintained by force, under the forms of legislation. We suppose every one will admit this. We understand, at the same time, that *"the Free Democracy"* deny the validity of such legislation, as being destitute of any authority over the slave, or over the conscience of any class of men. We believe that even Gerrit Smith regards the Free Democracy as going this length; but he objects, that in another part of the platform, there are admissions which militate against this doctrine; such, for instance, as the following resolution:

> *That no permanent settlement of the Slavery question can be looked for except in the practical recognition of the truth, that Slavery is sectional and Freedom national, by the total separation of the General Government from Slavery, and the exercise of its legitimate constitutional influence on the side of Freedom, and by leaving to the States the whole subject of Slavery and the extradition of fugitives from service.*

Now, admitting that this is an unsound plank in the Pittsburgh platform, there is an explanation by which, in truth, this resolution does not belong at all to the platform. The fact is, that a resolution asserting precisely what this resolution now asserts, at least asserting that which makes this resolution objectionable, was almost unanimously voted down, and cast out of the platform; it must therefore be plain that the present resolution holds its place in the series of resolutions purely by accident or oversight, not by design. Any other supposition would stamp the Pittsburgh Convention as meanly paltering in a double sense. Nevertheless, there are persons in *"the*

Free Democracy" whose sentiments are expressed in this resolution; and it will, in the circumstances, be claimed by all such, as a part of the platform; but in the light of the explanation we have given, it does seem that it ought not to be made a barrier against the union of *Liberty Party* men and *Free Democrats;* certainly not, when it is remembered that the right of discussion is secured, and the means of enlightenment are at hand.

Now let us see the principles laid down by the Free Democracy. Here are their resolutions on slavery:

> *Having assembled in National Convention as the delegates of the Free Democracy of the United States, united by a common resolve to maintain Right against Wrongs and Freedom against Slavery; confiding in the intelligence, the patriotism and the discriminating justice of the American People; putting our trust in God for the triumph of our cause, and invoking his guidance in our endeavors to advance it, we now submit to the candid judgment of all men the following declaration of principles and measures:*
>
> *1. That Governments deriving their just powers from the consent of the governed, are instituted among men to secure to all those inalienable rights of life, liberty and the pursuit of happiness, with which they are endowed by their Creator, and of which none can be deprived by valid legislation, except for crime.*
>
> *2. That the true mission of American Democracy is to maintain the Liberties of the People, the Sovereignty of the States and the perpetuity of the Union, by the impartial application to public affairs, without sectional discriminations, of the fundamental principles of equal rights, strict justice, and economical administration.*
>
> *3. That the Federal Government is one of limited powers, derived solely from the Constitution, and the grants of power therein ought to be strictly construed, by all departments and agents of the government, and it is inexpedient and dangerous to exercise doubtful constitutional powers.*
>
> *4. That the Constitution of the United States is ordained to form a more perfect union, to establish justice, and secure the blessings of liberty, or property, without due process of law; and therefore, the government, having no more power to make a slave than to make a king, and no more power to establish slavery than to establish a monarchy, should at once proceed to relieve itself from all responsibility for the existence of slavery, wherever it possesses constitutional power to legislate for its extinction.*
>
> *5. That to the persevering and importune demands of the Slave Power for* more Slave States, new Slave Territories, and the nationalization of Slavery, *our distinct and final answer is no more Slave States, no*

Slave Territory, no nationalized Slavery, and no legislation for the extradition of Slaves.

6. That slavery is a sin against God and a crime against man, which no human enactment nor usage can make right, and that Christianity, Humanity and Patriotism alike demand its abolition.

7. That the Fugitive Slave Act of 1850 is repugnant to the Constitution, to the principles of the common law, to the spirit of Christianity, and to the principles of the civilized world. We, therefore, deny its binding force upon the American people, and demand its immediate and total repeal.

8. That the doctrine that any human law is a finality and not subject to modification or repeal, is not in accordance with the creed of the founders of our government, and is dangerous to the liberties of the people.

9. That the acts of Congress known as the Compromise measures of 1850, by making the admission of a sovereign State contingent upon the adoption of other measures by the special interest of Slavery by their omission to guarantee freedom in Free Territories; by their attempt to impose unconstitutional limitations on the power of Congress and the people to admit new States; by their provisions for the assumption of five millions of the State debt of Texas, and for the payment of five millions more, and the cession of a large territory to the same State, under menace, as an inducement to the relinquishment of a groundless claim; and by their invasion of the sovereignty of the States and the liberties of the people, through the enactment of an unjust, oppressive and unconstitutional Fugitive Slave Law—are proved to be inconsistent with all the principles and maxims of Democracy, and wholly inadequate to the settlement of the questions of which they are claimed to be an adjustment.

11. These resolutions speak for themselves, and need no comment. They are broad and comprehensive in their scope, clear in their aim, cover the whole ground of anti-slavery principle, and the party adopting them is pledged to unceasing warfare against slavery, and all its pretentions.

Other resolutions were adopted at Pittsburgh, in respect to other matters which commend themselves to our judgment; but, considering that the first work to be done is the abolition of slavery, we have waived other considerations in discussing the merits of the Free Democracy.

12. We confess ourselves pleased with the spirit of *"the Free Democracy,"* not less than with its principles. It has passed through a trying ordeal. Defeated in its first great purpose, by the treachery of those who, under the pretended pressure of danger to the union,

gave up the struggle and joined the enemy; deserted by States that had avowed themselves favorable to the ends sought by the Buffalo Convention, with ranks thinned by repeated defection; their organization rudely broken up, where it at one time seemed strongest; the two great parties sallying forth to battle against them under one banner and in one cause; scattered and disjointed, yet they gather at the ancient trumpet call of freedom, and with undaunted spirit they meet and arrange themselves for a renewal of the conflict as if confident of a final victory. There is evidence here of an unconquerable spirit, and a firm resolve to fall or flourish with their convictions.

No man with proper feeling could behold without admiration the Pittsburgh Convention, a body of intelligent men thoroughly in earnest, scorning to remain with party and power, when their principles had been put under the ban—"great, glorious and free," though small in numbers and held in derision by the proud and the prudent. A noble, manly, independent, yet sympathizing spirit, diffused throughout their ranks without question drew us to their company, and compelled us to cast in our lot with them. *"These are the friends of God's suffering poor,"* came upon us with irresistible force, silencing all cavil.

Let the candidates then speak the same word, and breathe the same spirit, and the men of New York will stand by them, and for them, and against all who oppose them. Liberty will again be united against slavery, the friends of the slave will then join hands and present an undivided front, not merely defending the sacred cause of liberty, but boldly assailing the stronghold of the enemy.

IV THE TURN TO VIOLENCE

Benjamin Quarles

SHOCK THERAPY AND CRISIS

In a number of distinguished studies, Benjamin Quarles has enlarged understanding of the American past by tracing the historical experience of black Americans. Included among his works are a biography of Frederick Douglass and accounts of black participation in the American Revolution and the Civil War. The following selection comes from Quarles's Black Abolitionists, *a book which helped restore the reputation of a group often overlooked by historians. It is perhaps in the setting of militant resistance to slavery by slaves and free blacks that John Brown's turn to violence seems most readily justified. Quarles is a professor of history at Morgan State College.*

> *Come thou, Sweet Freedom, best gift of God*
> *to man! Not in a storm of fire and blood*
> *I ask it, but still, at all events,*
> *and all hazards, come.—*
>
> William G. Allen, October 6, 1852

The interest that many Negroes showed in colonization in the fifties stemmed basically from the discriminations against them in the land of their birth. In the case of emigration to Africa there was an additional motive—a feeling of identity based on color and ancestry. As a result many Negroes came to view the land of their fathers in a fresh light, discarding the shibboleths as to its backwardness and stagnation. But such a more positive attitude toward Africa was far short of any Pan-Negro movement or black hands-across-the-sea. For the lure of Africa could never compare with that of an America in which slavery had been wiped out and its twin offspring—prejudice and discrimination—put on the run.

On the surface of things, such a brightening day was hardly on the horizon when Frederick Douglass made his plans to take a trip to Haiti. But by 1860 America was close to a civil war. This country's institutions, secular and religious, had failed to bring about the emancipation of the slaves without bloodshed. The power structure was unable to cope with slavery because slavery itself had become a key component of the power structure. Since American institutions therefore lacked the strength or will to subdue slavery, other and more revolutionary techniques would begin to take hold of men's minds. Thus in the two decades prior to 1860 the notion of an armed confrontation mounted in intensity, however inapparent on the surface. On the eve of the Civil War, then, the idea of physical violence to free the slave was far from new. Since the time of Nat Turner this idea of a showdown by force of arms had been a recurring theme in Negro thought. Black fire-eaters did not go out of style with David Walker. But for a time their tones were muted because black people had taken on new hope with the coming of the new abolitionists.

These new friends of the Negro were strongly pacifist in method, no matter how forthright in language. They proposed to rely on reason and moral truth, opposing any efforts by the slave to obtain his rights by physical force. In their famous Declaration of Sentiments, issued December 4, 1833, the new abolitionists made their position clear: "We reject and entreat the oppressed to reject the use of all carnal weapons for deliverance from bondage; relying solely upon those which are spiritual and mighty through God to the pulling down of strongholds." Five years later, the influential James G. Birney assured a Southern inquirer that he did not know of a single abolitionist who would incite the slaves to insurrections.

The new abolitionists were pacifists, a stance fully supported by William Lloyd Garrison, a name revered among Negroes. Garrison wielded great influence among Negroes down to 1840. Harriet Martineau asserted in 1837 that Garrison's strong hold on the Negro people was the explanation "that no blood has been shed from the time his voice began to be heard until now." After the abolitionist split in 1840 Garrison's influence among Negroes waned outside of New England and even there his word was no longer gospel although affection for him remained constant.

In the 1840s it was a Garrisonian, Charles Lenox Remond, who first voiced unpacific thoughts. In the British Isles to attend the World Anti-Slavery Convention of 1840, Remond told the Glasgow Anti-Slavery Society that he would welcome a war between the United States and England over the Canadian boundary inasmuch as such a development would bring about the freedom of the slaves. Remond was rebuked by *The Anti-Slavery Standard,* which called his language "hardly in accordance with the character of primitive abolitionism." In a later address to the Hiberian Anti-Slavery Society, the undeterred Remond said that the dissolution of the American Union would lead the outraged slaves to turn upon their then friendless and weakened torturers, measuring arms with them.

A year later the possibility of having to bear arms for the United States brought a cool response from a Negro weekly in New York, the *People's Press.* The United States and England were in dispute over the *Creole,* a ship which, like the *Amistad,* had been seized by its slaves, but which had put into port at Nassau. A diplomatic argument was inevitable, with America's Secretary of State, Daniel Webster, saying that she would demand indemnification. Negroes had little sympathy with any efforts made to repossess the 135 slaves of the *Creole.* Hence the *People's Press* pointed out that since the previous military services of black Americans had been repaid with chains and slavery, they should maintain an organized neutrality if war came. Such a position would be held until the laws, federal and state, should make the Negro a free and equal citizen.

A note of militancy was sounded at a meeting called by Negroes in Troy, New York, in March 1842 to discuss the decision of the Supreme Court in *Prigg v. Pennsylvania.* The ruling of the court did need a word of explanation. For although it held that a state law could not restrain a master in seizing his slave, it also declared that the state authorities were not bound to assist in such seizures. After weighing the decision the Negroes meeting at Troy passed a series of resolutions, one of which expressed a full concurrence "with the statement of Patrick Henry, and solemnly declare that we will have liberty, or we shall have death."

At the Troy meeting the chairman of the five-man committee drafting the resolutions was Henry Highland Garnet, then a local clergyman. This was the man, the grandson of a Mandingo chieftain and warrior, who the following year delivered the most forthright call for a slave uprising ever heard in antebellum America. It took place at a national convention for black men in Buffalo in August 1843. Although then having appeared on the public platform only three years, Garnet already had a reputation as an orator, particularly for having "the power to fire up his auditors in such a way as to make every man feel like daring to do."

To an audience including the more than seventy delegates and scores of white visitors, the twenty-seven-year-old Garnet delivered "An Address to the Slaves of the United States." The time has come, brethren, when you must act for yourselves, said Garnet. There was little hope of obtaining freedom without some shedding of blood. The way would not be easy but "you will not be compelled to spend much time in order to become inured to hardships."

As the audience listened, some in tears and others with fists clenched, Garnet proceeded to hold up some examples of a slave who struck a blow for freedom—Denmark Vesey of South Carolina, "patriotic Nathaniel Turner," Joseph Cinque of the *Amistad,* and Madison Washington of the *Creole.* Garnet brought his remarks to a close with a sustained exhortation, reading in part as follows: "Brethren, arise, arise. Strike for your lives and liberties. Now is the day and hour. Let every slave throughout the land do this and the days of slavery are numbered. *Rather die free-men than live to be slaves.* Remember that you are four millions."

When Garnet finished it would have been risky, according to a Buffalo reporter, for any slaveholder to have been present. The deeply moved delegates, recovering from the powerful outburst, proceeded to give it an unprecedented amount of attention. Those opposing it included William Wells Brown, Frederick Douglass and Amos G. Beman, the last named speaking for over an hour. The convention turned the address over to a revision committee to soften its language, but even this toned-down version was rejected, although by a single vote.

Garnet's address hardly sat well with white abolitionists, particularly the Garrisonians. The latter called attention to the 1833 Declaration of Sentiments abjuring the use of force. They asked Garnet whether he, as a clergyman, found the gospel in harmony with his address to the slaves. Maria Weston Chapman deplored the kind of advice that Garnet had been getting: "Trust not in counsels that lead you to the shedding of blood."

In a sharp reply to Mrs. Chapman, Garnet said that she wished him to think as she did, thus reducing him again to the level of the slave. Rejecting her contention that he had received bad advice, he retorted that he was capable of thinking on the subject of human rights without any help "from the men of the West or the women of the East." Be assured, he concluded, "that there is one black American who dares to speak boldly on the subject of universal liberty."

Despite the criticisms of the Garrisonian press, Garnet's address to the slaves left its stamp on Negro thought. A national convention of Negroes at Troy in October 1847, the first since the Buffalo meeting four years earlier, did disapprove of physical violence—"we frown down any attempt to confide in brute force as a reformatory instrumentality." But a few months later Garnet published his 1843 address, combining it with a sketch of David Walker and the text of his forceful "Appeal to the Colored Citizens of the World." In January 1849 a convention of the Negroes of Ohio passed a resolution recommending that five hundred copies of this 1848 Garnet publication "be obtained in the name of the Convention and gratuitously distributed." This resolution was not carried out but the militant spirit it reflected is unmistakable.

Five months later Frederick Douglass gave a speech at Boston, one which indicated that he had abandoned the pacific stance he took at the Buffalo convention six years earlier. To a packed audience at Faneuil Hall, Douglass closed a lengthy address with the remark that he would welcome the news that the slaves had risen and "that the sable arms which have been engaged in beautifying and adorning the South were engaged in spreading death and devastation there." Although this remark occasioned "marked sensation," Douglass continued in the same vein. Saying that a state of war existed in the South, he asserted that Americans should welcome a successful slave uprising just as they had recently hailed the news that the French citizens had overthrown the monarchy. Douglass took his seat amid great applause but not without some hissing.

With the coming of the 1850s the militant tone among Negroes grew louder, spurred by the Fugitive Slave Law and their growing belief that liberty and slavery could not escape a head-on collision. By the summer of 1853 the clergyman Jermain W. Loguen was of the opinion that slavery would be done away with either by agitation or bloodshed, adding ominously, "and I sometimes think that I care not which." A year later H. Ford Douglas declared that he could join a foreign enemy and fight against the United States without being a traitor inasmuch as "it treats me as a stranger and an alien." In 1856 John S. Rock urged Negroes to undertake some daring or desperate enterprise in order to demonstrate their courage. Rock had been stung by a remark of Theodore Parker to the effect that if Margaret Garner, an escaped slave who put one of her daughters to death when facing recapture, had been Anglo-Saxon, the 400,000 white men in Ohio would have arisen in her defense. . . .

Throughout the North the strong denunciation of the Dred Scott decision did much to raise the threshold of incipient violence. Certainly, among Negroes the spirit of militancy became more pervasive and insistent. At a convention of Ohio Negroes in 1858, William H. Day, after reviewing the plight of the colored people, declared that resistance by force of arms was their right and duty. John I. Gaines, a boat-storekeeper from Cincinnati, criticized Day as being impractical, Negroes being "a weak, enslaved and ignorant people."

But however impractical, Negro public speakers were preparing their addresses around highly militant figures and themes. James T. Holly lauded Toussaint L'Overture, Haitian liberator, in a speech entitled, "The Auspicious Dawn of Negro Rule." Holly ended his lecture with the assertion that it was far better "that his sable countrymen should be *dead freemen than living slaves.*" J. Sella Martin, pastor of the Joy Street Baptist Church in Boston, drew large audiences for his prepared address on a Baptist exhorter of an earlier day, Nat Turner. Blunt-spoken William J. Watkins toured the abolitionist circuit with a lecture on the "irrepressible conflict."

The new climate of impending physical confrontation inevitably produced its own energizers. Of the abolitionist figures thrust up by the undercurrents of violence, one stands in a class by himself—John Brown of Osawatomie. To Brown, slavery itself was a species of warfare, demanding a counter resort to arms. Brown's daring sweep into Virginia in October 1859, his capture and his execution constituted a national shock from which there would be no recovery. Abolitionists hitherto of a pacifist orientation found reason to reverse themselves as the whole atmosphere became charged.

Brown's relationships with Negroes had been close, continuous, and on a peer basis, a pattern which no other white reformer could boast. Apparently no Negro who ever knew Brown ever said anything in criticism of his attitude or behavior toward colored people. Brown's attitude toward slavery and his grim and forceful response to it were shaped by many things, of which his own personal experiences with Negroes was not the least.

The reciprocal relations between John Brown and the blacks began long before five of them accompanied him to Harpers Ferry and four of them to his doom. Brown's interest in colored people dated back to 1834 when he proposed "to get at least one Negro boy or youth, and bring him up as we do our own." Fifteen years later Brown moved his family to North Elba, New York, expressly to settle among Negroes, most of them recipients of land grants from Gerrit Smith. Brown attempted to assist his Negro neighbors in business matters, and he invited them to his weekly sessions in the study of the Bible. Richard Henry Dana, paying a farewell call to John Brown at North Elba on a morning in late June 1849, noted that at the breakfast table eating with the family were the hired hands, including three Negroes.

Brown's attempt to spur Negroes on led him in 1848 to contribute a lengthy article to the *Ram's Horn,* a short-lived weekly. Entitled "Sambo's Mistakes," this article lampoons the habits of the Negro. Brown felt that the colored people were not doing all that they themselves could do in self-improvement. Hence in "Sambo's Mistakes" he makes his points by posing as a Negro who is offering to his fellows the benefit of his experience in life. A typical passage reads as follows:

> *Another error of my riper years has been, that when any meeting of colored people has been called in order to consider any important matter of general interest, I have been so eager to display my spouting talents, and so tenacious of some trifling theory or other that I have adopted, that I have generally lost all sight of the business [at] hand, consumed the time disputing about things of no moment, and thereby defeated entirely many important measures calculated to promote the general welfare; but I am happy to say I can see in a minute where I missed it.*
>
> *Another small error of my life (for I never committed great blunders) has been that I never would (for the sake of union in the furtherance of the most vital interests of our race) yield any minor point of difference. In this way I have always had to act with but a few, or more frequently alone, and could accomplish nothing worth living for; but I have one comfort, I can see in a minute where I missed it.*

If few men knew the Negro's shortcomings as perceptively as Brown, there were even fewer who were as distressed by color prejudice as he. One of his followers relates that while walking in Boston in April 1857 Brown was greatly annoyed at the rude language addressed to a colored girl, language of the type, Brown said, that would not have been directed to a white girl. Entering the Massasoit House in Chicago for breakfast on April 25, 1858, Brown was told that the Negro member of his party, Richard Richardson, a fugitive slave, could not be served. Brown marched out, although not before subjecting the proprietor to "a little bit of terse logic."

Aside from his equalitarian principles, Brown was interested in the welfare of the colored people because he had something for them to do. His all-consuming passion was the abolition of slavery, an end which he proposed to accomplish by enlisting a semimilitaristic group of followers ready for direct action. Brown's role for the Negro was implicit in an organization he formed in January 1851 at Springfield, Massachusetts, the United States League of Gileadites. Formed to resist the Fugitive Slave Law, the Gileadites pledged themselves to go armed and to shoot to kill, a pattern of conduct that would characterize Brown's later operations in Kansas and at Harpers Ferry. The forty-four colored men and women who signed the agreement apparently had little call for action. Moreover, in March 1851, Brown, the original man-in-motion, left for Ohio.

Brown was interested in recruiting Negro leaders and the black rank and file. Prominent figures sought out by Brown included Frederick Douglass, Martin R. Delany, Stephen Smith, Jermain W. Loguen, Henry Highland Garnet, William Still, and Charles H. Langston. His contacts with Douglass, whom he desperately wished to win over, stretched over a longer time-span and were more numerous than with any other Negro leader. Brown's acquaintance with Douglass went back to the spring of 1848 when the latter, at Brown's request, visited him at Springfield. In the spring of 1858 Brown paid two visits to the Douglass home in Rochester, New York, one of them extending over a period of two weeks. While a guest of Douglass, Brown met a fugitive slave, Shields Green, who would accompany him to Harpers Ferry.

Shortly before Brown got ready to make his raid into Virginia he arranged to meet Douglass at Chambersburg, Pennsylvania, some twenty miles from the site of the planned foray. Douglass brought a letter for Brown from Mrs. J. N. Gloucester, a Brooklyn woman of means, with $25 enclosed. Douglass was accompanied by Shields Green, the two of them being led to Brown's hideout by Harry Watson, a Negro underground railroad operator at Chambersburg. For three days Brown tried to persuade Douglass to join the expedition. Douglass steadfastly refused, discretion having formed his decision.

Not a single other Negro leader would join Brown, all of them considering his venture imprudent. On May 17, 1859, Brown wrote to Loguen: "I will just whisper in your private ear that I have no doubt you will soon have a call from God to minister at a different location." Despite the language, the Negro clergyman remained unconvinced. Loguen, like other Negroes, admired Brown for his antislavery exploits in Kansas and his daring excursion into Missouri in which he had freed eleven slaves by a show of force. However, as much as they revered Brown for his courage, Negro leaders thought that the proposed seizure of Harpers Ferry was inordinately risky, if not foolhardy.

Brown's most ambitious attempt to enlist the Negro rank and file was the holding of a convention at Chatham, Ontario, in early May 1858. Brown's own party of twelve was present, as were thirty-four Negroes. These included the presiding officer, a Negro clergyman, William C. Munroe, the poet James Madison Bell, and Martin R. Delany, the last named then practicing medicine at Chatham, having come at the urgent personal invitation of Brown himself. The chief work of the convention was the adoption of a provisional constitution of the United States, a document which avowed the Declaration of Independence and condemned slavery.

The Chatham convention lacked follow-up. With Brown gone and with no action of any kind forthcoming for more nearly seventeen months, the enthusiasm of the Chatham signers abated, never to be rekindled. But at Chatham, Brown for the first time had met Harriet Tubman. He had thought of her as the shepherd of the slaves that he would shake loose. Brown's tête-à-tête with Harriet confirmed his already high opinion of her. But neither she nor Delany would be with him at Harpers Ferry. Brown, however, had not left Chatham empty-handed. A young printer's devil, Osborne Perry Anderson, had been impressed by the convention and by its convener; he would be the only black survivor of Harpers Ferry.

By the autumn of 1859 Brown was ready to seize the government arsenal at Harpers Ferry, a prelude to establishing a stronghold in the mountains and thus liberating the slaves on a mounting scale of operations. Late in the night of October 16 Brown moved into the town, leaving three of his party at the Kennedy Farm, the base of operations in Maryland. Marching into the darkened Harpers Ferry behind Brown were eighteen followers, five of them Negroes, Osborne Perry Anderson, Shields Green, Dangerfield Newby, like Green an escaped slave, and two recruits from Oberlin, Ohio—John A. Copeland, Jr., and Lewis S. Leary, his uncle. Copeland, a former student in the preparatory department at Oberlin College and the most articulate of the five, had joined Brown "to assist in giving that freedom to at least a few of my poor and enslaved brethren who have been most foully and unjustly deprived of their liberty."

John Brown was hardly a battlefield tactician; lacking a clear and definite plan of campaign, his raid was quickly suppressed. The first of the five fatalities inflicted by Brown's men was on a free Negro, Heywood Shepherd, baggage master of the train depot, a contretemps which seemed to set the stage for a military fiasco. Ten of Brown's band were killed, Newby first and Leary later. Copeland and Green were among the seven who were captured, and Anderson was among the five who escaped.

Brown and his captured followers were imprisoned in Charleston. Brown was tried first, and on October 31 the jury returned with a verdict of guilty. Two days later the judge pronounced a sentence of death by hanging. During the thirty-day interval between the sentence and the execution, Brown bore himself with fortitude and serenity.

Brown's inner peace was not shared by his countrymen, particularly those in the North. For his act, however rash and wrongheaded, had dramatized the issue of slavery, forcing neutrals to abandon their fence-sitting posture and giving to the abolitionists a martyr figure of unprecedented proportions. Charles H. Langston, like half a dozen white abolitionists, felt the necessity of issuing a "card of denial" stating that he had had no hand in the Harpers Ferry affair. "But what shall I deny," added Langston. "I cannot deny that I feel the very deepest sympathy with the immortal John Brown in his heroic and daring effort to free the slaves." Langston's sentiment of sympathy and esteem mirrored the reaction of the overwhelming majority of black Americans.

During Brown's month in jail innumerable prayer and sympathy meetings were held throughout the North. None were more fervent than those called by Negroes. *The Weekly Anglo-African* for November 5 carried a guest editorial by James W. C. Pennington entitled, "Pray for John Brown." Such advice was hardly needed. On the day after Brown was sentenced a group of Providence Negroes, meeting at the Zion Church, expressed their full sympathy for Captain John Brown. Despite their "abhorrence to bloodshed and civil war," they referred to Brown as "hero, philanthropist and unflinching champion of liberty," and pledged themselves to send up their prayers to Almighty God on his behalf. A group of Chicago Negroes, meeting later that month, drafted a letter to Brown assuring him of their deep sympathy and their intention to contribute material aid to his family: "How could we be so ungrateful as to do less for one who has suffered, bled, and now ready to die for the cause?" At the Siloam Presbyterian Church in Brooklyn, a prayer meeting cutting across denominational lines was led by the pastor, A. N. Freeman, assisted by fellow clergymen Henry Highland Garnet, James N. Gloucester, and Amos G. Beman.

Colored women sent letters of esteem to the jailed Brown. A group of Brooklyn matrons wrote that they would ever hold him in their remembrance, considering him a model of true patriotism because he sacrificed everything for his country's sake. From Kendallville, Indiana, Frances Ellen Watkins sent a letter on behalf of the slave women, an admixture of Christian faith in the future and symbolic references to the past—"You have rocked the bloody Bastille," and, "The hemlock is distilled with victory when it is pressed to the lips of Socrates." A group of women from New York, Brooklyn, and Williamsburg sent Mrs. Brown a letter on November 23, its content summarized in the lines, "Fear not, beloved sister. Trust in the God of Jacob."

As John Brown stepped from the jail on the last morning of his life, "no little slave-child was held up for the benison of his lips, for none but soldiers were near and the street was full of marching men." However, as Brown was led to the gallows, a slave woman said, "God bless you, old man; if I could help you, I would." Brown went to his death with dignity, and the day concluded, wrote one who was present, "with the calm & quiet of a New England Sabbath."

If December 2, 1859, was also a quiet day in abolitionist circles, it was due to the nature of its observance. Throughout the North reformers held prayer meetings or meetings with a religious orientation. At Boston, where all Negro businesses were closed, the colored people, wearing arm bands of black crepe, held three prayer meetings—morning, afternoon, and night—at Leonard Grimes's Twelfth Baptist Church. Many persons stayed from one meeting to the next, not needing to go out for meals on a day of widespread fasting. One of these all-day sojourners was Lydia Maria Child, who had journeyed from Wayland, fifteen miles away, to spend the solemn day with Negroes. She therefore had to miss the much larger meeting at Tremont Temple arranged by the white abolitionists but with Negroes attending in large numbers and with J. Sella Martin as one of the featured speakers. But perhaps it was just as well that Mrs. Child did not go to the crowded Temple, for thousands were turned away.

Martyr Day, as some black abolitionists called it, was appropriately observed by New York Negroes at a meeting at Shiloh Church beginning at ten in the morning and with a period of silent prayer at noon. Of the six clergymen on the program, William Goodell, the only white speaker, differed from two of his colleagues on one point. When James N. Gloucester endorsed John Brown's course, Goodell dissented on the grounds that the weapons of the abolitionists were moral and religious rather than carnal. Sampson White took issue, informing Goodell that George Washington, whom Americans revered, had not taken the position that "our weapons are not carnal" when he led the new nation in its struggle against English oppression. Washington and the Americans of his day had acted on the premise that "resistance to tyrants was obedience to God." White, somewhat carried away, said that he had an arm which he felt duty-bound to use when his God-given rights were invaded.

Philadelphia Negroes, like those in Boston, observed Martyr Day by closing down their businesses. Public prayer meetings were held at two churches—Shiloh and Union Baptist. Hundreds of colored men and women went to National Hall to hear Robert Purvis and white William Furness. Pittsburgh's black community held a meeting addressed by native son George Vashon. At Detroit the colored people gathered at the Second Baptist Church where they passed a resolution vowing to venerate Brown's character, regarding him as "our temporal leader whose name will never die."

On Martyr Day at Cleveland the two thousand who managed to get into crowded Melodeon Hall included almost as many whites as blacks, with almost as many equally mixed milling around outside, unable to get in. Judges and members of the state legislature were among the platform guests flanking the presiding officer, Charles H. Langston. The walls were draped in black and the stage was hung with large-lettered, framed quotations from John Brown's writings and conversations. Negroes in lesser towns throughout the North—from Worcester, Massachusetts, to Galesburg, Ohio—likewise paused on December 2, 1859, to honor John Brown on the day of his death.

Negroes felt that they had an especial obligation to assist in the efforts to give financial aid to John Brown's widow. Their donations would not be large, but they would represent a more widespread giving than their modest totals might indicate. The John Brown Relief Fund of New Haven raised $12.75 for Mary Brown. Philadelphia Negroes sent her $150 and the recently formed John Brown Liberty League of Detroit donated $25. Some Negroes, such as Francis Ellen Watkins, sent personal contributions. Mrs. Brown's letters of acknowledgement were brief, but gracious and inspirational.

The sympathy that Negroes felt for Mrs. Brown extended to Mrs. Mary Leary, widow of Lewis S. Leary. The wife and seven children of the other Negro who fell at Harpers Ferry, Dangerfield Newby, were in slavery, and neither of the two Negroes who were hanged, John A. Copeland or Shields Green, was married. Boston Negroes raised $40 for Mrs. Leary and her child, and $10 to go toward erecting a monument to the memory of the heroes of Harpers Ferry. The colored women in Brooklyn and New York sent Mrs. Leary a total of $140, bringing from her the reply that her loss had been great but she hoped that her husband and his associates had not died in vain in their "attack on that great evil—American Slavery."

Negroes did not wait for history to pass the verdict on John Brown. He was the greatest man of the nineteenth century, ran a resolution adopted by a group of New Bedford Negroes two days after he mounted the scaffold. This evaluation was echoed by Frederick Douglass in a letter to Brown's associate, James Redpath, on June 29, 1860. Brown's portrait graced the wall of the Purvis diningroom at Byberry, Pennsylvania; in Troy, New York, the black children pooled their pennies so that they might buy a picture of him for their school. A Negro weekly compared him with Nat Turner, discovering that both were idealistic, Bible-nurtured, tenacious of purpose, swayed by spiritual impulses, and calm and heroic in prison.

The evaluation of Brown by Negroes was uncritical, since he perhaps "was worth more for hanging than anything else." But as prophets, Negroes did better. For with the ensuing rapid current of national events Brown's fate became a rallying cry and his name a legend. It is true, wrote John A. Copeland, as he sat in the jail awaiting the hangman's noose, that the outbreak at Harpers Ferry did not give immediate freedom to the slave but it was the prelude to that event. . . .

"Our National Sin has found us out," ran an editorial in *Douglass' Monthly* for May 1861. In this Old Testament sense, war had indeed come as sort of an atonement for a fall from grace, an act of redemption, no matter how untoward its expression. But in a sense less retributive and more peculiarly American, the Civil War was a phase of the continual striving for the goals for which this country had been conceived. The downfall of slavery would thus bring additional strength for the tasks ahead. Viewed in this light, the abolitionist crusade itself was but a continuing phase of the revolution of 1776, an attempt to put into practice the doctrine of man's essential equality.

"We have good cause to be grateful to the slave for the benefit we have received to *ourselves,* in working for *him,*" wrote Abby Kelley. "In striving to strike *his* chains off, we found, most surely, that *we* were manacled ourselves." Miss Kelley's sentiment bespoke a largeness of mind and of spirit. But, written in 1838, it did not fully encompass the role of the black American in the abolitionist crusade. More than an unhappy pawn, he had known that he must work to forge his own freedom. And to this task he had brought special skills. The struggle to make man free was a grim business, but he was accustomed to grim businesses. The struggle to make men free might entail armed resistance, but he was crisis-oriented from birth. To the extent that America had a revolutionary tradition, he was its protagonist no less than its symbol.

John Brown

SPEECH TO THE COURT

After Brown's capture, the public paid close attention to his various statements in an effort to understand his seemingly mad venture. Brown's speech to the court at the time of his sentencing, November 2, 1859, won admiration even among the many Northerners who deplored his action. The accompanying letter was part of a large correspondence carried on by Brown during his imprisonment before his execution on December 2.

I have, may it please the Court, a few words to say.

In the first place, I deny everything but what I have all along admitted,—the design on my part to free the slaves. I intended certainly to have made a clean thing of that matter, as I did last winter, when I went into Missouri and there took slaves without the snapping of a gun on either side, moved them through the country, and finally left them in Canada. I designed to have done the same thing again, on a larger scale.[1] That was all I intended. I never did intend

From F. B. Sanborn, ed., *John Brown: Liberator of Kansas and Martyr of Virginia: Life and Letters* (Cedar Rapids, Iowa: The Torch Press, 1910), pp. 584–585.

[1] In explanation of this passage, Brown three weeks afterward handed to Mr. Hunter this letter:—

Charlestown, Jefferson County, Va., Nov. 22, 1859.

Dear Sir,—I have just had my attention called to a seeming confliction between the statement I at first made to Governor Wise and that which I made at the time I received my sentence, regarding my intentions respecting the slaves we took about the Ferry. There need be no such confliction, and a few words of explanation will, I think, be quite sufficient. I had given Governor Wise a full and particular account of that; and when called in court to say whether I had anything further to urge, I was taken wholly by surprise, as I did not expect my sentence before the others. In the hurry of the moment I forgot much that I had before intended to say, and did not consider the full bearing of what I then said. I intended to convey this idea,—that it was my object to place the slaves in a condition to defend their liberties, murder, or treason, or the destruction of property, or to excite or incite slaves to rebellion, or to make insurrection.

I have another objection: and that is, it is unjust that I should suffer such a penalty. Had I interfered in the manner which I admit, and which I admit has been fairly proved (for I admire the truthfulness and candor of the greater portion of the witnesses who have testified in this case),—had I so interfered in behalf of the rich, the powerful, the intelligent, the so-called great, or in behalf of any of their friends,—either father, mother, brother, sister, wife, or children, or any of that class,—and suffered and sacrificed what I have in this interference, it would have been all right; and every man in this court would have deemed it an act worthy of reward rather than punishment.

This court acknowledges, as I suppose, the validity of the law of God. I see a book kissed here which I suppose to be the Bible, or at least the New Testament. That teaches me that all things whatsoever I would that men should do to me, I should do even so to them. It teaches me, further, to "remember them that are in bonds, as bound with them." I endeavored to act up to that instruction. I say, I am yet too young to understand that God is any respecter of persons. I believe that to have interfered as I have done—as I have always freely admitted I have done—in behalf of His despised poor, was not wrong, but right. Now, if it is deemed necessary that I should forfeit my life for the furtherance of the ends of justice, and mingle my blood further with the blood of my children and with the blood of

if they would, without any bloodshed; but not that I intended to run them out of the slave States. I was not aware of any such apparent confliction until my attention was called to it, and I do not suppose that a man in my then circumstances should be superhuman in respect to the exact purport of every word he might utter. What I said to Governor Wise was spoken with all the deliberation I was master of, and was intended for truth; and what I said in court was equally intended for truth, but required a more full explanation than I then gave. Please make such use of this as you think calculated to correct any wrong impressions I may have given.

Very respectfully yours,

John Brown.

Andrew Hunter, Esq., Present.

FIGURE 5. The Arraignment of John Brown before a Virginia Court. Brown is the figure in the foreground. Other prisoners are his associates in the Harpers Ferry Raid. Drawing by Porte Crayon, *Harper's Weekly* (November 12, 1859). (*Boston Public Library*)

millions in this slave country whose rights are disregarded by wicked, cruel, and unjust enactments,—I submit; so let it be done!

Let me say one word further.

I feel entirely satisfied with the treatment I have received on my trial. Considering all the circumstances, it has been more generous than I expected. But I feel no consciousness of guilt. I have stated from the first what was my intention, and what was not. I never had any design against the life of any person, nor any disposition to commit treason, or excite slaves to rebel, or make any general insurrection. I never encouraged any man to do so, but always discouraged any idea of that kind.

Let me say, also, a word in regard to the statements made by some of those connected with me. I hear it has been stated by some of them that I have induced them to join me. But the contrary is true. I do not say this to injure them, but as regretting their weakness. There is not one of them but joined me of his own accord, and the greater part of them at their own expense. A number of them I never saw, and never had a word of conversation with, till the day they came to me; and that was for the purpose I have stated.

Now I have done.

Tilden G. Edelstein

JOHN BROWN AND HIS FRIENDS

In the following essay, Tilden G. Edelstein analyzes the historiography and mythology of John Brown's Raid and argues that Brown is not a suitable hero for American liberals or nonviolent radicals. The essay raises critical questions concerning the intentions of Brown and those abolitionists who helped him prepare for the raid. Edelstein, who teaches at Rutgers University, is the author of Strange Enthusiasm, *a biography of Thomas Wentworth Higginson, one of the "Secret Six."*

A Virginia jury on October 31, 1859, found John Brown guilty of murder, treason and conspiring with slaves and others to rebel. Since that time, questionable logic and the omission and distortion of historical evidence have enabled many advocates of racial equality

This essay, originally presented as a lecture at Amherst College, has been revised by the author for publication in this form, and is used with his permission.

to say that John Brown was not only innocent but also one of the greatest heroes and martyrs of history. His most militant ante-bellum allies have been praised similarly for their unselfish nobility.

The painful slowness with which black Americans are achieving their civil rights appears to reaffirm in the minds of numerous champions of racial equality the need for faith in John Brown and his fellow conspirators. Though Brown is a more fitting symbol for revolutionaries, many nonviolent radicals and liberals—black and white—have idolized him. For example, a writer in the May 1962 issue of *The Crisis,* the NAACP magazine, argues that "the souls of most white Americans are too lacking in the sense of identification" with Brown. While the hateful mob violence of twentieth-century bigots is condemned, the violence of Brown and his supporters is viewed as humanitarian activism. Even the eloquent voice for nonviolence of Martin Luther King uncritically praised Brown. Necessary agitation for racial equality has helped to obscure the historical facts about Brown and to obscure what it means to glorify the Harpers Ferry Raid.

Supporting Brown's use of violence, Henry Thoreau asserted: "The method is nothing; the spirit is all." This argument has been restated by Louis Ruchames, one of Brown's recent and persistent defenders, in the Introduction to his anthology, *A John Brown Reader.* He proposes that John Brown, like the other abolitionists and the Founding Fathers, was devoted "to the highest ideals of equality and democracy" and "the best in the Judaeo-Christian tradition." That Brown frequently practiced the ruthless and relentless use of deception and violence as a means of operation is considered irrelevant, therefore, for judging Brown and his "spirit."

The Abolitionist John Greenleaf Whittier, a staunch ante-bellum supporter of Afro-Americans, was unsure about the ultimate destination toward which John Brown's soul was marching. After the Harpers Ferry Raid, Whittier said: "I have just been looking at one of the *pikes* sent here by a friend in Baltimore. It is not a Christian weapon; it looks too much like murder." Later, Whittier moved closer to praising the spirit of John Brown.

Perish with him the folly
That seeks through evil, good;
Long live the generous purpose
Unstained with human blood!

Not the raid of midnight terror,
But the thought which underlies;
Not the outlaw's pride of daring,
But the Christian sacrifice.

Confusion about achieving a sense of identification with Brown has never been limited to white Americans. The day after he was sentenced, notes Benjamin Quarles in *Black Abolitionists,* a group of Afro-Americans in Providence expressed its "full sympathy" with Brown; it simultaneously declared "abhorrence to bloodshed and civil war." Such specious reasoning is not present in C. Vann Woodward's "John Brown's Private War." Woodward suggests that Brown's "doctrine that the end justifies the means had arrived pretty close to justifying the liquidation of an enemy class." Brown's defenders largely ignore the issue of separating means from ends.

From 1859 to the present, a teleological assumption and a belief in the inevitability of historical events have helped Brown's defenders to feel secure in separating means from ends and also have served to give the Harpers Ferry Raid a disproportionate importance. Brown's supporters have relied upon the often unexpressed assumption that there is a purpose and design in nature that works itself out with or without the help of man. The Civil War is seen as a necessary condition for emancipation. Too frequently it has been assumed with certitude that since the war ended slavery and since John Brown brought war, then it is sound history to assert, by syllogism, that John Brown deserves a place as the emancipator of the slaves. Violence is judged, in retrospect, as *absolutely* the only way slavery could have ended.

Much of the praise for Brown has depended upon another kind of questionable logic, a kind which perhaps can be termed the *worth by association* fallacy. Throughout our history men committed to a pluralistic society and to freedom of association have fought against the repressive practice of employing the guilt by association concept to silence and condemn people with ideas and associations corresponding at certain points with those held by men far more extreme. But they have been less vigilant about the dangers of worth by association. To join with people of different views can be justified, of course, on ideological and practical grounds; but it is intellectually unsound for men to hold in uncritical high regard and to embrace as indistinguishable compeers individuals whose ideas and associations only partly correspond with their own. This sort of weakness has had an enormous influence in raising the reputation of John Brown far beyond the level justified by his deeds. Often Brown has received praise primarily because he associated with humanitarian abolitionists and because he desired to end slavery. But the fallacy of such gratuitous praise becomes apparent by recalling the number of demagogues, tyrants, dictators, incendiaries and assassins who offered their lives trying to bring into being what they believed to be a better society. That a man joined a group which aided runaway slaves, which spoke against slavery, or which fought against the South does not automatically make his motives idealistic, establish his contribution to these causes, nor equalize his role with all others in the group. Receiving this undeserved immunity from careful scrutiny, the story of what Brown was, said, and did often is allowed to remain hidden behind the colorful rhetoric spun by John Brown and his defenders.

The journalist Oswald Garrison Villard, in 1910, published his *John Brown: A Biography Fifty Years After.* A heavily documented book of 738 pages, for sixty years it had been considered the most complete and accurate account of the deeds of Brown and his ante-bellum allies. A grandson of William Lloyd Garrison, the author was the son of Fanny Garrison Villard who was a leader in American peace movements, and of Henry Villard, railroad magnate and newspaper publisher. By the time he began writing his Brown biography, Villard was an active liberal spokesman. Not only had he been an articulate pacifist since the Spanish-American War, but from 1908–1910, while completing his book, Villard led an attack against the leadership of Booker T. Washington and the policy of accommodating and appeasing Southern racism. Villard, along with W. E. B. Du Bois, sought to establish a new and aggressive organization to fight for the civil and political rights of Afro-Americans. His efforts led directly to the formation, in 1910, of the NAACP. Villard, Flint Kellogg notes, "hoped that the celebration by the colored people of the fiftieth anniversary of John Brown's death might inspire its [the NAACP's] birth."

In the Preface to his biography Villard promised a study "free from bias . . . and from the blind prejudice of those who can see in

Brown nothing but a criminal." This goal could be attained, he was sure, by setting forth "the essential truths of history." Though deploring Brown's wholesale use of violence in the chapter titled "Murder on the Pottawatomie," Villard produced a warmly sympathetic account of his life. First, he acquits Brown of criminality and then in his concluding chapter, "Yet Shall He Live," he explains: "In Virginia, John Brown atoned for Pottawatomie by the nobility of his philosophy and his sublime devotion to principle even to the gallows."

Despite the author's intention to write sound history, his fight against Booker T. Washington's excessive gradualism and his commitment to pacifism appear to have led to severe omissions and distortions of the Brown tale. Seeking to condemn Washington's appeasement of Southern racism by contrasting it with Brown's militancy, while simultaneously trying to maintain his own pacifism, induced Villard to cover Brown and the Harpers Ferry Raid with an heroic mantle. Upon Villard's book much of the subsequent defense of Brown has depended for its historical foundation.

Until 1971 James Malin's *John Brown and the Legend of Fifty-Six* (1942) stood as the most extensive scholarly effort to confront Villard and those who before and after him have perpetuated the Brown cult. Malin, primarily treating Brown's efforts in Kansas, suggests that "the business of stealing horses under the cloak of fighting for freedom" was both a major and profitable enterprise for Brown and his men. After thirty-five years and the successive failures of most of his twenty different business enterprises, several of which, according to Malin, were marked by "flagrant dishonesty," John Brown moved into the antislavery business. Imbued with a sincere hatred of slavery, Brown acquiesced to the hard fact that monetary profits were not imminent. He appeared able to envision, however, his future elevation to Commander-in-Chief of a postrevolutionary nation shorn of slavery, which would provide him with both power and financial security. Entering a market where the demand for revolutionaries was modest and the supply even more modest, and understanding that the new calm in Kansas left radical abolitionists in a quandary about where to invest money for antislavery action, Brown combined real entrepreneurial skill and antislavery zeal in raising resources for his projects. But he scarcely can be described as "noble and good" and possessing the "highest idealism."

I have shown in *Strange Enthusiasm: A Life of Thomas Wentworth Higginson* (1968) that Brown's striving to procure money and arms from that group of prominent Northerners who called themselves the Secret Six reveals a man adept at playing upon the guilt felt by middle-class and militant abolitionists who talked of revolution but were not prepared to take part personally in the bloodshed. In making one of his many requests for money from Franklin B. Sanborn, a disciple of Emerson and principal of a Concord private school, Brown suggested that Sanborn and his friends become "conscious that I am performing that service which is equally the duty of millions who need not forego a single hearty dinner by the efforts they are called on to make."

Carefully pitting his key supporters against each other to give each one the feeling of being the closest confederate, Brown wrote to one member of the Secret Six, the celebrated radical minister, Theodore Parker, to assure him that "none of them understand my views as well as you do." Both to Parker and to another abolitionist clergyman, T. W. Higginson, he expressed doubt about the abolitionist earnestness of Sanborn and of another confederate, the affluent Boston manufacturer George L. Stearns. Brown did this in the face of the fact that Sanborn and Stearns were his staunchest supporters while Parker and Higginson had been skeptical about supplying large amounts of money and arms. Such strategy was a major factor in increasing Brown's resources. Higginson was flattered when Brown confided in him that Stearns and Parker "overrated the obstacles," lacked "courage" and "were not men of action." Writing about Brown's way of dealing with fellow conspirators, Higginson said: "The sly old veteran . . . appeared to acquiesce [to the others] far more than he really did. . . . But he wishes me not to tell them what he had said to me."

That Higginson called Brown "the sly old veteran" is important not only for what it discloses about a militant abolitionist's estimate of Brown's character prior to Harpers Ferry, but also for what it reveals about Villard's biography. Higginson's statement is reprinted with the omission of the adjective "sly." Despite the great clarity of

Higginson's handwriting, and though Higginson frequently was consulted during the writing of the book, the biographer still found the word "illegible." Seeking to raise the reputation of Brown to heroic heights, Villard appears to have feared that Brown's character could not be compared favorably with martyrs of world history. And in the views of Brown's future friends the "illegible" word or a comparable characterization has continued to elude mention. Such friends, be they sympathetic historians or platform orators, have remained worshipful of an uncomplicated Brown, a martyr of purity and guilelessness.

If Brown callously used and manipulated the Secret Six—and to Woodward the truth of this is further indicated by his shrewdly leaving behind in the Maryland farmhouse where he must have known they would be found, private papers and letters implicating his absent Northern allies—there is still another side of Brown's relationship with his Northern supporters which deserves attention. Ten days before the raid, Sanborn informed Higginson that "an eager youth" of twenty-two would come to see him. The young man was en route, said Sanborn, to join Brown to contribute his services along with $600 of his own gold. Higginson was shocked when he met Francis Merriam, a nephew of the Boston abolitionist Francis Jackson; Merriam was frail, was totally blind in one eye and seemed to be either mentally unbalanced or somewhat retarded. Earlier, Merriam had written to Wendell Phillips about a desire to give money for "stealing slaves down South" and to partake in such action. Confessing that Southerners "might kill me, of which I should be glad although I am a coward, and do not know how much I should dare do, even in that Cause," he asked Phillips: "Could poison or a deadly weapon be passed to a prisoner caught in the South for stealing slaves?"

When Higginson complained about the fitness of this recruit, Sanborn, three days before the raid, sent him a revealing letter which Villard copied from the original manuscript but chose not to mention in his book:

> *'tis a virtue posted in numbskulls to give money freely. . . . I consider him about as fit to be in this enterprise as the devil is to keep a powder house; but everything has its use & must be put to it if possible. Out of the mouths of babes and sucklings come dollars by the hundred, and*

> *what is wisdom compared to that? I do not expect much of anybody. . . but when a plum drops in your mouth shall you not eat it because it is not a peach or a pumpkin?*

On October 16, John Brown invaded Virginia and within thirty-six hours was subdued by troops under the command of Brevet-Colonel Robert E. Lee. Brown's revolutionary activities had ended permanently, but his Northern supporters still sought to use him as their expendable instrument. During the time preparations were being made for Brown's trial, Higginson wrote: "I don't feel sure that his acquittal would do half as much good as his being executed. . . ." Brown was less eager for execution. His request for legal counsel included the admonition: "Do not send an Ultra-Abolitionist."

Later, when Brown became reconciled to his fate, he had to battle against Abolitionists' desire to send his wife to visit him in jail to gain public sympathy. He was forced to have a telegram sent North. Anticipating great expense and a painful scene, he next sent a letter. "I . . . was feeling quite cheerful before I heard she talked of *coming* on. I can certainly judge better in this matter than ANYONE ELSE." But Mrs. Brown was sent. Also, despite his firm opposition to plans to try to free him forcefully, plans were made to free him; insufficient funds prevented the attempt when the rescuers demanded monetary compensation for their prospective widows and fatherless children. Even at the point of death, John Brown had to strive to avoid being manipulated by his offstage supporters. After the execution, as preparations were being made to move the body to his home in North Elba, New York, the Brown family was asked by some Northern conspirators to make one more sacrifice. But the Browns refused. They denied a request to move John Brown's body to a grave in Mt. Auburn Cemetery in Cambridge.

Thirty years later, Garrison's son, Wendell Phillips Garrison, confidently posed this question: "What would John Brown have been without Boston?" Whether Brown duped his Northern supporters (as Woodward has emphasized) more than they used him, indeed is open to question. Certainly the relationship was less than noble. Brown freely deceived and manipulated the Secret Six. Deserving still greater emphasis, however, is that they showed few compunctions about sending him and his undermanned force to almost certain death. To Brown's eleventh-hour plea that they join him, they responded by staying home and sending Sanborn's "plum," Francis Merriam. After the raid their eagerness for self-sacrifice did not increase.

In 1943, thirty-three years after his book had first appeared, Oswald Garrison Villard published "a new and revised edition." Actually, an Addenda summarizing some manuscript material uncovered since 1910, an additional bibliography, and a new Preface were the only changes in the book. But the Preface, if not the text, showed that the author's views had been influenced by Malin's *John Brown and the Legend of Fifty-Six* and affected even more profoundly by the movement of world events since 1910. Having equally condemned Stalin and Hitler, and having maintained his pacifist position, Villard—the one-time liberal reformer—turned by 1937 to support Republican conservatism and isolationism. Only after Pearl Harbor did he approve America's military efforts. Writing his Preface during the war, Villard still could praise Brown's "spirit and courage in the face of certain death," but now was greatly troubled by Brown's "resort to murderous violence and the armed revolt against his government." Unlike 1910, he said that "there were no proslavery crimes to justify Pottawatomie massacres. . . . Nothing could have excused Brown and his sons for taking the law into their own hands and stabbing men with broadswords, just when they were denouncing the proslavery forces for violating the Constitution and overriding the laws of the country."

Villard, however, despite new reservations about Brown's morality and despite Malin's research, would not surrender unconditionally. In a book review of Malin's work, he argued:

> *But Professor Malin to the contrary notwithstanding, there must have been something in this man to seize the imagination of great sections of the American people, to stir the hearts of men like Channing, Emerson, John A. Andrew, Thomas Wentworth Higginson, Wendell Phillips, and numerous others who flowered and led in New England. Granted that his hands were blood-stained; that his business record was one succession of failures and defaults; that the amount of insanity in his family was appalling and that he received credit for many things he did not do, and was not adequately scourged for sins and crimes, he still becomes a symbol and remains an imperishable figure in our history.*

Says Villard in exclamation, "Surely, no man who was merely a midnight assassin and a horse-thief could have become that!"

What Villard now granted, of course, was enormous; what remained of his case was tenuous. If it is acknowledged that men often become heroic symbols and imperishable historical figures for reasons having more to do with excessive presentism, questionable logic and historical inaccuracy, than with historical fact, Villard's final argument depends solely upon the reliability of popular sentiment and upon the testimony of prominent ante-bellum character witnesses. For Villard, and for all others who have similarly defended Brown, to use such evidence as proof neglects another crucial part of the Harpers Ferry story. Robert Penn Warren's *John Brown: The Making of a Martyr* (1929) noted, and even Brown's supporters generally have agreed, that the prisoner's final trial speech was pivotal in bringing many ante-bellum men to praise the life and work of John Brown. This extraordinarily moving speech indicated to Northerners who previously had been critical or cool to him, the high courage Brown possessed in the face of death. More important, as Warren stressed, the speech denied that Brown had any intention of either spilling blood at Harpers Ferry or of fomenting a slave insurrection in the South. With fine rhetorical skill Brown dropped the role of the vengeful soldier of the Lord who sought to punish the forces of slavery and instead slipped into the garments of a merciful son of God. John Brown's execution, concluded Emerson, "will make the gallows glorious, like a cross."

But by what kind of marvelous alchemy was John Brown transformed into the Prince of Peace? Brown had revealed plans in 1858 for a slave insurrection in his "Provisional Constitution and Ordinances for the People of the United States," a document reprinted in full in the 1860 Report of the Senate Investigating Committee. Knowledge about the contents of the "Provisional Constitution" should have convinced more men that the raid never was intended to be merely a nonviolent expedition where slaves would join Brown without their masters' forcible resistance, live peacefully in the mountains of Virginia, and be inconspicuously sent on their way to Canada. How, furthermore, can peaceful intentions be reconciled with Brown's collection of two hundred rifles, two hundred revolvers, and nine hundred and fifty steel-tipped pikes specially chosen for slaves to use in insurrection, or with his seizure of a United States arsenal, a federal armory and a rifle works? And how are peaceful intentions reconciled with his previous Kansas record of homicide, or with his killing of four residents of Harpers Ferry, the first of whom was a black freeman?

Brown's closest conspiratorial supporters played a major part in encouraging men to evade such questions. These men first helped Brown toward insurrection and then they helped to erase some of his deeds and theirs from the pages of history. (Not until after the Harpers Ferry investigations, however, did they know about Brown's participation in the massacres at Pottawatomie.) Before the failure of the Harpers Ferry venture became apparent, they had openly advocated and encouraged plans for a slave insurrection. As early as May 1857, Higginson told the annual meeting of the American Anti-Slavery Society that "the question of slavery is a stern and practical one. Give us the power, and we can make a new Constitution, or we can interpret the old one. How is that power to be obtained? By politics? Never. By revolution and that alone." And in September of the same year Sanborn understood that Brown was "as ready for revolution as any other man. . . ." "I could not wonder," said Sanborn in February 1858, "if his plan contemplated an uprising of slaves. . . ." Three months later, Higginson again spoke from the public platform and this time joined the issue of insurrection with an estimate about the behavior of the black slave. "We white Anglo-Saxons," said this descendant of the first minister in the Massachusetts Bay Colony, "are too apt to assume the whole work is ours. Behind all these years of shrinking and these long years of cheerful submission [by the slave] . . . there may lie a dagger and a power to use it when the time comes. . . . We speak of the American slave as if he were never to do anything for his own emancipation." Slavery, he predicted, "is destined, as it began in blood, so to end." And when the anarchist, Lysander Spooner who was uninformed about Brown's plans suggested to Higginson, in late November 1858, that a new Northern organization be formed to go South and foment insurrection, Higginson replied that such plans already were launched, apologizing for not being "at liberty to be more explicit." But he did reveal that insurrection would come "by the action of the slaves themselves, in certain localities, with the aid of *secret* cooperation from the whites." While other antislavery men looked hopefully to the new Republican party which opposed the extension of slavery, Higginson said: "Had there been an insurrection every year since the American Revolution, I believe slavery would have been abolished ere this. . . .A single insurrection, with decent temporary success would do more than anything to explode our present political platforms." Finally, when the first bits of exaggerated news about the raid reached Massachusetts, he joyfully referred to "the most formidable slave insurrection that has ever occurred. . . ."

But as soon as it became apparent that Brown's assault had ended in complete disaster for the abolitionist forces, Higginson and the other conspirators joined the retreat. Sanborn, quickly deciding to forego the opportunity to lead his Concord students on their annual chestnut-hunting excursion, fled toward the Canadian border. "According to advice of good friends and my own deliberate judgment," wrote this zealous advocate of revolution, "I am to try a change of air for my old complaint. . . ,whether my absence will be long or short will depend on circumstances. . . . Burn this. . . ." Stearns and Samuel Gridley Howe joined the migration north. Frederick Douglass, who previously had planned to visit England, now saw his trip as a means of refuge from arrest. Gerrit Smith, the Syracuse philanthropist who had given Brown more money than any other man, stayed in the country but required temporary shelter at the New York State Asylum for the Insane at Utica.

Putting the John Brown tale into verse, Stephen Vincent Benet reflected the judgment of past historians: "Only the tough, swart-minded Higginson/ Kept a grim decency, would not deny." And it is true that Higginson neither denied complicity nor fled the country. However, like all other close ante-bellum supporters of Brown except Parker, Higginson denied in another way. He would never again say that John Brown and his Northern allies had been looking forward to a slave insurrection. Instead, some forty years after the raid, Higginson claimed that he had known in 1859 that "the delicate balance of the zealot's mind" had been "somewhat disturbed."

Wendell Phillips did say that "the lesson of the hour is insurrection," but he then added: "I ought not to apply that word to John Brown of Osawatomie. . . . It is a great mistake to call him an insurgent." Frederick Douglass mentioned "future insurgents" and "the insurrection test" but did not link Brown with plans for violent slave insurrection. "Hiding places" for runaway slaves amidst the "lofty peaks of the Alleghenies" was what Brown sought, according to Douglass. James Redpath, an abolitionist journalist and companion of both Brown and Merriam, wrote a series of newspaper articles during late October 1859 which he variously titled "Reminiscences of the Insurrection" and "Notes on the Insurrection." He categorically stated: "Brown believed that slavery must be abolished by a servile insurrection." But after Brown's trial speech expressing abhorrence of bloodshed and insurrection, Redpath also changed his mind. He even took a step backward. His book, *The Public Life of John Brown,* published soon after Brown's death, made no mention of slave insurrection. Brown wanted "not revolution, but justice," wrote Redpath. The author, aware of the massacre at Pottawatomie, refrained from connecting Brown's deeds in Kansas with those at Harpers Ferry. "For such a notion," Redpath shrewdly conceded in private, "degrades him from the position of a Puritan 'warrior of the Lord' to a guerrilla chief of vindictive character." Brown's defenders, from Emerson to the present day, generally have been as understanding as Redpath.

No defender of Brown's purity and nobility is Stephen B. Oates' *To Purge This Land With Blood* (1971), the first full length scholarly Brown biography ever published by a professional historian. Oates accepts neither Allan Nevins' view of Brown as a madman nor James Malin's portrait of a Kansas horse thief who had been a blatantly dishonest businessman. Brown simply was "a bit more reckless and incompetent than the average western speculator" according to Oates' evidence. Throughout life, Brown was "negligent, careless and inept." At Harpers Ferry, the culmination of his career, his insurrectionary efforts were hampered by a profusion of tactical blunders including having collected the wrong caliber ammunition for some of his guns.

In recent years, John Brown has been enlisted again to provide a viable tradition for nonviolent civil rights agitation. Exonerated posthumously from the guilt of murder by his deeds being contrasted with the greater guilt of slaveholders, Brown has become identified with men of good will. But it should be remembered that his ante-bellum allies, black and white, hesitated about supporting him until his execution day drew near and memories of his deeds became blurred. And there is real doubt whether John Brown, their expendable warrior, ever identified with these men who were sure of their next "hearty dinner." It is also doubtful whether today's activists for racial equality who oppose using guns, bombs and torches should imagine that John Brown, the apostle of violence, would have identified with them. Brown's place is more properly among those who have emerged from obscurity to make history as insurrectionists or assassins.

V THE HISTORIANS' SEARCH FOR NEW PERSPECTIVES

Motivations: Personal and Institutional

Avery Craven

THE NORTHERN ATTACK ON SLAVERY

A noted advocate of the view that the Civil War was a great national tragedy, Avery Craven, of the University of Chicago, presents his evaluation of abolitionists, especially William Lloyd Garrison, in the following selection from his The Coming of the Civil War *(1942). Craven was one of the first historians to suggest psychological maladjustment as a partial explanation for abolitionists' activities, and his interpretation has been widely influential.*

Removing motes from a brother's eye is an ancient practice. The urge to make over other individuals and to correct real or fancied evils in society operates with unusual force in certain individuals. This used to be ascribed to a peculiar sensitiveness of wrongdoing —a willingness to sacrifice personal comfort for a larger good. Perpetual reformers, though resented as meddlers by those they disturbed, have been hailed as pioneers and martyrs who have unselfishly helped to usher in new eras and a better world.

The modern psychologist is somewhat skeptical of such explanations. He talks of youthful experiences, maladjustments, inferiority complexes, and repressed desires. He is not so sure about the sources of the reform impulse or the unselfish character of the reformer. The student of social affairs is likewise less inclined to grant unstinted praise to the fanatic and is not certain about the value of the contribution. He views him as a normal product of social phenomena acting on certain types of personality. He sees the triumph of emotion over reason in the extremist's course and sometimes wonders if the developments of history might not have been more sound without him. He talks with less assurance about "progress" in human affairs.

From Avery Craven, *The Coming of the Civil War* (New York: Charles Scribner's Sons, 1942), pp. 117–118, 134–138, 149–150. Reprinted by permission of the author. Footnotes omitted.

At all events, recent historians have been inclined to reconsider the part played by the abolitionists in the coming of the War Between the States. They have judged the reformer and his efforts to be open fields for new study. The old assumptions that the movements against slavery arose entirely from a disinterested hatred of injustice and that their results were good beyond question can no longer be accepted without reservations. Those who force the settlement of human problems by war can expect only an unsympathetic hearing from the future. Mere desire to do "right" is no defense at the bar of history. . . .

The abolition movement was . . . closely related in origins, leadership, and expression to the peace movement, the temperance crusade, the struggles for women's rights, prison and Sabbath reform, and the improvement of education. It was not unrelated to the efforts to establish communities where social-economic justice and high thinking might prevail. It was part of the drive to unseat aristocrats and reestablish American democracy according to the Declaration of Independence. It was a clear-cut effort to apply Christianity to the American social order.

The antislavery effort was at first merely one among many. It rose to dominance only gradually. Fortunate from the beginning in leadership, it was always more fortunate in appeal. Human slavery more obviously violated democratic institutions than any other evil of the day; it was close enough to irritate and to inflame sensitive minds, yet far enough removed that reformers need have few personal relations with those whose interests were affected. It rasped most severely upon the moral senses of a people whose ideas of sin were comprehended largely in terms of self-indulgence and whose religious doctrines laid emphasis on social usefulness as the proper manifestation of salvation. And, what was more important, slavery was now confined to a section whose economic interests, and hence political attitudes, conflicted sharply with those of the Northeast and upper Northwest.

Almost from the beginning of the new antislavery movement, two distinct centers of action appeared, each with its distinct and individual approach to the problem. One developed in the industrial areas of New England. Its most important spokesman was William Lloyd Garrison, founder and editor of a Boston abolition paper called the

Liberator. Garrison at first accepted the old idea that slavery was an *evil* to be pointed out and gradually eradicated by those among whom it existed, but he shifted his position in the early 1830s and denounced slavery as a damning crime to be unremittingly assailed and immediately destroyed. The first issue of his paper announced a program from which he never deviated: ". . . *I do not wish to think or speak or write with moderation.* I will not retreat a single inch, and I will be heard." The problem, as Garrison saw it, was one of abstract right and wrong. The Scriptures and the Declaration of Independence had already settled the issue. Slavery could have no legal status in a Christian democracy. If the Constitution recognized it, then the Constitution should be destroyed. Slaveholders were both sinners and criminals. They could lay no claim to immunity from any mode of attack.

The character of this movement and its leadership is strikingly revealed in an incident related by one of Garrison's traveling companions:

> *As we rode through the [Franconia] Notch after friends Beach and Rogers, we were alarmed at seeing smoke issue from their chaise-top, and we cried out to them that their chaise was afire! We were more than suspicious that it was something worse than that, and that the smoke came out of friend Rogers' mouth. And so it turned out. This was before we reached the Notch tavern. Alighting there to water our beasts, we gave him, all round a faithful admonition. For anti-slavery does not fail to spend its intervals of public service in mutual and searching correction of the faults of its friends. We gave it soundly to friend Rogers—that he, an abolitionist, on his way to an anti-slavery meeting, should desecrate his anti-slavery mouth . . . with a stupefying weed. We had halted at the Iron Works tavern to refresh our horses, and while they were eating walked to view the Furnace. As we crossed the little bridge, friend Rogers took out another cigar, as if to light it when we should reach the fire! "Is it any malady you have got, brother Rogers," said we to him, "that you smoke that thing, or is it habit and indulgence merely?" "It is nothing but habit," said he gravely; "or I would say, it was nothing else," and he significantly cast the little roll over the railing into the Ammonoosuck.*
>
> *"A Revolution!" exclaimed Garrison, "a glorious revolution without noise or smoke," and he swung his hat cheerily about his head. It was a pretty incident. . . . It was a vice abandoned, a self indulgence denied, and from principle. It was quietly and beautifully done. . . . Anti-slavery wants her mouths for other uses than to be flues for besotting tobacco-smoke. They may as well almost be rum-ducts as tobacco-funnels. . . .*

> *Abolitionists are generally as crazy in regard to rum and tobacco as in regard to slavery. Some of them refrain from eating flesh and drinking tea and coffee. Some of them are so bewildered that they want in the way of Christian retaliation . . . they are getting to be monomaniacs, as the Reverend Punchard called us, on every subject.*

The extreme and impractical nature of the Garrison antislavery drive served to attract attention and arouse antagonism rather than to solve the problem. It did, however, show how profoundly the conditions of the time had stirred the reform spirit and how wide the door had been opened to the professional reformers—men to whom the question was not so much "how shall we abolish slavery, as how shall we best discharge our duty . . . to ourselves." Garrison may be taken as typical of the group. His temperament and experiences had combined to set him in most relationships against the accepted order of things. His life would probably have been spent in protesting even if slavery had never existed. From childhood he had waged a bitter fight *against* obstacles and *for* a due recognition of his abilities. A drunken father had abandoned the family to extreme poverty before William was three years old, and the boy, denied all but the rudiments of an education, had first been placed under the care of Deacon Bartlett, and then apprenticed for seven years to one Ephraim Allen to learn the printing trade. His first venture after his apprenticeship was over failed. His second gave him the opportunity to strike back at an unfair world. He became an editor of the *National Philanthropist,* a paper devoted to the suppression of "intemperance and its Kindred vices." This publication served also as a medium through which to attack lotteries, Sabbath-breaking, and war. A new Garrison began to emerge. His personality, given opportunity for expression, asserted itself. Attending a nominating caucus in Boston, he made bold to speak, and, being resented as an upstart, he replied to his critic in a letter to the Boston *Courier:*

> *It is true my acquaintance in this city is limited. . . . Let me assure him, however, that if my life be spared, my name shall one day be known to the world—at least to such an extent that common inquiry shall be unnecessary.*

To another critic he reiterated this statement, adding these significant words: "I speak in the spirit of prophecy, not of vainglory—

with a strong pulse, a flashing eye, and a glow of the heart. The task may be yours to write my biography.

Antislavery efforts entered the Garrison program when Benjamin Lundy, the pioneer abolitionist, invited him to help edit the *Genius of Universal Emancipation* in Baltimore. Hostile treatment there, climaxed by imprisonment for libel, together with the influence of extreme British opinion, changed a moderate attitude which admitted "that immediate and complete emancipation is not desirable . . . no rational man cherishes so wild a vision," into the extreme and uncompromising fanaticism expressed only two years later in the *Liberator.* From that time on Garrison was bothered only by the fact that the English language was inadequate for the expression of his violent opinions. Southerners in Congress were desperados.

> *We would sooner trust the honor of the country . . . in the hands of the inmates of our penitentiaries and prisons than in their hands . . . they are the meanest of thieves and the worst of robbers. . . . We do not acknowledge them to be within the pale of Christianity, or republicanism, or humanity!*

Hatred of the South had supplanted love for the Negro!

In such an approach as this, there could be no delay, no moderation. Right was right, and wrong was wrong. The slaveholder could not be spared or given time to learn the evil of his ways. Action immediate and untempered was demanded. . . .

Two principal assumptions stood out in this antislavery indictment of the slaveholder. He was, in the first place, the arch-aristocrat. He was the great enemy of democracy. He was un-American, the oppressor of his fellow men, the exploiter of a weaker brother. Against him could be directed all the complaints and fears engendered by industrial captains and land speculators. He, more than any other aristocrat, threatened to destroy the American democratic dream.

In the second place, he was a flagrant sinner. His self-indulgence was unmatched. His licentious conduct with Negro women, his intemperance in the use of intoxicating liquors, his mad dueling, and his passion for war against the weak were enough to mark him as the nation's moral enemy number one! The time for dealing moderately had passed. Immediate reform was imperative.

Thus it was that the slaveholder began to do scapegoat service for all aristocrats and all sinners. To him were transferred resentments and fears born out of local conditions. Because it combined in itself both the moral and the democratic appeal, and because it coincided with sectional rivalry, the abolition movement gradually swallowed up all other reforms. The South became the great object of all efforts to remake American society. Against early indifference and later persecution, a handful of deadly-in-earnest men and women slowly built into a section's consciousness the belief in a Slave Power. To the normal strength of sectional ignorance and distrust they added all the force of Calvinistic morality and American democracy and thereby surrounded every Northern interest and contention with holy sanction and reduced all opposition to abject depravity. When the politician, playing his risky game, linked expansion and slavery, Christian common folk by the thousands, with no great personal urge for reforming, accepted the abolition attitudes toward both the South and slavery. Civil war was then in the making.

Martin B. Duberman

THE ABOLITIONISTS AND PSYCHOLOGY

Martin B. Duberman began his scholarly career in a period when important post-Freudian psychological theories offered new concepts for examining human behavior and when the struggle for civil rights encouraged a new imaginative identification with abolitionists. He has turned both these factors to advantage in the following article. Duberman is the author of Charles Francis Adams, 1807–1886, *and* James Russell Lowell.

Out of their heightened concern with the pressing question of Negro rights, a number of historians, especially the younger ones, have begun to take a new look at the abolitionists, men who in their own day were involved in a similar movement of social change. About both them and ourselves we are asking anew such questions as the

From Martin B. Duberman, "The Abolitionists and Psychology," *Journal of Negro History* 47 (July 1962): 183–191. Reprinted by permission of the publisher, the Association for the Study of Negro Life and History, Inc.

proper role of agitation, the underlying motives of both reformers and resistants, and the useful limits of outside interference. From this questioning a general tendency has developed to view the abolitionists in a more favorable light than previously. As yet, however, it is a tendency only, and hostility to the abolitionists continues to be strong among historians.[1]

Perhaps one reason why no fuller reevaluation has taken place is that historians have been made cautious by the fate of previous "revisionist" scholarship. We have seen how current preoccupations can prompt dubious historical reevaluations. But this need not always be the case. Contemporary pressures, if recognized and contained, can prove fruitful in stimulating the historical imagination. They may lead us to uncover (not invent) aspects of the past to which we were previously blind.

If historians need more courage in their re-consideration of the abolitionists, they also need more information. Particularly do they need to employ some of the insights and raise some of the questions which developments in related fields of knowledge have made possible. Recent trends in psychology seem especially pertinent, though historians have not paid them sufficient attention. It is my hope in this paper to make some beginning in that direction.

It might be well to start by referring to one of psychology's older principles, the uniqueness of personality. Each individual, with his own genetic composition and his own life experience, will develop into a distinctive organism. There are, of course, certain universal processes common to the species—that cluster of basic drives and reflexes which are more or less "instinctive." There are also a variety of common responses conditioned by our membership in a particular group, be it family, class, church or nation. These similarities among human beings make possible such disciplines as sociology, anthropology and social psychology, which concern themselves with patterns of behavior, and demonstrate that no man is *sui generis.*

[1] I deliberately refrain from citing specific works and authors. In suggestions as tentative as mine, I have not thought it profitable to take issue with individuals. I wish to make clear that I am not suggesting that *all* historians have viewed the abolitionists without sympathy or understanding. Men such as Louis Filler, Dwight Dumond, Irving Bartlett, Leon Litwack, Ralph Korngold, Louis Ruchames, Oscar Sherwin, and David Davis have, in varying degrees, and with varying effectiveness, demonstrated their sympathy. But they have not, in my view, as yet carried the majority of historians along with them.

But it does not follow that the qualities which are uniquely individual are mere irrelevancies. As Gordon Allport has said, ". . . all of the animals in the world are psychologically less distinct from one another than one man is from other men."[2]

This is not to question, of course, the validity of attempts, whether they be by sociologists, psychologists or historians, to find meaningful similarities in the behavioral patterns of various human groups. The point is to make certain that such similarities genuinely exist, and further, to be aware that in describing them, we do not pretend to be saying *everything* about the individuals involved. Historians, it seems, are prone to ignore both cautions—their treatment of the abolitionists being the immediate case in point.

With barely a redeeming hint of uncertainty, many historians list a group of "similar traits" which are said to characterize all abolitionists: "impractical," "self-righteous," "fanatical," "humorless," "vituperative," and,—if they are very modern in their terminology—"disturbed." The list varies, but usually only to include adjectives equally hostile and denunciatory. The stereotype of the "abolitionist personality," though fluid in details, is clear enough in its general outlines.

But did most abolitionists really share these personality traits? The fact is, we know much less about the individuals involved in the movement than has been implied. Some of the major figures, such as Joshua Leavitt, have never received biographical treatment; others—the Tappans, Edmund Quincy, and Benjamin Lundy, for example—badly need modern appraisal. And the careers and personalities of the vast majority of significant secondary figures—people like Lydia Maria Child, Sidney Gay, Maria Weston Chapman, Henry B. Stanton, and Abby Kelley Foster—have been almost totally unexplored. Whence comes the confidence, then, that allows historians to talk of "the abolitionist personality," as if this had been microscopically examined and painstakingly reconstructed?

Certainly the evidence which we do have, does not support such confident theorizing. In order to adhere to this conceptual straitjacket, it is necessary to ignore or discount much that conflicts with it—the modesty of Theodore Weld, the wit of James Russell Lowell,

[2] Gordon W. Allport, *Becoming, Basic Considerations for a Psychology of Personality* (Clinton, 1960), p. 23.

the tender humanity of Whittier, the worldly charm of Edmund Quincy. This does not mean that we need leap to the opposite extreme and claim all abolitionists were saints and seraphs. But if some of them were disagreeable or disturbed, we want, instead of a blanket indictment, to know which ones and in what ways; we want some recognition of the variety of human beings who entered the movement.

It seems to me that what too many historians have done is to take William Lloyd Garrison as a personality symbol for the entire movement (at the same time, ironically, that they deny him the commanding leadership which he was once assumed to have had). Fixing on some of the undeniably "neurotic" aspects of his personality (and bolstered, it should be said, by the eccentric psychographs of other abolitionists—a Gerrit Smith say, or a Stephen Foster), they equate these with the personality structures of all the abolitionists, and conclude that the movement was composed solely of "quacks." In doing so, they fail to do justice to the wide spectrum of personality involved; in fact, they do not even do justice to Garrison, for to speak exclusively of *his* oracular and abusive qualities is to ignore the considerable evidence of personal warmth and kindliness.

It may be that when we know more of other abolitionists, we may with equal certainty be able to single out qualities in them which seem palpable symptoms of "disturbance." But let the evidence at least precede the judgment. And let us also show a decent timidity in applying the label "neurotic." Psychiatrists, dealing with a multitude of evidence and bringing to it professional insights, demonstrate more caution in this regard than do untrained historians working with mere traces of personality. If the disposition to be hostile exists, "neurosis" can almost always be established. Under the Freudian microscope, it would be a rare man indeed whose life showed no evidence of pathological behavior. (Think, for one, of the admirable William James, who, as his devoted biographer, Ralph Barton Perry, has shown, was subject to hypochondria, hallucinations, and intense oscillations of mood.) I am not suggesting that all men's lives, if sufficiently investigated, would show equally severe evidence of disturbance. I mean only to warn that, given the double jeopardy of a hostile commentator and the weight of a hostile historical tradition, we must take special precaution not to be too easily convinced by the "evidence" of neurosis in the abolitionists.

And even were we to establish the neurotic component of behavior, the story would certainly not be complete. To know the pathological elements in an individual's behavior is not to know everything about his behavior. To say that Garrison, in his fantasy world, longed to be punished and thus deliberately courted martyrdom, or that Wendell Phillips, alienated from the "new order," sought to work out his private grievances against the industrial system by indirectly attacking it through slavery, is hardly to exhaust the range of their possible motives. We know far too little about why men do anything —let alone why they do something as specific as joining a reform movement—to assert as confidently as historians have, the motives of whole groups of men. We may never know enough about the human psyche to achieve a comprehensive analysis of motivation; how much greater the difficulty when the subject is dead and we are attempting the analysis on the basis of partial and fragmentary remains.

Our best hope for increased understanding in this area—aside from the artist's tool of intuition—is in the researches of psychology. But at present there is no agreed-upon theory of motivation among psychologists. Gordon Allport, however, summarizing current opinion, suggests that behavior does not result solely from the need to reduce tension, but may also aim (especially in a "healthy" person) at distant goals, the achievement of which can be gained only by maintaining tension.[3] Allport does not press his views, realizing the complexity of the problems at issue. But his hypotheses are at least suggestive as regards the abolitionists, for their motives, rather than being solely the primitive ones of eliminating personal tension (under the guise of ethical commitment), may also have included a healthy willingness to bear tension (in the form of ostracism, personal danger and material sacrifice) in order to persevere in the pursuit of long-range ideals.

Acceptance of these suggestions runs into the massive resistance of neo-Freudian cynicism.[4] How old-fashioned, it will be said, to talk in terms of "ideals" or "conscience," since these are only unconscious rationalizations for "darker" drives which we are unable to

[3] Ibid., pp. 65–68.
[4] Based largely on what people think Freud said, rather than what he actually said. See Philip Rieff, *Freud: The Mind of the Moralist* (New York, 1959).

face. How old-fashioned, too, to talk as if men could exercise choice in their conduct, since all our behavior is determined by our antecedents.

But the surprising fact is that such views are not old-fashioned. On the contrary, they have recently returned to favor in psychoanalytical circles.[5] Increasing dissatisfaction with the ability of behaviorist theory fully to explain human action, has led to a reconsideration of the role of reason and the possibilities of purposive, deliberate behavior. The result is the influential new school of "ego psychology," which views man as endowed with a considerable margin of freedom and responsibility, and which has restored to the vocabulary such "old-fashioned" terminology as character, will-power and conscience. Moral earnestness, moreover, is no longer equated with self-deception. As Allport has said, the very mark of maturity "seems to be the range and extent of one's feeling of self-involvement in abstract ideals."[6] Some of these new emphases had been prefigured in the work of such philosophers as Sartre, who have long stressed social action as a sign of "authenticity" in man.

But although all of this makes a reevaluation of the abolitionists possible, it does not make one necessary. Men may now be thought capable of impersonal devotion to ideals, but this does not mean that the abolitionists were such men. Maturity may now be defined as the ability to commit ourselves objectively to ethical values, but it does not follow that every man who makes such a commitment does so out of mature motives.

Yet at least some doubts should be raised in our minds as to whether we have been fair in regarding the abolitionists as psychologically homogeneous, and at that, homogeneous in the sense of being self-deceived. My own feeling goes beyond doubt, into conviction. I do not claim, to repeat, that because the abolitionists fought in a noble cause, their motives were necessarily noble—that is, "pure" and "unselfish," unrelated in any way to their own inner turmoil or conflicts. A connection between inner problems and outer convictions probably always exists to some degree. But an individual's public involvement is never completely explained by discussing

[5] See, for example, O. Hobart Mowrer, "Psychiatry and Religion," *The Atlantic* (July 1961).
[6] Allport, op. cit., 45.

his private pathology. Yet it is just this that historians have frequently done, and to that degree, they have distorted and devalued the abolitionist commitment.

To provide a concrete example, by way of summary, consider the case of James Russell Lowell, whose biography I am writing, and about whom I can talk with more assurance than I might some other figure.

His history seems to me convincing proof that at least *some* people became abolitionists not primarily out of an unconscious need to escape from personal problems, but out of a deliberate, rational commitment to certain ethical values—recognizing, as I have said, that the two are never wholly unrelated. Lowell's active life as a reformer came during the period of his greatest contentment—secure in a supremely happy marriage, and confident of his talents and his future. His contemporaries agree in describing him as a gay, witty, warm man, without serious tensions or disabling anxieties. I have come across so little evidence of "pathology" in the Lowell of these years that when the standard picture of the abolitionist as a warped eccentric is applied to him, it becomes absurd.

And he *was* an abolitionist, though various arguments have been used to deny this. Lowell, it has been said, came to the movement late—and only at the instigation of his bride, Maria White, who was a confirmed reformer, never fully committed himself to abolition, and finally left the ranks in the early 1850s. There may be some justice to these charges, but on the whole the argument is not persuasive. Given Lowell's youth (he was born in 1819) he could not have joined the movement much earlier than he did (which was around 1840), and there is evidence that he was involved in the cause before he met Maria White. The important point is that for roughly ten years he was unquestionably a serious abolitionist, both as an active member of the Massachusetts Anti-Slavery Society, and as a frequent contributor to abolitionist periodicals. The reasons for his drifting out of the movement are complex, but turn largely on the fact that his wife's death in 1853 destroyed the structure of his life and left him apathetic to public issues. (Might not this give added weight to the argument that it takes a reasonably contented man to interest himself in the problems of others?)

Even when it is admitted that Lowell was an abolitionist, he is dismissed as not having been a "typical" one. But who was the typical abolitionist? Is the standard of measurement meant to be some outstanding individual—Garrison, say, or Theodore Weld—and is everyone else to be considered more or less of an abolitionist depending on how closely he approximated the personality structure of the model? But a man may be prominent in a movement without necessarily typifying it. And which of several leading—and very different—figures should be chosen as the model? The decision is likely to be arbitrary (and unconscious), varying with each historian.

Or is the standard of measurement meant to be some composite group of traits which accurately describe the large number of abolitionists, so that when any single individual fails to exhibit these traits, he may justifiably be dismissed as "the exception which proves the rule?"[7] This approach is more reasonable, but here again we run up against the old difficulty of drawing a genuinely valid group portrait. We know so little about the individual personalities and careers of the majority of abolitionists that it seems like putting the cart before the horse to even talk about a composite portrait. Certainly the one which is now commonly accepted ("impractical"; "self-righteous," etc.) fails adequately to describe many of the abolitionists about whom we do have information. I mean here not only Lowell, but a number of others. What I have seen in my researches into the papers of people like Edmund Quincy, Lydia Maria Child or Maria Weston Chapman (to name only a few of the more prominent), has created the strong suspicion in my mind that if their personalities were to be investigated in depth, they too would be found to deviate from the accepted portrait in so many significant ways as further to undermine its reliability.

A conceptual scheme may yet be devised which adequately describes the motives and actions of most of the abolitionists. But if so, it will not be of the primitive kind thus far suggested. There is no reason why historians cannot legitimately investigate group patterns, but to do so meaningfully, they must become skilled in the techniques of sociology and other related disciplines. This takes

[7] It is interesting that in its original form, the aphorism read: "is this the exception which *probes* the rule?"

time and inclination, and the historian, busy with his special interests and orientated towards the particular, rarely has either. Unfortunately this does not always prevent him from trying his hand, though the result has too often been the elementary kind of categorizing used to describe the abolitionists.

Opinions will continue to differ as to the best way of achieving desired social change. Our own generation's confrontation with segregation has made this clear. Many of us feel as strongly about the evil of that practice as the abolitionists did about the institution of slavery. Like them, too, we have scant faith in Southern voluntarism or the benevolent workings of time; patience and inactivity have not done their work. Naturally we would like to believe that our sense of urgency comes from concern for the Negro rather than from a need to escape from some private torment of our own. Because of this we are admittedly prone to credit our historical counterparts with the kind of "good" motives we would like to impute to ourselves. Our wish to think well of these people may account for our doing so. But as Erich Fromm has said, "the fact that an idea satisfies a wish does not mean necessarily that the idea is false."[8] There is much in the new psychology to encourage the belief that the idea is not false. At any rate, if we are to find out, we need less dogma, more research, and a chastening sense of wonder at the complexities of human nature.

[8] Erich Fromm, *Psychoanalysis and Religion* (Clinton, 1959), p. 12.

Stanley M. Elkins

SLAVERY: A PROBLEM IN AMERICAN INSTITUTIONAL AND INTELLECTUAL LIFE

Stanley Elkins is a historian known for his willingness to use the concepts and methods of the social sciences. In a fruitful collaboration, he and Eric McKitrick have produced a series of studies presenting fresh approaches to several areas of American history. The volume from which the following selection is taken applies concepts of sociology, cultural anthropology and social psychology to historical problems concerning slavery and antislavery. This excerpt presents in highly condensed fashion Elkins's theory that abolitionists acted as they did because of the nature of American society, notably its lack of institutions and its exaggeration of the importance of the individual. It would have been better, he contends, if abolitionists had seen slavery as an institution "mutable like others." Elkins teaches history at Smith College.

It was inherent in the state of sensibility which Western civilization had attained by the nineteenth century that slavery, involving the most basic values of humanity, should at that time become morally absorbing to both Europeans and Americans. Englishmen, Frenchmen, Spaniards, and Portuguese each responded to the oppressive subject at various levels of intensity in thought and action; out of their complex experience each could focus upon slavery a variety of resources in order that they might judge its evils, mitigate its abuses, and finally abolish it altogether. There is a certain sense in which the same might be said of the Americans. Yet the simple and harsh moral purity of our own antislavery movement, from the 1830s on, gave it a quality which set it apart from the others. The theory of society which was its backdrop, the intellectual expressions upon which it drew, the slogans which it sent to the market place, the schemes for practical action which it evolved—every phase of the movement combined to produce in our abolitionists that peculiar quality of abstraction which was, and has remained, uniquely Ameri-

Reprinted from *Slavery: A Problem in American Institutional and Intellectual Life* by Stanley M. Elkins by permission of The University of Chicago Press, pp. 27–37, 175–178, 183–185, 189–193. Footnotes omitted.

can. For them, the question was *all* moral; it must be contemplated in terms untouched by expediency, untarnished by society's organic compromises, uncorrupted even by society itself. It was a problem of conscience which by mid-century would fasten itself in one form or another, and in varying degrees, upon men's feelings everywhere.

But while our thinkers and reformers considered the issue in such abstract purity, in such simple grandeur, there was, in principle if not in fact, an alternative philosophical mode. Slavery might have been approached not as a problem in pure morality but as a question of institutional arrangements—a question of those institutions which make the crucial difference in men's relationships with one another, of those arrangements whereby even so theoretically simple a connection as that between master and slave might take any of a dozen forms among which the sharpest and finest of moral distinctions might be made. This approach was of course never taken, and to expect it of nineteenth-century Americans would be to make impossible demands upon their experience. It is, however, still of interest to ask why this should be so. Why should the American of, say, 1830 have been so insensitive to institutions and their function?

Consider the seeming paradox of how by that time, in the very bright morning of American success, the power of so many American institutions had one by one melted away. The church had fallen into a thousand parts. The shadow of an Anglican church, disestablished in the wake of the Revolution and its doom forever sealed by the yearly anarchy of the camp meeting, was all that remained in the South of vested ecclesiastical authority; and in New England the Congregational church, which had once functioned as a powerful state establishment, was deprived of its last secular supports early in the century. It was not that religion itself was challenged—quite the contrary—but that as a source both of organized social power and internal discipline the church had undergone a relentless process of fragmentation. Religious vitality everywhere was overwhelming, but that vitality lay primarily in demands for individual satisfaction which took inevitable and repeated priority over institutional needs. The very ease with which the great evangelical sects could divide, by a sort of cellular fission, into myriads of tiny independent units, showed that the institutional balance between official coercion and individual self-expression had completely broken down.

As for the bar, the very profusion of lawyers on the American scene, their numbers daily increasing, made a central focus of traditional and vested power among them out of the question; no such continuing structure as the English bar, with its institutional self-awareness, its standards of competence and discipline, its stabilized recruitment, its Temples and Inns of Court, could exist in America. There was a brief period, in the later eighteenth century, when organizations of the bar in our eastern cities did appear capable of providing such a nucleus of stability. But here too, as with the church and the ministry, the great expansion getting under way after the War of 1812, bringing so widespread a demand for services of whatever quality, soon made it clear that individual drives rather than institutional needs would prevail. With the democratization of the bar and its inevitable decline in standards, came a deterioration of whatever institutional bulwarks the bar might have developed.

In our politics, as elsewhere, the old organizational balance was dissolving; something new and unprecedented was emerging in the shape of mass parties. In a way, of course, the sheer formlessness of the new system would cloak an inscrutable logic; its very innocence of principle would foster a special conservatism; its apparent lack of focus would be its own protection, enabling it to act as a kind of super-institution absorbing the functions of a dozen institutions which no longer existed. Yet in its very birth it was necessary that an older, a more stable and traditional conception of political responsibility should disappear. The Federalist party, even in New England, was by 1830 utterly dead. The Federalists, though in actual policy hardly different from their successors, had assumed and embodied certain traditional attributes of political life which later establishments did not and could not provide. They took their impulse and *esprit* from the Fathers themselves, and their very aura of exclusiveness made possible a certain sharpness of focus. They took for granted the tradition that politics was an occupation for men of affairs, property, and learning. The Federalist party, by its very air of vested interest, came closer than any of its successors to providing a clear institutional nucleus for the loyalty and commitment of other vested interests in society—the intelligentsia, the ministry, the bar, the propertied classes. But the wide democratization of politics in the 1820s ordained that political life in the United States should assume a completely new tone, one quite different from that imagined by the Fathers. Even the Jeffersonians, following the Federalists, had moved more or less instinctively to establish institutional safeguards for political leadership, discipline, and power; yet they too, in the 1820s, saw their special creation, the congressional caucus, swept away and damned as an engine of aristocracy and privilege.

Even in the country's economic activity this breakdown of structural equilibrium was quite as evident as it was in other sectors of public life. The reasonably stable economic organizations maintained by the great trading families of the East were being challenged by a rising class of petty industrialists everywhere. It need not be supposed that these mercantile and banking structures were in a state of decline; yet in a relative sense their power and leadership, amid the proliferation of the small enterprise, no longer carried the decisive weight of former times. The very tone of business life assumed a character peculiarly indicative of what was happening. Its keynote was the individual confronted with boundless opportunity; a veritable new culture-hero was being fashioned on the frontier of the Old Northwest: the young man on the make, in whose folklore the eastern banker, bulwarked by privilege and monopoly, would become a tarnished symbol. The one really effective economic institution that did exist—the second Bank of the United States—was consigned to oblivion amid the cheers of the populace. Capitalism was burgeoning indeed, but in anything but a conservative way; its very dynamism was breaking old molds. Whatever institutional stability American capitalism could conceivably develop was at its lowest possible ebb in 1830.

And yet it was a society whose very energy and resources had themselves become a kind of stability. For such a society, traditional guaranties of order had become superfluous. Its religion was so dynamic that it needed no church; its wealth and opportunity were so boundless that a center of financial power could lose its meaning; and in its need for politicians and lawyers by the thousands it could do without a governing class and ignore many an ancient tradition of bench and bar. Thus for the American of that day it was the very success of his society—of capitalism, of religious liberalism and political democracy—that made it unnecessary for him to be concerned with institutions. Had he a "past"? Yes; it was already two hundred years old, but he could afford to forget it. Had he once known "institutions"? Yes, of a sort, but he could now ignore their meaning; *his* style of life did not depend upon them. His new system of values could now question "society" itself, that very society which had made success possible and which offered him his future. Because he no longer seemed to need it, it became an abstraction which even bore certain allusions to the sinister. He was able to imagine that "stability" resided not in social organization but in "human nature." He no longer appeared to draw from society his traditions, his culture, and all his aspirations; indeed he, the transcendent individual—the new symbol of virtue—now "confronted" society; he challenged it as something of a conspiracy to rob him of his birthright. Miraculously, all society then sprang to his aid in the celebration of that conceit.

We may suppose that such was not merely the general sense but one shared by those men who in other societies would be called "intellectuals"—those men whose traditional preoccupation is to reflect and express in various ways the state of society at large, its tensions, its ills, its well-being. So we should also ask about the consequences which such a happy state of things might have had for intellectual activity. Might there not have been (in spite of everything) a price? Where, for instance, in such a setting were art and learning to find their occupation? "No author, without a trial," wrote the lonely Hawthorne in his preface to *The Marble Faun,* "can conceive the difficulty of writing a romance about a country where there is no shadow, no antiquity, no mystery, no picturesque and gloomy wrong, nor anything but a commonplace prosperity, in broad and simple daylight, as is happily the case with my dear native land." This society with few problems and few visible institutions set the American intellectual, such as he was, peculiarly on his own and made him as susceptible as anyone else to the philosophy of self-help. In the America of the 1830s and 1840s there was no other symbol of vitality to be found than the individual, and it was to the individual, with all his promise, that the thinker, like everyone else, would inexorably orient himself. Every reward which the age offered seemed pointed out by the way of self-reliance. But the thinker, thus oriented, left himself without a specific and concrete sense of society as such and without even a strong sense of himself as belonging to a community of other men of intellect. He was involuntarily cut off from the sources of power (the political, ecclesiastical, and financial power had become more and more diffuse), so that he could no longer operate, as it were, in the midst of things. For Americans of this generation the very concept of power—its meaning, its responsibilities, its uses—was something quite outside their experience. This intellectual disengagement from problems of power had a great deal to do with the peculiar abstractness of our thought on the subject of slavery.

Such was the state of mind in which Americans faced the gravest social problem that had yet confronted them as an established nation. Theirs had been, considering the bulk of their achievement, a mild existence in which the stimuli of chronic and complex institutional tensions had been absent; it was in such a setting that their habits of thought had been shaped; such was the experience with which they might approach the ills of society and deal with serious questions of morality.

By the 1830s slavery had come to offend the sensibilities of all Christendom. It was a problem partaking of the Christian conception of sin. Mortal sin lay in the path of all who dealt in slaves, and it was so defined and given meaning by the Christian church in countries where the church had power. Slavery, by its very age, had almost assumed the character of original sin, entailed as it was upon living generations by their predecessors. In America, slavery was unique among the other institutions of society. In one section of the country it had existed for over two centuries, having become interwoven with the means of production, the basic social arrangements, and the very tone of Southern culture. Slavery in the South, instead of diminishing, had spread. Though it had been a source of discomfort there a generation before, men could now see it, under pressure, as the keystone of a style of life in a sense that was not true of any other institution in American society. Conversely, it was at this very time that Americans of the North found themselves suddenly confronted, as it were, with slavery's full enormity.

"No picturesque and gloomy wrong"—Hawthorne here referred to a society which, distinguished from the civilizations of Europe, was not concretely acquainted with sin. The innocence of America and the wickedness of Europe would form one of the great themes of nineteenth-century literature, but of all the writers who used it, perhaps it was Hawthorne's most distinguished biographer, Henry James, who best understood how even "sin," in European culture, had been institutionalized. There, an actual place had been made for it in life's crucial experience. It had been classified from time out of mind and given specific names; the reality of "lust," "avarice," and "oppression" had given rise to the most intricate of social arrangements, not for eliminating them, but for softening their impact and limiting their scope—for protecting the weak and defining the responsibilities of the strong. One powerful social agency in particular had made of iniquity its special province and had dealt with it in a thousand forms for centuries. All this may well have been in James's mind when he exclaimed of America: *"no church."*

What, then, might be expected to happen if sin *should* suddenly become apparent, in a nation whose every individual was, at least symbolically, expected to stand on his own two feet? The reaction was altogether destructive. The sense of outrage was personal; the sense of *personal* guilt was crushing. The gentle American of mild vices was transformed into the bloody avenger. It would seem that the reaction of a society to sin (as well as to any other problem) depends on the prior experience of that society; whether the wrong shall be torn out root and branch, or whether terms are to be made with it, depends on how intimate that society is with evil in all its forms. The outraged innocent can be a thousand times more terrible than the worldly temporizer. By 1830 the spread of slavery had begun to force upon Americans a catalogue of unsuspected revelations. And accordingly, their guilt and outrage were harassed and quickened from the days of Garrison's first blasts in 1831—"harsh as truth, uncompromising as justice"—until the upheaval of 1861 in which slavery was destroyed with fire and sword.

The sharpest spokesmen of North and South, more and more inclining to stand at polar opposites on all questions touching slavery in the thirty years before the Civil War, had at least a feature of style in common: each expressed himself with a simple moral severity. Each in his way thought of slavery as though it were a gross fact with certain universal, immutable, abstract features unalloyed by considerations of time and place. To the Northern reformer, every other concrete fact concerning slavery was dwarfed by its character as a moral evil—as an obscenity condemned of God and universally offensive to humanity. The Southerner replied in kind; slavery was a positive moral good—a necessary arrangement sanctioned in Scripture and thus by God Himself, in which an inferior race must live under the domination of a superior. "Slavery, authorized by God, permitted by Jesus Christ, sanctioned by the apostles, maintained by good men of all ages, is still existing in a portion of our beloved country." "As a man, a Christian, and a citizen, we believe that slavery is right; that the condition of the slave, as it now exists in slaveholding states, is the best existing organization of civil society." These were characteristic replies to sentiments such as those of the abolitionist George Bourne, who in 1834 had written, "The Mosaic law declares every slaveholder a *thief;* Paul the Apostle classes them among the vilest criminals. . . . To tolerate slavery, or to join in its practice is an insufferable crime, which tarnishes every other good quality. *For whosoever shall keep the law and yet offend in one point, he is guilty of all.*" Neither antagonist, in short—burning with guilt or moral righteousness, as the case may have been—could quite conceive of slavery as a social institution, functioning, for better or worse, by laws and logic like other institutions, mutable like others, a product of human custom, fashioned by the culture in which it flourished, and capable of infinite variation from one culture to another.

There is, in justice, little reason to expect that the question should have been argued otherwise than it was, in view of the intellectual setting available to the pre-Civil War generation. . . .

The anti-institutionalism so characteristic of the Transcendentalists reached heights of extravagance in the speeches and writings of the radical abolitionists. "The difficulty of the present day and with us is," declared Wendell Phillips, "we are bullied by institutions." They attacked the church both North and South as the "refuge and hiding-place" of slavery; the sects—particularly the Methodist—were denounced singly and severally, and Stephen Symonds Foster condemned the entire clergy as a "brotherhood of thieves." Foster also reviled both Whig and Democratic parties for countenancing slavery; Edmund Quincy, Wendell Phillips, and William Lloyd Garrison repudiated the Constitution itself; resolution after resolution was passed in various societies condemning the Union ("No Union with Slaveholders"); and Garrison actually "nominated Jesus Christ to the Presidency of the United States and the World."

> *No matter [wrote Garrison], though . . . every party should be torn by dissensions, every sect dashed into fragments, the national compact dissolved, the land filled with the horrors of a civil and a servile war—still, slavery must be buried in the grave of infamy, beyond the possibility of a resurrection. If the State cannot survive the anti-slavery agitation, then let the State perish. If the Church must be cast down by the strugglings of Humanity to be free, then let the Church fall, and its fragments be scattered to the four winds of heaven, never more to curse the earth. If the American Union cannot be maintained, except by immolating human freedom on the altar of tyranny, then let the American Union be consumed by a living thunderbolt, and no tear be shed over its ashes. If the Republic must be blotted out from the roll of nations, by proclaiming liberty to the captives, then let the Republic sink beneath the waves of oblivion, and a shout of joy, louder than the voice of many waters, fill the universe at its extinction.*

An anti-institutional attitude so pronounced as this could hardly be confined merely to doctrine. It was bound to have disintegrating effects on the organizational development of the very societies which promoted it. Whereas such societies did indeed flourish and expand in the early and middle 1830s, the truth is that the life of *institutional* antislavery was doomed to brevity: the story of abolitionism's spread is not, after all, that of the strengthening of the societies as such. On the contrary, the national organization, after a luminous but short career, was all but extinguished during the Depression years of the late thirties and never really recovered. The story of the movement is to be found elsewhere.

We have elsewhere noted that the democratization of all the major institutions once familiar to American life had to a profound degree worked to undermine those same institutions, and that in a larger sense such institutional breakdown was the very condition, or price, of national success. But, in at least one area, the price of democracy was very high. For a fatal process was at work, and that process was nothing less than the very democratization, North and South, of the controversy over slavery. The tragic flaw of an otherwise singularly favored society was the absence of mechanisms for checking such a development—the absence of mechanisms which might permit a range of alternatives in sentiment and idea to be crystallized and maintained and which might prevent the development of a lowest common denominator of feeling in each section, widely enough shared as to provide a democratic ground for war. . . .

It might well be said that the theme which dominated the declining phase of *nationally organized* abolition activity was, after all, that of Garrisonian individualism triumphant. Garrison and his methods were peculiarly suited not only to stamping the movement in his image and giving it his tone but also to splitting the movement's institutional structure. "Garrisonism" was in the last analysis deeply subversive of antislavery's efforts to develop and consolidate organized power. The man himself, with his egocentric singleness of mind, antagonized most of those who tried to combine with him in any action requiring concerted effort. As a result virtually all such enterprises with which his name was connected acquired, as Theodore Weld wrote, a "vague and indefinite odium." Garrison's own New England Anti-Slavery Society, which had never in any case been much concerned with field operations, split wide apart over the venom of his attacks on the clergy, and the movement all over New England fell into disrepute. By the late thirties the vitality of the American Anti-Slavery Society itself had been sufficiently sapped by Garrison's reputation that it was quite unable to weather out the depression years which followed the 1837 panic. By a touch of irony the meeting of 1840, at which the society's final dissolution was to have taken place, was captured by Garrison with a boatload of hastily commissioned "delegates" brought down from Lynn on an outing. Nearly all the state auxiliaries promptly withdrew, but this did not disturb Garrison; he was at last in full control. Yet the society which he had thus "rescued" was by then nothing more than a name.

Garrison's personal legend had been built up at the expense of organized antislavery. It is thus that one may deny his having "represented" in any functioning sense the majority of abolitionists and at the same time exhibit him as the living symbol of abolitionism, so far as the country at large was concerned. He had alienated hundreds by personal contact; his name was deeply distasteful to most middling citizens of the North and anathema to the entire South. But this very fact had made him famous; to think of abolitionism was to think of Garrison. Besides, he had spoken out early; he did have a vocal personal following, and for thousands of local abolitionists who had never seen him and who cared nothing for societies, his name was magic. It was a personal notoriety; he was profoundly the individual, anything but the organizer. As Gilbert Barnes writes, "He was equipped by taste and temperament for free-lance journalism and for nothing else. As a journalist he was brilliant and provocative; as a leader for the antislavery host he was a name, an embodied motto, a figurehead of fanaticism."

"Garrisonism" might thus carry a number of meanings—radical doctrines, intransigence, intolerance, fanaticism—but what is chiefly of interest here is the way it symbolizes the direction in which antislavery, Garrison or no Garrison, was bound to move, even as it spread. That direction was from complexity of doctrine to simplicity, from organization to fragmentation, from consolidated effort to effort dispersed, diffuse and pervasive. Whatever institutional character antislavery might have had, either as colonization or abolition, had broken down by the 1840s. Nor was this the only institutional breakdown of the period, for it was also in the 1840s that whatever last opportunity there may have been, in the interest of the slave, to exploit the power of the national church organizations disappeared forever. By that time the Methodists and Baptists had quarreled over slavery and split into sectional wings, Northern and Southern.

But while antislavery sentiment and action were thus becoming less and less institutional they were becoming at the same time—almost in inverse ratio—more widely shared. It had been made increasingly clear that the societies conceived their fundamental purpose to be that of spreading the antislavery gospel rather than of striking for the most vulnerable spots in slavery itself. There were now forces at work which made for a diffusion of the issue in such a way that it no longer needed to be carried by the societies; the ground upon which one might conceivably hold antislavery views was being tremendously broadened. The mechanism whereby this was brought about has been denoted in our own time, quite accurately, as the "fellow-traveler" principle.

The process operated somewhat as follows: Relatively few were actually prepared to take unequivocal abolitionist positions, but moral pressures, coming from everywhere in the civilized world and reflected intensely from our own abolitionists, were more and more insistent that Northerners recognize in some form the evils of slavery. Functional substitutes for abolitionism, that is, were coming increasingly into demand. And this growing need for some satisfactory mode of self-expression was in fact being provided for by the appearance of other issues and other forms of action—in some cases broader, and in all cases more acceptable—to which abolitionism could be linked but in which more and more persons could participate. . . .

Finally, the broadest of all such issues, emerging after the Mexican War, was that of "free soil"—an antislavery position so widely shared that by 1860 it could command political majorities in every Northern state but one. It was with this issue that the democratization of antislavery had become complete.

The remainder of our paradigm of antislavery thought with its four explanatory categories—anti-institutionalism, individualism, abstraction, and guilt—is speedily traversed. Various implications of the first of these, anti-institutionalism, have already been noted, and in the process certain things have been said of its counterpart, individualism. As more and more individuals entered the antislavery movement at one level or another, the movement became less and less institutional in character; moreover, between institutional solidarity on the one hand and individual satisfaction and self-expression on the other, the balance would invariably swing to the latter.

Now this very individualism also penetrated, in spite of itself, to the debate over the slave. That debate, focusing as it did upon the Negro's "nature" and "innate capacities," in effect bypassed the nature of the institution within which he acted out his daily life. "The negro is a child in his nature," an anonymous Southerner had written in 1836, "and the white man is to him as a father." He was cheerful and gay, a trait which John Pendleton Kennedy called "constitutional and perennial"; he was imitative and adaptable ("The African adapts himself with greater readiness to circumstances than the white man"), docile and lacking in pride and courage: "The slave, besotted, servile, accustomed to degradation, and habituated to regard his master with deference and awe, does not presume to dream of contending with him." He was lazy and dishonest: "All history proves that idleness and vice is the only liberty the African aspires to, either in his own country or as a slave in Christian lands."

He was irresponsible ("the most improvident race in the world, and must have a superior mind to guide them"), and yet in the last analysis affectionate and loyal. "They look up to their liberal and generous masters, and their mistresses, with a feeling absolutely fond and filial." Slavery, in short, was really the only state in which such a creature could exist. "He is happier . . . as a slave," wrote the Southerner of *The South Vindicated,* "than he could be as a freeman. This is the result of the peculiarities of his character."

The Northern reformer accepted the argument on the Southerner's terms by reversing it, and attempted to refute it with that logic of individual perfectibility upon which the humanitarianism of the day drew so deeply. Lydia Maria Child admitted the existence of ignorance among the Negroes, but insisted that their desire to be otherwise would increase "just in proportion as they are free. The fault is in their *unnatural* situation, not in themselves." Mrs. Child, pointing to the existence of numerous merchants, priests, and doctors in Brazil who had once been slaves, drew the inference not that this was due to institutional differences between American and Brazilian slavery but rather that it was simply freedom which had made the difference. She thought that freedom, followed by universal education, was the remedy and that it was only prejudice that prevented "the improvement of a large portion of the human race." Emancipation, according to William Jay, would have instant salutary effects upon the Negroes; it would "stimulate their morals, quicken their intelligence, and convert a dangerous, idle, and vicious population into wholesome citizens." The transition from slave to free labor might, he thought, be "effected instantaneously, and with scarcely any perceptible interruption of the ordinary pursuits of life." S. B. Treadwell wrote:

> *If all the slaves in the United States should have their shackles knocked off, and endowed with the privileges of freemen tomorrow, and barely paid a fair compensation for their labor (which would also be far better for their masters) they would at once be as capable, from the honest avails of their labor of supporting themselves and their families, in their accustomed mode of living, as any class of people in the world. Of this there can be no question.*

It was, and is, perfectly possible to accept both the descriptive accuracy of what the Southerner saw and the attainability, in theory, of what the Northerner hoped for. But not at the level of "the individual and his innate capacities"; to argue it out at that level (innate racial inferiority versus innate human perfectibility) was not only to freeze all hope of mutual understanding but actually to rule out of the argument a formidable social institution. Here was the antebellum form of a now-venerable debate—the debate over "Sambo." Finally, the controversy, never very concrete, was raised to empyrean heights of abstraction as both sides resorted to Bible criticism. Each searched the sacred texts, one to show slavery as "consistent with the precepts of patriarchs, apostles, and prophets," the other to prove "The Book and Slavery Irreconcilable," and of course each found the appropriate passages.

What it came down to, after all, was a problem of morality whose intellectual content had become more and more attenuated. It was really the abolitionist, with guilt as both powerful stimulus and powerful weapon, who understood most surely—if only by instinct—the means which would carry the issue furthest. Alternately he writhed and thundered. "My brother," wrote Weld with quiet intensity to James G. Birney,

> *God's terrors have begun to blaze upon the guilty nation. If repentance, speedy, deep and* national *do[es] not forestall Jehovah's judgments, they will break upon us from the thickening air and the heaving earth and the voice of a brothers blood crying from the ground will peal against the wrathful heavens and shake down ruin as a fig tree casteth her untimely fruit. May God purify us, gird us for the conflict, give us faith and then we shall stand unscathed by the flames which blaze around us.*

"How ought I to feel and speak?" Garrison demanded meanwhile, in apocalyptic accents.

> *My soul should be, as it is, on fire. I should thunder—I should lighten. I should blow the trumpet of alarm, long and loud. I should use just such language as is most descriptive of the crime. I should imitate the example of Christ, who, when he had to do with people of like manners, called them sharply by their proper names—such as, an adulterous and perverse generation, a brood of vipers, hypocrites, children of the devil, who could not escape the damnation of hell.*

The Southerner of course, whose own moral tradition was not so very different from Weld's and Garrison's, also writhed. "If you would reform the Southern man," protested Joseph Stiles, "say, if you please, that his explanations do not entirely satisfy you; but say something of them; give them some regard, some weight. For he knows, and so do you, that his views and feelings are such as an intelligent and honest man may well entertain." But the Southerner's guilt could do little other than turn defensive. Nehemiah Adams, a Northern minister who returned from a Southern visit with greatly modified views on Southern morals, had conversed with a slave-holder "of liberal education and great influence at the south, and withal an extreme defender of the system of slavery." Adams was much impressed by this man's words: "If the north had directed its strength against the evils of slavery instead of assailing it as a sin *per se,* it could not have survived to the present day." While doubtless not worth much as *post hoc* prediction, the statement is an admirable little map of what had happened to Southern squeamishness on the subject of slavery.

Bertram Wyatt-Brown

ABOLITIONISM: ITS MEANING FOR CONTEMPORARY AMERICAN REFORM

The following essay analyzes trends in recent historical writings on abolitionists as well as the connections between abolitionism and the civil rights movement of the 1960s. Biographer of the abolitionist Lewis Tappan, Wyatt-Brown pays closest attention here to William Lloyd Garrison, with whom Tappan differed strongly and often. The author finds the abolitionists more willing to rely on institutions than Elkins imagined and calls them essentially "liberal nineteenth-century reformers." Wyatt-Brown teaches at Case Western Reserve University.

Some historians are like the gentleman of Cambridge who heard Wendell Phillips address the Harvard faculty in 1881: he applauded the veteran abolitionist but was overheard to exclaim, "the damned

Reprinted by permission of the publisher from the *Midwest Quarterly* 8 (October 1966): 41–55.

old fool, the damned old fool." These historians may also applaud the cause of Negro Rights, but they cannot help muttering an uncharitable phrase or two about the pioneers of the abolitionist movement.

There are a number of explanations for this attitude. Old historical traditions do not die easily. One of them holds that abolitionists plunged the nation into civil war simply to gratify their own bloodlusts. Black Reconstruction was the result. Scholars may claim their emancipation from this apology for the Old South, but regional folklore remains in unswept corners of the most sophisticated minds. A similar interpretation was expressed by the late James G. Randall, whose biography of Abraham Lincoln reflected his sympathy for a conservative approach to slavery. Moreover, Randall, like some other historians writing between the two world wars, considered violent conflict an ineffectual and immoral means to settle national and international disputes. In consequence, he held that *war,* not slavery, was the compelling sin of mid-nineteenth-century America. Abolitionists, therefore, were harpies of destruction rather than prophets of freedom. Another tradition has grown out of Charles A. Beard's theory of American history, which, with its emphasis upon class and economic issues, undercut the moral significance of the abolitionists' role. By implication at least, they became apologists for wage-slavery and Yankee industry. Despite their oversimplifications, these familiar interpretations have colored our attitudes toward the movement.

The real trouble, however, is our inability to understand the nineteenth-century reformer. Some historians are not very fond of *any* of them. Scholars have taken to hauling all sorts of groups before the bar of history: Jeffersonians, Jacksonians, Civil Service reformers, suffragettes, Populists, and Progressives. Twenty years ago most of them were in good favor, but since the 1950s they have sometimes been accused of status insecurity, opportunism, censoriousness, narrow vision, chauvinism, hypocrisy, and occasionally, racial and religious bigotry. It would seem that John Brown (or Jeff Davis) is not the only one hanging on the sour-apple tree of history.

According to C. Vann Woodward, however, recent authors have exonerated the abolitionists from these charges. As a result, he maintains, an "Antislavery Myth" continues to flower among the Yankee legends of the "Underground Railroad" and the "North Star"—a growth presently watered by a constant flow from the pens of journalists and uncritical scholars. Certainly, it is unfair to transform all abolitionists into heroes and moral giants. After all, they, like other crusaders, had to pay a high price for the weakness of moral arrogance. Humility was a rare virtue in their movement. "The Holy Spirit did actually descend upon men and women in tongues of flame," wrote Lydia Maria Child, recalling her early antislavery days, "and mortals were never more sublimely forgetful of self than were the abolitionists." The tragic cost was their misunderstanding of both the sinners and those sinned against. In their minds the slaveholder was totally depraved, while the Negro was a helpless creature, stunted in soul and mind by the cruel system. These Sunday school simplicities about the "poor slave" and his fate reinforced the popular stereotype of him as a docile and childlike creature. Ironically, the abolitionists' propaganda arising from their moral indignation, helped to prepare the way for their own and the postwar nation's disillusionment with the freedman and a confusion about his needs.

Obviously, Woodward has good reason to question the historical judgment of those who would ignore the abolitionists' weaknesses. As he recognizes, some writers such as Dwight L. Dumond run a risk of surrendering their critical faculties by readopting the moral fervor and sometimes the language of the ante-bellum crusade. Abolitionism is, however, so integral a part of our history that it can withstand objective and discerning criticism.

Although Woodward has done much to illuminate the myth-making process in American historiography, there is reason to doubt his claim that with respect to slavery and antislavery "the orthodox text is obviously still the gospel according to Mr. Dumond." Recent developments indicate a contrary trend. William and Jane Pease and John L. Thomas have attacked the white abolitionists, even William Lloyd Garrison himself, for monopolizing the cause to the neglect of Negro orators and workers, taking too complacent a view of racial, as distinct from slave, prejudice, and even harboring a race-consciousness incompatible with their professed principles. Influenced perhaps by the rising militancy of the Negro Rights movement of today, these writers and others soon to appear in print, find the antislavery standards of a century ago hypocritical, insufficiently egalitarian, and timidly conservative.

Yet, there are a number of historians who avoid polemics. Guided by the hopes arising from the successful outcome of the war against German and Japanese militarism, Allan Nevins, Russel B. Nye, and Louis T. Filler have been basically sympathetic with the Civil War's aims and outcome, but they have not surrendered their critical judgment. A younger group of scholars have carried on that liberal trend: Irving Bartlett, Martin B. Duberman, Larry Gara, Leon Litwack, James McPherson, and Willie Lee Rose. McPherson's study of the abolitionists during and after the war has added a new dimension to our understanding of their work since most accounts end with the firing on Fort Sumter. Instead, he points out that vigorous agitation continued, not just for abolition, but also for the later protection of the freedman in his new status. Thus, McPherson challenges those critics who claim that the Emancipation Proclamation left the abolitionists with nothing further to say. Willie Lee Rose in her prize-winning *Rehearsal for Reconstruction* analyzes an abolitionist enterprise for raising free cotton and educating exslaves on the Sea Islands of Georgia and South Carolina. Without resort to easy judgments or sociological jargon, she explains with subtlety and discrimination the complexities of the situation, which the abolitionists and indeed the Negroes and Southerners had hardly anticipated. Her geographical setting is small, but the themes apply to an entire nation grappling with its conscience and its inadequacies of thought and spirit. All these scholars, especially Mrs. Rose, demonstrate that the abolitionists, like the rest of us, had a liberal share of common humanity.

Even after painful thought and research, the historian should have as much difficulty in proving deceit, malice, and venomous prejudice in a man as in finding evidence of his sainthood. David Knowles, in *The Historian and Character* (1955), has said that in times of religious zeal "conscious or unconscious hypocrisy is peculiarly difficult to recognize. The novelist or dramatist can easily unmask a Tartuffe or Trusty Tomkins or the Rev. Mr. Stiggins, but Torquemada and Oliver Cromwell and Henry Edward Manning and Mr. Gladstone are far more difficult problems." It could be that these historians are heralds of a time when a righteous defense of abolitionism and a fierce indictment of it are equally superfluous.

In the meantime, however, criticisms of a belligerent nature continue. At one time, it was easy enough to separate the pro-Southern and the antislavery myth-makers, for they applied their moral judgments with abandon. According to Fawn Brodie, however, the pro-Southern bias has recently gone underground to be replaced by "Olympian detachment" and an "ironic dismissal of 'moral issues.' " While a new group has arisen to call into question the sincerity of the abolitionists' egalitarianism, the historians whom she criticizes still dominate the field. By using the instruments of psychology, sociology, and political science, they have clothed old vices in new and scientific terms. Undoubtedly the wise application of behavioral techniques will add to historical knowledge. In the dissection of abolitionists, however, these scalpels have thus far proved to be double-edged.

Using the manner of a sociologist, David Donald in his essay "Toward a Reconsideration of Abolitionists" in *Lincoln Reconsidered* (1956) has to some degree reconfirmed the position of his mentor, James G. Randall of the University of Illinois. In Donald's opinion, antislavery agitators belonged to a declining New England class of pious farmers and country clergymen. Unable to adjust to the fast-rising industrial order, these misguided rustics took out their social and psychological frustrations first on Southern slave-holders and later on President Lincoln, whose conservatism displeased them. As a group, Donald concludes, they showed signs of "some deep-seated malaise." In rebuttal, one can ask for an example of a reform movement with genuine merits which did not attract a few misfits and undesirables. Maria Weston Chapman once remarked, "The good Lord uses instruments for His purpose I would not touch with a fifty foot pole." In other words, abolitionists themselves were sometimes embarrassed by the exotic souls who occasionally drifted into their ranks.

Abolitionists were determined to be individualists, with the result that they defy sociological pigeon-holing. While some were eccentric, others were at least generally sensible. Take, for instance, Lewis Tappan, a leader of the evangelical wing. Contrary to Donald's proposition that abolitionist leaders were usually ineffective in harsh day-to-day transactions, Tappan demonstrated that business and professional men could be and sometimes were abolitionists. After several years in the silk trade in New York City, Tappan founded in 1841 the nation's first credit-rating agency, now known as Dun & Bradstreet. As an enterprising reformer, he played a leading part in the founding of the American Missionary Association, which helped to establish Berea College, Fisk and Howard Universities, and other Negro schools. There were others like him. These men had no social axe to grind, yet they favored immediate and uncompensated emancipation. Although some were prevented by their professional and personal inclinations from being as aggressive as the salaried agitators, they cannot be excluded from any full discussion of the cause. In this group were William Jay, son of Chief Justice John Jay; James G. Birney, a former slaveholder and Presbyterian elder; such leading counsellors of Massachusetts and New York as Ellis Gray Loring, Samuel E. Sewall, John Jay, and Hiram Barney; William Henry Furness, clergyman of Philadelphia; O. B. Frothingham, James Freeman Clarke, and Samuel J. May, liberal ministers of New England; Francis Jackson, Arthur Tappan, and Duncan Dunbar, businessmen; Edmund Quincy and Thomas Wentworth Higginson, writers; and Henry Ingersoll Bowditch, Joseph Parrish, and Abraham Liddon Cox, physicians. Even the distinguished Unitarian preacher, William Ellery Channing, was compelled by humanitarian logic to support abolitionism in spite of his distaste for controversy.

It is not surprising that men of this character, as well as their more countrified antislavery friends, should hold very traditional views about the social classes. It is true, as Donald says, that abolitionists did not always overcome the current prejudices against the white-skinned poor. Nor were they entirely free of racial bias, particularly in the earliest days of the cause when discretion in the face of mobs prevented full espousal of the goal of equality for all. But, after all, they were generally rural folk like nearly everybody else. Even if they lived in cities all their lives, they seldom lost their country habits. Instead, they tried to solve social problems with time-honored means—the Bible, the sermon, and the New England code of hard work. Samuel Eliot Morison has described the men of New England well: "A race whose typical member is eternally torn between a passion for righteousness and a desire to get on in the world." Abolitionists by and large belonged to this race, and perhaps they were impatient with those who did not live up to that impossible duality. Moreover, they could not fully escape the times in which they lived, and if Americans felt the Negroes to be degraded people, something of that sentiment might appear in the abolitionists' patronizing, uncomfortable manner of dealing with them.

If a reformer turned his back on a sweat shop or passed out religious tracts instead of welfare checks and voter registration blanks, there is supposed to be something hypocritical about him. E. M. Forster (*Marianne Thornton,* p. 54) has observed that while English abolitionists were myopic about conditions around them, the "really bad people . . . are those who do no good anywhere" and thus "slip through their lives unnoticed and so escape the censure of historians." Many American abolitionists may have been just as indifferent toward poverty (and indeed toward some aspects of racial discrimination) as their English friends, but after all, both groups were far ahead of others on the matter of slavery.

David Donald's essay first appeared in 1956, just as a Second Reconstruction was dawning. Three years later, Stanley Elkins's *Slavery* was published, and it soon overshadowed the concurrent additions to the "antislavery myth," although these works harmonized with contemporary racial goals. Despite his persuasive analysis of slavery, his institutional approach to abolitionism in his final chapter is less successful. He reflects contemporary concern with the stability and operation of American corporate life and therefore looks back to the ante-bellum period and marvels at the scarcity of visible links in the nation. The canal barge, the local church, the courthouse, and that single symbol of federal power, the post office—how weak these organs seem compared with those of nineteenth-century England or modern mass society. Puny though these institutions were, Elkins observes, a group of intellectuals, anxious to absolve their feelings of guilt over slavery, risked their destruction by attacking it.

Elkins seems to suggest that if the abolitionist intellectuals, the Transcendentalists of New England in particular, had not been alienated from centers of power, they would have worked for practical, peaceable reforms. Instead, he believes that their thought became "anti-institutional, individualistic, abstract, and charged with guilt," thus shutting "off all concrete approaches to the problems of society" (p. 206). American reformers, he claims, grant "a disproportionate role" to their sense of guilt, which "becomes aggressive, unstable, hard to control, often destructive" (p. 161). Indeed, it may be hard to discover what amount of guilt is proportionate in dealing with the monolithic character of slavery and what is not. He finds the answer, however, in his proposition that English abolitionists were more judicious in handling their emotions and in managing their cause than the Concord elite. But surely the British movement is hardly analogous to the American. West Indian Emancipation, unlike the question of American Negro slavery, at no time jeopardized civil peace. Yet, Elkins asks, in contrast to the antislavery Clapham Sect of William Wilberforce, "who was poor Garrison? . . . What plans had he, what were *his* resources—other than the impotent fury of his own poisoned pen?" (pp. 204–205). Yet, in spite of these faults, one is hard pressed to know what chance gradual reform or benevolent feelings toward the slave–holder ever had.

As a challenge to this thesis, one must ask for an accurate analogy. Certainly, West Indian Emancipation will not serve, for Parliamentary action in freeing a black population on distant colonial islands was not comparable to the American situation. If the British, however, had freed the southern Irish from imperial rule without bloodshed and a century of agitation and violence, then Elkins would have a point. It is true that Garrisonians did not use their knowledge to work out acceptable schemes of gradual emancipation. Instead, they threw their books in the air and took to shouting on street corners about the sin of slaveholding, an approach as concrete perhaps as any then available. "The work of the agitator," says Richard Hofstadter, "consists chiefly in talk; his function is not to make laws or determine policy, but to influence the public mind in the interest of some large social transformation" (*American Political Tradition,* p. 138). Moreover, once the war began, Garrisonians and evangelical abolitionists constantly urged plans and measures upon their friends in Congress and the Administration designed to hasten a recognition of the rights of Negroes. As J. Miller McKim declared in 1863, "We have passed through the *pulling down* stage of our movement; the *building up*—the constructive part remains to be accomplished." Congress and the Northern public hardly fulfilled all that the abolitionists wished to do, but a refusal to use institutional channels was not one of their failings.

Elkins's criticism is actually an indictment of William Lloyd Garrison whose opinions did so much to shape the movement. Certainly, Elkins is not unique in deploring his influence. Perhaps no one in American history has been so universally condemned as Garrison, except in the very first studies of the movement following the war. Of course, one of the major reasons for misunderstanding his role was the peculiarity of his philosophy of prewar agitation. He and his followers rejected the church, the state, and the use of force on the grounds that all these elements of national life condoned and even upheld the sin of slaveholding. Since social institutions were basically coercive, they argued, they denied freedom and the pursuit of individual perfection. "Come-outerism," as it was called, seemed at the time a radical, frightening, and even insane proposition. So, too, it might appear quixotic and lunatic to historians today.

Another powerful influence on our view of Garrison is the interpretation of Gilbert H. Barnes, even though he wrote *The Antislavery Impulse* thirty years ago. According to Barnes and his militant disciple Dwight L. Dumond, Garrison played neither an appreciable nor an ethical role in the cause. They complained that his romantic, nonresistant philosophy disrupted and demoralized the crusade. Radicalism, they assure us, had no place in the cause.

Following the interpretation of Barnes and Dumond, historians and textbook writers have usually stressed his apocalyptic ultraism, as if he were, as Southerners claimed, the archpriest of chaos. At the very least, his critics blame him for alienating the moderates of the nation—that great mass of citizens with vague, well-meaning aims and no convictions. Garrison's influence on this group was incalculable, because he goaded less radical abolitionists and hence ordinary citizens to adopt more forceful antislavery positions. After the war was under way, he constantly urged forceful antislavery action upon the Republican party, having gradually relinquished his opposition to political efforts even before Southern secession. But his greatest contribution to awakening the moderates to the evil of slavery was his own respectability. For thirty years Garrison was living proof that the radical American agitator was not an advocate of violence. He had never sent a *Liberator* to the slaves of the South.

He never said, "Slaves, arise, you have nothing to lose but your chains." He never urged military action against the South until the Civil War had begun. Southerners were the ones to abandon political solutions in the final analysis.

It might be said that Garrison's pacifism was a hoax. Words can, after all, be as insurrectionary as arms and abolitionists. A handful of them did support John Brown's plans, but the raid on Harpers Ferry simply demonstrated the lack of appeal of Brown's method for most Americans, most antislavery men, as well as most Garrisonians. John Brown, however, offered one alternative to Garrison's "shocking" but harmless burning of the Constitution and the Fugitive Slave Law—Yankee filibusters into the South. There were other possibilities—slave insurrections, sabotage, antislavery propagandists operating in slave areas, assassination of prominent proslavery politicians to call attention to the movement. Towards the close of the 1850s a few hotheads such as Lysander Spooner suggested some of these measures, but Garrison and his pacifist colleagues rejected them, even considering the use of Sharp's rifles in Kansas a dangerous and immoral precedent unworthy of Christians and humanitarians. Yet, abolitionists might easily have brought on by these means a martyrdom and persecution that would have shocked the nation into either an earlier civil war or an era of rampant tyranny in North and South.

Why did Garrison and his disciples choose another course? Primarily, because they were liberal nineteenth-century reformers, for all their heady talk about Christian perfection. For instance, one of his followers named Adin Ballou declared that disunionism of the Garrisonian stamp was concerned with "individual, moral, peaceable withdrawal from political covenant with slaveholders," not with "state dissolution of the Union." The latter, after all, was "sedition," but the former, he concluded was the duty "of every conscientious man" (*Liberator,* May 28, 1844). In other words, even their perfectionism had its limitations. Actually, they were little different from others of their kind—John Bright, Richard Cobden, Elizabeth Fry, and William Wilberforce. Like them, they tried to reach the great middle-class by using the tactics of shock and exaggeration. Only through such means could the discrepancy between national principles and national practices be brought to public attention.

On the other hand, the Garrisonians might have adopted the

means of their counterparts on the continent. Although engaged in a revolutionary cause, they were not, like Mazzini, Garibaldi, Orsini, Louis Blanc, and German university students, revolutionaries at heart. Instead of throwing bombs, seizing arsenals, or organizing guerrilla forces and raising up barricades, Garrison and his associates were satisfied with platform soldiery, the ridicule of politicians and voting, and irreverent barbs at stodgy clerics. They even shied away from civil disobedience, except to challenge the unpopular fugitive slave laws and to supply Kansas free-soilers with defensive weapons. In spite of Garrison's Northern secessionism, he never advocated the overthrow of state or national government by force. Nor did he even refuse to pay taxes in the fashion of Henry Thoreau. If abolitionism had really been synonymous with the anti-institutionalism of Mikhail Bukanin and other nineteenth-century anarchists and revolutionaries, then American historians might have good reason to question the abolitionists' values, their sanity, and their integrity.

Rather than finding them a vengeful, unstable, and neurotic lot it could be said that they were one of the happiest sets of reformers in American history. They were generally a solemn and earnest group, of course, for their happiness was chiefly discernible in their boundless optimism. It was a source of strength as well as a weakness. Hope served them well during the bleak and bloody days of the 1830s. Although Negro slavery had existed since the Middle Ages, they expected it to fall within the lifetime of their children if not their own. In 1834 one of them, Elizur Wright, criticized his friends for thinking that slavery would only last another five years, while he admitted, "it may be that I shall live long and still die before the happy jubilee comes, but come it will." Such a faith as this nourished the cause throughout periods of crisis. Unfortunately, this optimism had its darker side, too. Once the institution was gone, the millennium which they expected did not arrive. The abolitionists' nineteenth-century concepts of society and economy did not prepare them or anybody else for the racial prejudice and violence which followed. Under these conditions, visionary idealism became wishful thinking or turned sour in disillusionment.

In summary, let us consider the most important contributions which the abolitionists have made to our reform tradition. First, it should be said that among their gifts was that of institutional approaches to agitation. A large number of abolitionists tried to convert their congregations, ministerial associations, ladies' groups, political parties, and so forth. American reform has generally followed these lines. Secondly, the radical approach of Garrisonian pacifism has been an addition to American reform methods. A later advocate of non-violent agitation, Leo Tolstoy, once pointed out that Garrison, one of the foremost "champions of true human progress," was the first "to proclaim" the principle of non-resistance. This technique has been reintroduced to the Negro Rights movement of today, a strange international lineage extending from Garrison and Thoreau to Tolstoy and Ghandi and finally to Martin Luther King. It is, of course, possible that frustrations and failures through pacific and institutional action may break the links with the abolitionist past, but such a chain of events cannot be blamed upon the pioneers of the cause of a century and a quarter ago.

The vital contribution of abolitionism, however, has been its help in the development of our guilty conscience about race. In 1831, Garrison peered through his steel-rimmed glasses at a Negro gathering in Philadelphia. "I never rise to address a colored audience," he declared, "without feeling ashamed of my own color; ashamed of being identified with a race of men who have done you so much injustice." The heritage of guilt had existed before Garrison's time, but he was the first to use it as a basis for agitation. The guilt-stricken conscience is the most powerful weapon the abolitionists could have passed along. Without this belief, successful non-violence in the 1850s or the 1960s would be absolutely impossible.

Perhaps the time will come when these reformers will earn our respect, if never our affection. Cantankerous, incorrigible, self-satisfied, moralistic, and irascible, they were tough old birds. They do not need us at all. In fact, they enjoyed unpopularity. Elizur Wright, when asked what he cherished most in his long career, replied, "Well, I have been mobbed; what more could a man ask?" There is no need to pity their psychological problems, to scold them for their bumptious dismissal of our institutions, or to frown at their naiveté and outmoded prejudices. Nor should we forget their faults of character, their religiosity and sentimentality, and their defects of vision and thought. Above all, we ought not to feel sorry for them—only for ourselves if we can no longer appreciate their contribution to our reform tradition.

Racism and the Re-examination of Abolitionists' Ends

C. Vann Woodward

THE NORTHERN CRUSADE AGAINST SLAVERY

Drawing on historical studies published mostly after Wyatt-Brown wrote the foregoing article, C. Vann Woodward emphasizes the Northern racism that coexisted with the antislavery crusade. Abolitionists themselves often revealed covert racial bias, and they underestimated the persistence of racism among their countrymen. From this perspective, many of the earliest charges against abolitionists of self-righteous meddling appear to have continued validity. Woodward, whose studies of Southern history have shown great sensitivity to inter-sectional and inter-racial relationships, is a professor at Yale University.

From the opposite ends of American history has come evidence of white racism, of both its antiquity and its persistence. Winthrop D. Jordan unearthed its origins in Elizabethan England and sixteenth-century Europe and traced its growth as the functional rationale of white supremacy and American identity down to 1812. The Kerner Report spelled out the disastrous consequences in the violence and riots in contemporary America.[1] But what of the period between? Was there not, as legend has it, an interlude of redeeming virtue in the mid-nineteenth century when white Americans, inspired by the antislavery crusade, put aside their racism, rededicated themselves to their ideals of equality, and waged a heroic war for freedom and a

[1] Winthrop D. Jordan, *White Over Black: American Attitudes Toward the Negro, 1550–1812* (Chapel Hill, N.C., 1968), and *Report of the National Commission on Civil Disorders* (Washington, D.C., 1968).

temporarily successful campaign for racial equality? Or was the crusade itself corrupted and frustrated by a sickness endemic among the crusaders?

Answers to these questions are obscured by time and propaganda, by vested interests of racial and national pride. For one thing, the justification of the bloodiest war in national history, a war resulting in the sacrifice of 600,000 lives, more than the number of Americans killed in two world wars, is at stake. Answers will be slow in coming and may never be perfectly clear. From time to time, however, additional insights are provided by historians, even when they have other purposes and problems in mind.

One illuminating source of insight is Aileen S. Kraditor's study of the abolitionist strategy and tactics.[2] To her surprise she came out with a new and favorable revision of the prevailing interpretation of William Lloyd Garrison. She began with the received opinions, presented most recently in two able biographies of Garrison, both published in 1963.[3] As she says, whatever respect they inspire for their subject is "more than balanced by the conviction that he was bullheaded, arrogant, vindictive, and incredibly blind to some obvious truths." For more than a generation it has been the practice, even among the most strongly proabolitionist historians, to protect the reputation of the movement by disavowing Garrison's importance or centrality in it. Dwight L. Dumond, for example, though an ardent champion of abolitionists, puts Garrison down as "insufferably arrogant" and (in italics) "a man of distinctly narrow limitations among the giants of the antislavery movement."[4]

Miss Kraditor does not contend that Garrison was a typical abolitionist or that he represented majority opinion on antislavery strategy. Nor does she deny his personal idiosyncrasies and foibles (though she does put in a timid and not too convincing claim for his sense of humor). But she is "struck by the logical consistency of his thought on all subjects," granted his principles, with which she finds

[2] Aileen S. Kraditor, *Means and Ends in American Abolitionism: Garrison and His Critics on Strategy and Tactics, 1834–1850* (New York, 1969).
[3] John L. Thomas, *The Liberator: William Lloyd Garrison, A Biography* (Boston, 1963), and Walter M. Merrill, *Against the Grain: A Biography of William Lloyd Garrison* (Cambridge, Mass., 1963).
[4] Dwight L. Dumond, *Antislavery: The Crusade for Freedom in America* (Ann Arbor, 1961), pp. 173–174.

herself usually in agreement. She admits that he changed his opinions from time to time but holds that "the changes themselves represented a logical development." Though she does not use the terms, she sees Garrison as the "hedgehog" (in Sir Isaiah Berlin's sense) among the "foxes," the man who "knows one big thing." His big thing was that abolitionism was a *radical* and not a *reform* movement. It is a bit anomalous to find a Marxian historian applying the term "radical" to a bourgeois thinker like Garrison, who never questioned the capitalist system, "free enterprise," or "free labor." What she means is that Garrison, unlike his opponents, believed that slavery and the racial dogmas which justified it so thoroughly permeated American society and government, North as well as South, that the eradication of the institution and its ideological defenses—and the racism of the latter was as important to him as slavery—was a root-and-branch operation. On that he never equivocated.

Garrison's abolitionist opponents were reformers, not real "radicals," even in the limited sense of the term. They believed in constitutional means and political strategy. They professed to be "realists" and sought to attract moderates rather than repel them by extremism and "extraneous" issues. They believed that American society, government, and institutions were fundamentally sound and that once the alien institution of slavery was removed, all would be well. Hence they were appalled at Garrison's intransigent denunciation of the Constitution as "a covenant with death, and an agreement with hell" which "should be immediately annulled." They deplored his demand for disunion, along with sundry "extraneous" demands, such as no government, no church, and no party. Moderates believed him capable of following to its conclusion "every corollary, and every corollary of every corollary of a syllogism." To them there were limits to logic.

To the incorrigible radical, logic has few limits. Slavery was a sin and that was that, and the only thing to do about sin was to stop sinning. Now! As for the impracticability of his demands, his answer was that politics was the art of the possible, and that his role was agitation, the art of the desirable. To ask the agitator to trim his demands for the sake of expediency was to miss the point. Garrison's ends were much too radical for political and parliamentary means. In his opinion American society was not fundamentally sound but thoroughly corrupt, top to bottom. Down with it, root and branch. He would not trim, he would not compromise, he would not vote for corrupt politicians or support corrupt governments and churches, and he would not temper his means to his ends.

The old Liberator will find more unqualified admirers on the contemporary scene than he would have a few years ago. But even the most hot-gospel root-and-brancher of today will have difficulties with the Garrisonian rhetoric and premises. As Miss Kraditor says, "The key to Garrison's ideology is perfectionism." He believed implicitly in the perfectibility of man. Modern man does not. Or if he does, he should have his head examined. Modern libertarians will also balk at his puritanical rigidity on morals and stimulants, all the way down to and including a cup of tea. There are numerous other difficulties, including those "personal idiosyncrasies." William Lloyd Garrison was a strange and difficult man.

Miss Kraditor appears to believe, however, that history has in a measure vindicated Garrison. "The policy of the 'realistic' political abolitionists [his opponents] did not, after all, produce peaceful abolition, and the alternatives that Garrison presented . . . were presented by life itself a score of years later." It did, after all, as she points out, take a revolution, a civil war, and a repudiation of the old Constitution, as well as some drastic shaking up of other institutions to abolish slavery. She goes further in a concluding passage "to speculate what the result would have been if a large part of the abolitionist movement had not weakened the moral force of its propaganda and accepted the compromises dictated by political expediency." She can not help wondering "whether the abolitionist movement did not yield too much when the major part of it, during the 1840s, played down the purely agitational sort of tactics in favor of political action that gave increasing emphasis to pragmatic alliances with politicians who would not denounce slavery in the abstract." She might have extended these speculations to ask whether those alliances and compromises did not burden the cause of emancipation so heavily with racist ideology and allies as to vitiate the cause itself. These are all the more interesting in view of a rich mine of recent scholarly investigation of white American attitudes toward race, race policy, and slavery in mid-nineteenth century

America that make such speculation more profitable and informed than it might otherwise have been. Several years ago Leon Litwack opened up this field with a stimulating survey.[5] Later studies get down to the particulars and the in-fighting. Only at this level can one assess the wisdom and the chances of success that the various alternative policies might have had and test the claim of historical vindication for Garrison.

In the first place, while conceding the sincerity of abolitionist hatred of slavery and concern for the welfare of the Negro, several historians have recently pointed out that race prejudice of various kinds was endemic among the white abolitionists themselves. This tendency has been spelled out most explicitly by William H. Pease and Jane H. Pease,[6] who find that "antislavery crusaders were beset by a fundamental ambivalence in their attitude toward the Negro himself." Abolitionist pronouncements cited to illustrate this attitude range from the crudely explicit to subtly implicit and often unconscious stereotypes. Of the more explicit examples, Theodore Parker, a supporter of John Brown, could write in 1860 that "the Anglo-Saxon with common sense does not like this Africanization of America; he wishes the superior race to multiply rather than the inferior." More often the attitude betrayed a romanticized racial "stereotype of the malleable, willing and docile colored man." Thus, the antislavery rebels of Lane Seminary concluded in their debates that Negroes "would be kind and docile if immediately emancipated"; J. Miller McKim praised "their susceptibility to control"; and Angelina Grimké wrote a Negro friend with staggering tactlessness that "your long-continued afflictions and humiliations was the furnace in which He was purifying you from the dross, the tin, and the reprobate silver. . . ." Abolitionists measured the Negro by white, middle-class standards and expected him to live up to those standards. They were careful to disclaim approval of adopting colored children, encouraging interracial marriage, or "exciting the people of color to

[5] Leon F. Litwack, *North of Slavery: The Negro in the Free States, 1790–1860* (Chicago, 1961).

[6] William H. Pease and Jane H. Pease, "Antislavery Ambivalence: Immediatism, Expediency, Race," *American Quarterly* 17 (1965): 682–695. See also Litwack, *North of Slavery,* pp. 216–230. Other historians such as Stanley Elkins, Larry Gara, and Louis Filler have referred to these attitudes among abolitionists.

assume airs." They debated endlessly whether and to what degree to admit Negroes to their antislavery societies without ever wholly resolving their doubts. As Mr. and Mrs. Pease write:

> *Never could the abolitionists decide collectively, and infrequently individually, whether the Negro was equal or inferior to the white; whether social equality for the Negro should be stressed or whether it should be damped; whether civil and social rights should be granted him at once or only in the indefinite and provisional future. . . . The abolitionists, furthermore, were torn between a genuine concern for the welfare and uplift of the Negro and a paternalism which was too often merely the patronizing of a superior class.*

The ambivalence and temporizing of abolitionists is better understood in the light of an excellent study of antiabolition mobs by Leonard L. Richards.[7] With its help, we can begin to understand what abolitionists were up against and the willingness of all but a few to temporize and compromise. Employing ingenious techniques and imaginative scholarship, Mr. Richards has studied "all the major and minor mobs, riots, disturbances, civil disorders, and the like" reported between 1812 and 1849. More than half of them, 115 out of 207, occurred in the 1830s and were concentrated in the middle years of that decade, and 48 of the incidents in the 1830s and 1840s were antiabolitionist and racial in character. As Lincoln pointed out, mob violence had become a feature of American life. Great and small cities, small towns and rural communities in all parts of the country fell under the mercy of the mob, some of them for days at a time.

The conventional picture of mobs, antiabolition and anti-Negro mobs included, is that they were lower class, spontaneous, unorganized, and indiscriminate in their violence. This picture bears no resemblance to the typical antiabolition mobs Richards has carefully analyzed. "They were neither revolutionary nor lower-class. They involved a well-organized nucleus of respectable, middle-class citizens who wished to preserve the status quo rather than to change it. They met purposefully and often formally, and they coordinated their actions several days in advance. Frequently, they had either the support or the acquiescence of the dominant forces in the com-

[7] Leonard L. Richards, *"Gentlemen of Property and Standing": Anti-Abolition Mobs in Jacksonian America* (New York, 1970).

munity. Sometimes they represented the Establishment. More frequently they *were* the Establishment." They were "usually led or engineered by the scions of old and socially dominant Northeastern families," by doctors and lawyers, merchants and bankers, judges and congressmen—"gentlemen of property and standing," in Garrison's own phrase. The collective wealth of mob members was appreciably greater than that of abolitionists of a given community. Yet subservience to Southern economic pressure was not a significant motive. "There were too many Northern mobs in cities and towns such as Montpelier, Utica, Lockport, Troy, and Granville—in places that had little or no dependence on Southern patronage." Fear and hatred of the black man played a part, to be sure, but "Negrophobia had been common for as long as anyone cared to remember," and blacks were no real threat to these disturbed gentlemen. Rather they saw the abolitionists as a symbol of all the dread forces of a new America that were challenging their elite status, the moral legitimacy of the established order, and threatening traditional means of social control. With their pressure groups, mass petitions, mass press, and free newspapers, the abolitionists, like so many other and even more powerful (but less vulnerable) subversive forces of centralization, were undermining the authority of local men of "character" and "respectability" who had dominated the old Northern Jacksonian society of gentlemen merchants. The abolitionists short-circuited these local elites, bypassed the city fathers, appealed over their heads directly to young and old, women as well as men, blacks as well as whites, to preach "amalgamation" and "leveling." The anti-abolition mobs were in part a reaction against this challenge to traditional prerogatives of community leaders.

Abolitionist organizations and activities declined sharply after the Panic of 1837 cut back their funds, reduced their agents and publications, and broke up their unity. Simultaneously the number of anti-abolitionist mobs declined sharply—the response with the challenge. Yet, paradoxically, antislavery converts then became more numerous and widespread. An important reason for this suggested by Mr. Richards was "that the ground upon which one might hold antislavery views was tremendously broadened in the late 1830s and 1840s." Abolitionism had become linked with other issues having little to do with its own validity—not only freedom of speech, press, and petition, but broadest of all with such issues as free soil. One could join the free soilers not only because he opposed slavery or its expansion, but also because he feared and hated Negroes. The antislavery leaders of the Free Soil Party in 1852 dropped the demand for equal rights for free Negroes of the North because, as Eric Foner has pointed out, they "realized that in a society characterized by all but universal belief in white supremacy, no political party could function effectively which included a call for equal rights [for blacks] in its national platform."[8] Under these conditions some of the bitterest antiabolitionists and even some of the mob leaders of the 1830s became prominent antislavery politicians in the 1850s and Radical Republicans later on.[9] The movement that eventually democratized antislavery sentiment contrived to make it respectable at the Negro's expense. This was not Garrison's movement, for he abhorred racism as much as he did slavery. The successful antislavery movement embraced anti-Negro recruits and their prejudices and triumphed over slavery in the name of white supremacy.

In no part of the country was the combination of these sentiments and the alliance of those holding them more evident than in the West. It is the thesis of Eugene H. Berwanger's *The Frontier Against Slavery* that "prejudice against Negroes was a factor in the development of antislavery feeling in the ante-bellum United States."[10] His study "concentrates on the ever-shifting frontier regions which became free states or territories by 1860" but which were threatened at some time with the legalization of slavery. This latest investigation of "frontier influences" offers cold comfort to Frederick Jackson Turner's hypothesis that the frontier experience was a major source and an ever-rejuvenating stimulus of the democratic impulse in American life—if democracy and American life included Negro people. Without explicitly making the comparisons suggested, Ber-

[8] Eric Foner, "Politics and Prejudice: The Free Soil Party and the Negro, 1849–1852," *Journal of Negro History* 50 (October 1965): 239–240.

[9] For example, John Parker Hale of Dover, New Hampshire, disrupted and broke up a series of antislavery lectures in 1835 by a speech in which he declared that Negro slaves *"are beasts in human shape, and not fit to live,"* adding in a barely audible voice, "free." Hale later became the standard bearer of the Liberty party in 1847 and the presidential candidate of the Free Soil party in 1852. Richards, *"Gentlemen of Property and Standing,"* pp. 163–164.

[10] Eugene H. Berwanger, *The Frontier Against Slavery: Western Anti-Negro Prejudice and the Slavery Extension Controversy* (Urbana, 1967).

wanger lends less support to Turner's thesis than to Tocqueville's observation that "the prejudice of race appears to be stronger in the states which have abolished slavery than in those where it still exists; and nowhere is it so important as in those states where servitude never has been known."[11]

Proslavery men kept up their fight for legalizing bondage in the Old Northwest until the 1830s, but by 1811 antislavery and anti-Negro forces of the Indiana territorial legislature had passed laws preventing Negroes from testifying in court against whites, excluding them from militia duty, and barring them from voting. Ohio in 1807 excluded Negroes from residence in the state unless they posted a $500 bond for good behavior. In 1813, Illinois ordered every incoming free Negro to leave the territory under a penalty of 39 lashes repeated every fifteen days until he left. The chief argument against slavery was that it would eventually produce a free Negro population. By the early 1830s all three states had adopted "almost identical statute restrictions against free Negroes." Michigan and Iowa followed suit in their turn, and Wisconsin joined them in voting down Negro suffrage by large majorities. Anti-Negro activity intensified in the 1840s and 1850s, when Illinois and Indiana wrote harsh free-Negro-exclusion provisions into their constitutions. John A. Logan of Illinois, future radical Republican leader, was the author of "the most severe anti-Negro measure passed by a free state."

The peak of the anti-Negro movement in the Middle West coincided with the height of agitation over the slavery-expansion issue, but Mr. Berwanger's evidence indicates that often the main concern was not so much over the expansion of slavery as the migration of Negroes. David Wilmot, author of the famous "Proviso" excluding slavery from new territories, avowed his object was to "preserve to free labor . . . of my own race and own color" those new lands. Horace Greeley declared that the unoccupied West "shall be reserved for the benefit of the white Caucasian race." Owen Lovejoy, congressman from the "most abolitionized" district of Illinois and brother of the martyred abolitionist Elijah, denounced the idea of Negro equality. Joshua Giddings, zealous antislavery congressman from Ohio, pronounced Negroes "not the equal of white men," and Benjamin F.

[11] Alexis de Tocqueville, *Democracy in America* (New York, 1904), I, 383.

Wade, another congressman of the same state and same persuasion called Washington "a Nigger-ridden place." Lyman Trumbull, Illinois Republican leader and a close friend of Lincoln, declared that "We, the Republican Party, are a white man's party."

The region that inspired these obsessions and phobias against Negro people never had a black population in this era exceeding one percent of the total. Yet the attitudes and laws developed in the Middle West became the models for new territories farther westward as Midwesterners followed the frontier to the Pacific. As Mr. Berwanger says, "These pioneers pushed westward with an increased determination to keep the Negro, free or slave, out of the new lands."

Before 1848, Californians under Mexican rule are said to have "accepted Negroes as equal individuals" and intermarried with them, but this situation quickly changed with the arrival of great numbers of Americans the following year. Delegates to the Constitutional Convention of California in 1849 voted without opposition and without debate to adopt the same constitutional restrictions on free Negroes in their fundamental laws that were found in the Middle West. A measure excluding free Negroes from the territory entirely was defeated only because of fear that this would delay congressional action on statehood. Californians voted down slavery, but an informed citizen said that "not one in ten cares a button for its abolition . . . all they look at is their own position; they must themselves swing the pick, and they won't swing it by the side of Negro slaves." The state legislature swiftly debarred blacks from testifying against whites in court and from intermarriage with whites, while local authorities segregated them. In 1857, the state prison director shipped black inmates of the prisons to New Orleans, where they were sold into slavery.

The Pacific Northwest in its turn duplicated the laws and racial customs of the Old Northwest and was settled in considerable measure from that region. The territorial legislature of Oregon subjected Negroes who refused to leave to periodic floggings and later substituted apprenticeship to white men. The constitutional convention for statehood in 1857 rapidly approved laws excluding Negroes from the militia and the polls. A popular referendum rejected slavery by a majority of 5,000, but approved exclusion of free Negroes from the state by a majority of 7,500—8,640 to 1,081. "Slavery and the Negro," it seems, "to the average farmer, were one and the same." Congress admitted Oregon in 1857, the only free state with a Negro exclusion clause in its original constitution ever admitted. "Oregon is a land for the white man," said the *Oregon Weekly Times.* "Refusing the toleration of Negroes in our midst as slaves, we rightly and for yet stronger reasons, prohibit them from coming among us as free Negro vagabonds."

"Bleeding Kansas" was the *cause célèbre* among Eastern antislavery radicals in the mid-1850s, but a census of 1856 showed that 83 percent of Kansas settlers had lived in the Old Northwest, or in Iowa, Kentucky, or Missouri. Mr. Berwanger proves that "a large group of settlers was more anti-Negro than antislavery." The population was, of course, divided politically and sometimes militarily between the proslavery and antislavery factions. But even among the latter, except for a minority in the area of Lawrence, reliable evidence shows that "anti-Negro sentiment was overwhelming among the antislavery settlers." A referendum which the proslavery people boycotted and which was confined to the antislavery population polled 1,287 for and 453 against excluding free Negroes from the territory. Thus three out of every four antislavery Kansans approved Negro exclusion. The antislavery heroes of the Western plains to whom Boston abolitionists were shipping "Beecher's Bibles" were at that time engaged in limiting suffrage, office holding, and militia service to white men. They were evidently more anti-Negro than they were antislavery. The same was true of Utah, Colorado, New Mexico, and Nebraska, which repeated the old story of discrimination, but with the added absurdity of having so few Negroes in their borders about whom to quarrel. With only 59 live Negroes in their territory to prove it, Mormons resolved that the race was inferior to whites even "in the next world." Nebraska had only 67 Negroes in 1860, yet Negro exclusion had been a hot issue in 1859.

The modesty and thoroughness of Mr. Berwanger's scholarship is indicated by his admission that "the exact extent of racial prejudice as a factor encouraging the limitation of slavery is indeterminable." But he adds cogently that "if 79.5 percent of the people of Illinois, Indiana, Oregon and Kansas voted to exclude the free Negro simply because of their prejudice, surely this antipathy influenced their decisions to support the nonextension of slavery." And surely any fair-minded reader will concede that he has a point there.

All writers on Midwestern attitudes toward slavery and the Negro point out that these attitudes may be partially accounted for by the considerable migration of nonslaveholding Southern yeomen into some parts of that region. What then of the attitudes in the Middle Atlantic and New England states, where the number of Southern migrants was negligible? In a less ambitious study than the previous one, Lorman Ratner treats the Northern states omitted by Berwanger—those of the Northeast.[12]

It is not difficult to establish that, in the period concerned, the great majority of people in the Northeast despised or opposed abolitionists and were hostile or indifferent to the antislavery cause. Mr. Ratner undertakes to go further, however, and explain why they had those attitudes. What he actually does is to tell us why they *said* they opposed the movement. What they said is of interest even if it does not explain. For example, two great theologians, Charles Grandison Finney and William Ellery Channing, and Noah Porter, later President of Yale, agreed that abolishing slavery would aggravate the race problem. Two powerful clergymen, Lyman Beecher and Horace Bushnell, were afraid that it would place Negroes on an equal basis with whites. James Fenimore Cooper, the novelist, and Francis Wayland, clergyman and authority on ethics, feared that free Negroes would be the prey of demagogues and subvert the state. Seth Luther and George Henry Evans, labor spokesmen, feared that abolition would result in unfair competition for white labor.

Everybody had reasons, all kinds of reasons, logical and frivolous reasons, informed and superficial reasons. Among churchmen, the Presbyterians, Congregationalists, Baptists, Methodists, Episcopalians, Lutherans, Unitarians, Catholics all took positions at one time "that placed the majority of their clerical leaders in opposition to the antislavery movement." This does not mean that these churches were necessarily dominated by proslavery men. Indeed, opponents of abolition were often opponents of slavery as well. They might deplore slavery but deplore abolition more and abolitionists even more than

[12] Lorman Ratner, *Powder Keg: Northern Opposition to the Antislavery Movement, 1831–1840* (New York, 1968).

that. The commonest reason given by churchmen when speaking for their churches was that abolition would disrupt their institutions by dividing the members—which it undoubtedly would in most instances.

All the Northeastern states had abolished or taken steps for the gradual abolition of slavery within their own borders by 1804, but racial discrimination, segregation, and injustice still flourished and often proliferated in those regions. Only the five states with the most insignificant numbers of blacks, all in New England, permitted them to vote. New York had property qualifications that withheld the ballot from nearly all of them. Massachusetts outlawed intermarriage and for a while tightened segregation, and the other states followed much the same policy. The Pennsylvania legislature formally refused the Negro the vote in 1837 and at the same time seriously debated, though did not pass, an exclusion bill of the Western type to prevent free Negroes from entering the state. Northeasterners of high and low status flaunted race prejudice openly. Negroes lived a thoroughly segregated existence, set apart in church, school, public services, and society, excluded from politics and handicapped in the courts of justice. They constituted, with few exceptions, a despised and ostracized caste.

Mr. Ratner is probably right that the "romantic image of the South" created by Northern novelists[13] fostered "northern respect and admiration, even pride in that region." This attitude toward the South doubtless affected Northern attitudes toward slavery and the Negro. As the sectional crisis intensified in the 1850s, however, the romantic image faded and the South, not the Negro, came to be regarded as the real menace to the North. Yet the North entered the Civil War as part of a slave republic to defend a Constitution that guaranteed slave property, led by a party with a platform pledged to protect slavery where it existed, and headed by a President who declared in his inaugural address that he had "no lawful right" and "no inclination" to interfere with slavery in the South. Congress followed this up three months after the war started with virtually unanimous resolutions viewing with horror any suggestion of permitting the war to interfere with "established institutions of those States."

The party that led the Northern crusade against slavery has not

[13] Analyzed by William R. Taylor, *Yankee and Cavalier: The Old South and American National Character* (New York, 1961).

come off well at the hands of the new revisionists who have been emphasizing the pervasiveness of anti-Negro sentiment in Northern society. Not only the conservative and the moderate, the ex-Whig and ex-Democratic Republicans, but the radical, antislavery, and abolitionist Republicans as well have been found wanting in their racial attitudes and policies. They have been caught mouthing the slogans of white privilege and white supremacy, appealing to race prejudices of the electorate, appeasing mass phobias, and condoning compromises with discriminatory and outrageously unjust anti-Negro policies and laws. This derogatory emphasis on the seamy side and the hypocritical aspects of the Republican party, especially the Radicals, is all the more striking because it follows hard upon a decade of historiography devoted to the rehabilitation and vindication of the Radical Republicans. In the hands of these historians, what had probably been until about 1960 "the best-hated men in American history" were on the way to becoming the most elaborately vindicated and widely venerated politicians in our history.[14] It was to be expected, therefore, that the new counterinterpretation emphasizing the retrograde and racist side of Radical Republicans would not long go unchallenged.

The first challenge of consequence comes from the pen of Eric Foner in a work on Republican ideology before the Civil War.[15] Conciliatory and low-keyed, his response is free of the sweeping tone of vindication and unqualified defense. Admitting that "racism and colonization were important elements of the Republican attitude toward the Negro," he contends that "they were by no means the entire story," and that those who take Republicans to task for racial prejudice "have carried a good point too far." He points out, for example, that even in the Middle West, enclaves of radical Re-

[14] Hans L. Trefousse, *The Radical Republicans: Lincoln's Vanguard for Racial Justice* (New York, 1969), attempts "to draw together the findings" of this school. While he admits that there was a "diversity of approaches to the race question" among radicals and cites evidence of their racial prejudices, his conclusions about the radicals are better reflected in the subtitle of his book. "The villains of yesteryear," he observes, "are the heroes of today." A briefer synthesis is Larry Kinkaid, "Victims of Circumstance: An Interpretation of Changing Attitudes toward Republican Policy Makers and Reconstruction," *Journal of American History* 57 (June 1970): 48–66. The assessment covers the historiography of vindication, but not the later literature that runs counter to it.

[15] Eric Foner, *Free Soil, Free Labor, Free Men: The Ideology of the Republican Party Before the Civil War* (New York, 1970).

publicanism, such as fourteen counties of northern Illinois and the Western Reserve of Ohio, consistently opposed black laws and exclusion laws. He believes that "a majority of Republicans [in the West] were ready to give some recognition to Negro rights" and that in Ohio "some Republican legislators favored Negro suffrage." Mr. Foner is able to list Republicans of high rank who advocated political rights for free Negroes, opposed exclusion laws, and defended and assisted fugitive slaves, and a few who fought for Negro suffrage. This alone, he thinks, "should be proof that there was more to Republican attitudes than mere racism." Out of experience and debate emerged "what may be called the mainstream of Republican opinion" on Negro rights. "Fundamentally it asserted that free Negroes were human beings and citizens" and deserved protection of life, liberty, and property. Although these rights were not extended to slaves, did not include equality or the right to vote and hold office, and were "not accepted by everyone in the party," they constituted "a distinctive Republican position." And in view of pervasive Northern racism, "the Republicans' insistence on the humanity of the Negro was more of a step forward than might appear."

This is not a very strong case for the defense, and was not intended to be. It relies heavily on the point that the Democrats were even worse, which is true. "To a large extent, these [Republican] expressions of racism were political replies to Democratic accusations rather than gratuitous insults to the black race." The case is further weakened by the admission that "inherent in the antislavery outlook of many Republicans was a strong overtone of racism" and that the party borrowed much from the "free labor" position that abhorred the black man about as much as the slave. It is further conceded that "no portion of the Republican party could claim total freedom" from racism. "Nevertheless," contends Mr. Foner, "by the eve of the Civil War there had emerged a distinctive attitude toward the Negro." This was best represented by Abraham Lincoln, who acknowledged the "universal feeling" against the Negro in the North and shared the opposition to Negro suffrage and Negro political and social equality, but who insisted on "the basic humanity of the Negro," his right to earn a livelihood and to have protection of his basic rights.

In spite of the Republican party's formal disavowal of any intention to interfere with slavery, within two years after the opening of the

Civil War the Union was formally committed to freedom as a war aim and later in some degree (so the present historian once maintained) to the far more revolutionary war aim of racial equality. By these commitments, a power struggle with the negative aim of preventing secession was metamorphosed into a war of ideologies, a moral crusade with divinely sanctioned ends. Exalted by the crusading spirit, many Union participants, especially in retrospect, hallowed their cause with a "common glory" and sanctified it as a holy war. Thus the American Civil War entered into legend and history with an aura of sanctity that few wars in history have enjoyed. The extent to which Union policies and attitudes toward the Negro justified this view of the war is subject to searching investigation by V. Jacque Voegeli.[16] He focuses his study on the Middle West, but his findings have wider import and deserve respectful attention.

Convincing evidence supports Voegeli's conclusion that the outbreak of the Civil War actually "increased the virulence of midwestern racism." For the war opened the prospect of an inundation of the North by fugitive or liberated Negroes. Thus the fears that motivated so much opposition to the *expansion* of slavery were now revived and intensified by the threatened *abolition* of slavery. Congressmen and editors gave full voice to these fears of "free Negroism," or "Africanization," fears of an invasion of blacks who would "fill the jails and poorhouses, compete with white labor, and degrade society." Ohioans were not prepared to "mix up four millions of blacks with their sons and daughters." The *Chicago Times* predicted that emancipation would flood the North with "two or three million semi-savages." Lincoln's own state, where the constitution and statutes already barred further Negro settlement, endorsed new Negro exclusion measures in a referendum of June 1862, by a vote of two to one.

The urgent question for the politicians was framed by a correspondent of Senator Ben Wade: "If we are to have no more slave states what the devil are we to do with the surplus niggers?" Lyman Trumbull, speaking for the West as a whole and for Illinois in particular, told the Senate, "Our people want nothing to do with the Negro." Salmon P. Chase urged General Ben Butler "to see that the blacks of the North will slide Southward, and leave no question to quarrel

[16] V. Jacque Voegeli, *Free but Not Equal: The Midwest and the Negro During the Civil War* (Chicago, 1967).

about." Others held out the hope that after slavery was abolished freedmen would want to stay in the South and Northern Negroes would actually prefer to live there. Hoping to placate Northern fears, Republicans made Negro deportation and colonization abroad the official policy of the party, and "openly avowed in Congress that deportation was designed partly to keep the freedmen out of the North." President Lincoln was a strong advocate of the policy. In view of the keen instinct for the practical and possible that Lincoln had, it is hard to believe his advocacy was other than political in motivation.

The backlash to emancipation was frightening. Lincoln thought his Proclamation had "done about as much harm as good." The Illinois legislature adopted a resolution denouncing it and debated enforcement of the state exclusion law with "thirty-nine lashes on the bare back." Anti-Negro violence erupted in Toledo, Chicago, Peoria and Cincinnati. At New Albany, Indiana, guards were stationed at ferries to prevent Negroes landing and a regiment of Indiana troops threatened to fire on Negroes and keep them from crossing the Ohio. Republican party leaders repeatedly disavowed intentions of permitting or encouraging Negro migration or tolerating Negro equality. The charge that "our volunteers are periling their lives to make the niggers equal" was denounced by the Indianapolis *Journal* as "a monstrous and villainous lie."

Deeds rather than words were required of the Republicans. The old clichés and promises were not enough. Everyone knew that hundreds of thousands of idle and helpless refugee freedmen were piling up behind the Union lines in the South. Secretary of War Edwin M. Stanton, seeing the need for labor in the North, blundered into shipping hundreds of blacks into Illinois, and then beat a hasty retreat when his action touched off a violent explosion of resentment. Lincoln's experiment with deportation and colonization of blacks in the Caribbean proved a failure. He began arming Negroes in spite of his "fear that in a few weeks the arms would be in the hands of the rebels," but the army could absorb only a fraction of the refugees. In March 1863, Lincoln placed the problem in the hands of General Lorenzo Thomas, a rather hapless old functionary. Speaking to Union troops in Louisiana the following month, "with full authority from the President," Thomas said of the refugees, "They are coming in upon us in such numbers that some provision must be made for them. You cannot send them North. You all know the prejudices of the Northern people. . . ." The policy decided upon, said the General, was deliberately to contain the Negroes in the South, put them to work on "the multitude of deserted plantations" he pointed to "along the river." The hope was to make them self-supporting, but at any rate to keep them down South. Mr. Voegeli concludes that the policy "effectually sealed the vast majority of them in the region," and that "the political motive was crucial" in the determination of the containment policy.

Northern racial phobias and "apprehensions of a black invasion" cooled somewhat after the policy of containment was publicized and its effectiveness became apparent. War service of the Negroes, their demands for justice, and their horrible persecution in the New York City riots gained some sympathy for them. The war then became "a limited crusade" in the eyes of many, "a struggle for God, mankind, liberty and Union." Combining "a mixture of idealism and vengefulness, innocence and arrogance" the limited crusaders saw the war as "a battle for cultural supremacy . . . the final confrontation of Puritan and Cavalier," in which "Southern vices . . . were to be supplanted by Northern virtues—industrialism, democracy, equality, prosperity, ingenuity, intelligence, and unselfish nationalism."

Several years ago, the present writer advanced the thesis that in this crusade phase a "third war aim," the boldly revolutionary aim of racial equality, was almost surreptitiously added by the radicals to the primary war aims of union and freedom. It was a qualified suggestion, later retracted.[17] Mr. Voegeli effectively attacks the original suggestion. I think he is right and I was wrong. Of course, some influential Northerners did want to make equality a war aim, and the postwar civil rights acts and constitutional amendments can be read as evidence of their success. But as I said at the time, "legal commitments overreached moral persuasion," and the Union "fought the war on borrowed moral capital" and then repudiated the debt. It was nevertheless misleading to equate Equality with the commitments to union and freedom, and Mr. Voegeli is right in saying "there is no reason to believe that full equality for Negroes ever became one of

[17] The thesis of "the third war aim" was suggested by the author in *The Burden of Southern History* (Baton Rouge, 1960), and retracted in a second edition of that work (p. 87) published in 1968.

their war aims." He is also right that there was "some bold talk . . . but little action," that "only a few of the innumerable extralegal devices which drew the color line in the Midwest were discarded during the war," that "on the whole, these changes scarcely scratched the surface of white supremacy," and that "in most places Negroes remained fundamentally as before—victims of discrimination . . . of social ostracism, and of economic subordination."

Sincerity of Union purpose may also be tested by federal race policy in the South after the war, and on this subject there is a revisionary work of superior quality by William S. McFeely.[18] It soon became apparent that Radical Reconstruction did not mean abandonment of the containment policy. Voegeli pointed out that an amendment to the Freedmen's Bureau bill sensibly providing for the organized dispersion of freedmen to jobs in the North was defeated in the Senate, where Senator Charles Sumner of Massachusetts called it "entirely untenable," and Senator Henry Wilson of the same state feared it would have "a bad influence." General Howard's mission was to solve the problem of freedmen within the South. All agreed then and still agree now that the one-armed "Christian General" was by all odds the best man for the job. He was given wide powers and a bill authorizing him to distribute "abandoned and confiscated land" to freedmen.

The freedmen never got the promised land to have and hold. It was taken away from them and returned to the planters, and General Howard painfully and personally presided over the restitution. It is one of the stranger ironies of historiography that for a hundred years the Freedmen's Bureau has been pictured by friend and foe alike as an instrument of radical policy. Actually it was skillfully employed by President Andrew Johnson with the compliance of Howard to subvert radical purposes and advance conservative ends. On the complaint by influential whites, the General eventually removed virtually every subordinate who sought to fulfill the original mission of the Bureau and help the freedmen. "The Freedmen's Bureau had not stopped the delivery of the Negro labor force into the hands of Johnson's planters and businessmen allies," writes Mr. McFeely. "On the contrary, it was used by the President to accomplish this purpose." In less skillful

[18] William S. McFeely, *Yankee Stepfather: A Study of General O. O. Howard and the Freedmen's Bureau* (New Haven, 1968).

hands, this important revision of history might have taken the tone of strident cynicism and exposure. Fortunately Mr. McFeely has the subtlety and grace to make his story "not an exposé of a knave, but rather a record of naïveté and misunderstanding." Thus he is able not only to grasp the tragedy of the freedmen, but the tragedy of General Howard as well, and to see both as the failure of America.

The findings of the revisionists might help with Miss Kraditor's speculations about history vindicating Garrison and what might have happened had abolitionists remained faithful to his ideals. History supports Garrisonian dogma that "reform" was not enough, that to be effective the eradication of slavery had to be root-and-branch, that the racist ideology supporting it permeated the country, and that abolishing slavery in alliance with racists and without eradicating their ideology would be largely an empty victory. To grant that agitation is "the art of the desirable" is to concede Garrison much. But when Garrison put aside his pacifism and many of his principles to support the Union cause and the Constitution on the ground that "death and hell had seceded," he shifted from agitation to politics, "the art of the possible." Of that art he was wholly innocent. The greatest artist of the possible in his time was now in charge, and Lincoln knew in his bones that unless he fought that war with the support of racists and in the name of white supremacy it would be *his* lost cause and not Jefferson Davis's.

To return finally to the questions raised at the beginning of this chapter, some of the answers still seem rather elusive and ambiguous. After an excursion through revisionary historical literature, however, it seems harder than ever to locate precisely that legendary "interlude of virtue" when Americans renounced their racial prejudices and rededicated themselves to their ideals of equality. The present seems depressingly continuous with the past. And now that the old policy of "containment" no longer holds, now that the fears of an inundation by Negro migrants from the South that obsessed the North of the 1860s have materialized a century later, the continuity of plantation and ghetto is borne in upon us. It also seems rather more difficult than it was before to be confident in justifying the sacrifice of those 600,000 lives. It was a crusade to be sure, but a "limited" one, and it does appear to have been corrupted and frustrated all along by an old sickness endemic among the crusaders.

James M. McPherson

SCHISM IN THE RANKS: 1864–1865

For many years, historians wrote as if abolitionists' efforts came to an end with the onset of the Civil War, or at least with the Emancipation Proclamation. As his many articles and books show, James McPherson has set himself the task of filling this gap in American historiography. Especially in his book The Struggle for Equality, *McPherson traces the efforts of abolitionists to make the war serve the antislavery cause and the attempts many of them made to keep faith with the former slaves during Reconstruction, often by themselves going into the South for freedmen's aid work. They came closer than any of their contemporaries, he argues, to transcending racism. The following excerpt suggests some of the dilemmas facing abolitionists early in 1865, when the war was ending and the Thirteenth Amendment promised an unquestionably antislavery Constitution. Was this enough? Should they continue active, or might they justifiably rest on their laurels? As so often in the past, abolitionists disagreed. McPherson teaches at Princeton University.*

In 1865 there occurred a schism in the Garrisonian abolitionist movement comparable in importance to the division of 1840. One of the main causes of the schism of 1865 was the sharp clash between the followers of Garrison and Phillips over the presidential election of 1864, but there were other causes, dating back many years. The controversy between Pillsbury and Foster, on the one hand, and Garrison on the other regarding the attitude of abolitionists toward the Republican party was long-standing and foreshadowed the conflict of 1864. During the early war years Wendell Phillips exercised a mediating influence between the two factions, but as the war progressed his increasingly revolutionary concept of reconstruction drove him closer to the Pillsbury-Foster camp.

Disputes among Garrisonians over the future of their antislavery societies broke out in the first year of the war. McKim's attempt to resign from the Pennsylvania Anti-Slavery Society and devote himself full-time to freedmen's aid work sparked the controversy. After Lincoln made emancipation an official war aim, the discussion of the

From James M. McPherson, *The Struggle for Equality: Abolitionists and the Negro in the Civil War and Reconstruction* (copyright © 1964 by Princeton University Press; Princeton Paperback, 1967), pp. 287–299. Most documentary footnotes omitted. Reprinted by permission of Princeton University Press.

fate of organized abolitionism became more heated. At the annual meeting of the Massachusetts Anti-Slavery Society in 1863, Garrison hinted that before another year went by abolitionists might be able to proclaim the jubilee and disband their societies. Stephen S. Foster and Charles Remond, a fiery New England Negro abolitionist, were angered by this kind of talk. After all, they argued, malignant prejudice and discrimination against the Negro would still exist after slavery was gone. One of the declared purposes of the antislavery societies was to end this discrimination. The societies could not consider their work done when slavery was abolished. Garrison agreed that abolitionists were pledged to remove racial discrimination, but maintained that "as Abolitionists, distinctively, our special work is . . . the utter annihilation of slavery." The work of educating, uplifting, and securing equal rights for the freedmen should be done through other organizations or through the established social and political institutions of the nation. The historic mission of antislavery societies, he asserted, would be fulfilled when slavery disappeared from the nation.

Many abolitionists could not see it this way. America's hostility to emancipation had compelled them to organize separately, and they anticipated as much opposition to their drive for equality as they had encountered in the struggle for liberty. Pillsbury and Phillips registered their protest against what they considered Garrison's conservatism by staying away from the Third Decade Anniversary Celebration of the founding of the American Anti-Slavery Society at Philadelphia in December 1863. This meeting was planned partly as a joyous jubilee anticipating the end of the antislavery crusade. Pillsbury and Phillips, ever-mindful of the dangers of a conservative reconstruction, could see little to be thankful for and hence stayed away. Aware of the reasons for their absence, Garrison tried to assuage the apprehensions of the Pillsbury-Phillips faction in his opening speech to the Philadelphia meeting. "We may now confidently hope that our labors are drawing near to an end, so far as the abolition of slavery is concerned," he said. "But our labors in the field of a common humanity, and in the cause of reform, are never to terminate here, except with our mortal lives." Emancipation would confront the nation with the task of lifting generations of enforced ignorance from the minds of the freedmen. "This is a work of mercy and benevolence, in the doing of which we believe the great mass of the people of all denominations, and parties, and sects will flow together."

Frederick Douglass was not entirely satisfied with Garrison's statement. "A mightier work than the abolition of slavery now looms up before the Abolitionist," he told the veteran crusaders at Philadelphia. "The work of the American Anti-Slavery Society will not have been completed until the black men of the South, and the black men of the North, shall have been admitted, fully and completely, into the body politic of America." A month later Douglass warned a New York audience of the reaction that usually followed revolutions. When the Confederacy was conquered and slavery abolished, there would be danger of a reaction that could rob the black man of his rights. "There never was a time when Anti-Slavery work was more needed than right now. The day that shall see the Rebels at our feet, their weapons flung away, will be the day of trial."

The controversy over presidential politics in 1864 intensified abolitionist differences, but other issues were also driving a wedge between the two wings of the Garrisonian movement. One of these issues was General N. P. Banks' freedmen's labor system in Louisiana. Many Louisiana planters within Banks' department had taken the oath of allegiance and were allowed to continue working their plantations with Negro labor. The Negroes were now free, but Banks had established a system of regulations to govern their conduct that, according to some abolitionists, left the planter-laborer relationship very little different from what it had been under slavery.

When he arrived in New Orleans in December 1862, Banks had found the contrabands in a pitiable condition, crowded into filthy camps and huts, living on half-rations handed out by the army. In an effort to get them back to work on the plantations, Banks issued a general order establishing rules and regulations for a system of labor on January 29, 1863, supplemented by an additional order of February 3, 1864. These orders were designed to put every able-bodied male Negro to work. All freedmen not assigned to plantations were required to labor on public works without wages. The Negro could choose his own employer, but once having chosen he must remain with him for one year. Banks' officers encouraged the Negroes to go to work for their old masters. The order regulated the wage scale by ability up to $10 a month, and stipulated that payment of half the wages would be reserved until the end of the year. Workers were promised "just treatment, healthy rations, comfortable clothing, quarters, fuel, medical attendance, and instruction for children." But plantation hands would not be allowed to leave the plantation without a pass, and provost marshals were ordered to enforce the "continuous and faithful service, respectful deportment, correct discipline and perfect subordination" of the freedmen.

Abolitionists denounced Banks' order of 1863 as an "execrable proclamation" and called Banks a "born slave-driver." A Massachusetts abolitionist stationed with the army in Louisiana declared that the Banks system was tantamount to a "reestablishment of slavery." Some of Banks' officers, he declared, were Negro-phobes and treated the freedmen with cruelty and contempt. Charles K. Whipple asserted that Banks' system "substitutes serfdom for slavery, and seems merely a modification of that intermediate state which Great Britain found to work so ill." A British abolitionist agreed that Banks' policy was similar to the West Indian apprenticeship system which had worked so badly "that it was obliged to be thrown to the dogs."

"It is not easy," wrote Theodore Tilton, "to conceive all the injustice, the oppression, the wrong to inalienable rights, the insult to men keenly capable of feeling it, the misery inflicted on those without redress or opportunity to appeal, [and] the general degradation of a race struggling up toward freedom" produced by Banks' system. Sydney Gay asserted in a *New York Tribune* editorial that Banks' labor system was little better than serfdom. "The negro bound to the soil for a year, compelled to work for wages two-thirds less than he could command in open market, not permitted . . . to have a voice in the contract by which he becomes bound, exposed to the tyrannous caprices of lifelong slaveholders. . . . Such is the serfage which predominates on the soil of Louisiana," wrote Gay angrily.

Abolitionist attacks on Banks found a sympathetic hearing among radical Republicans, but Lincoln supported the general's policy, and it was not substantially changed until after the end of the war. Banks defended himself publicly against radical attacks, and even persuaded some abolitionists, including Garrison, that his policy was humanely conceived and wisely carried out for the good of the freedmen. Garrison had never criticized Banks very sharply, and during 1864 he began to reexamine the Banks system more sympathetically. A major reason for this reexamination, of course, was Garrison's support of Lincoln. The President had authorized Banks' policy, and Garrison soon began to defend Banks as part of his effort to vindicate Lincoln. This angered the Phillips wing of the American Anti-Slavery Society and confirmed their belief that Garrison had unaccountably become conservative.

Garrison had several friends stationed with the Union forces in Louisiana who assured him of the essential benevolence of the Banks system. Two men in particular played an important role in shaping Garrison's thinking on this question: Major B. Rush Plumly and the Reverend Edwin Wheelock. Both were veteran abolitionists. Plumly served as special treasury agent in New Orleans and later as a major in the *Corps d'Afrique.* Wheelock had come South as chaplain of a New Hampshire regiment and on February 20, 1863, was appointed deputy superintendent of labor in Louisiana.

Plumly stated that he had been consulted by Banks before issuance of the labor orders, which were drafted primarily with an eye to the best interests of the freedmen. Before Banks came, said Wheelock, the freedmen had been huddled together in filthy camps, and some policy such as that initiated by Banks was absolutely necessary to save them from disease or starvation. Under the Banks system the planter had to provide his laborers with food, clothing, housing, and medical care plus a small plot of land on which the Negroes could grow some of their own food. As a deputy superintendent of labor, Wheelock was assigned to inspect conditions on the plantations. At first there was much disorder. The planters were wedded to their old ways and did not comprehend the revolution going on around them. They did their best to obstruct Banks' policy and make it fail. Wheelock reported planter abuses and obstructionism to Banks, who took prompt corrective action. Undesirable overseers and provost marshals were removed; some planters were fined or deprived of their plantations. Order gradually emerged from chaos, and by the end of 1863, Wheelock reported, the system had proved a success.

One abolitionist criticism of Banks' labor policy was its fixed rate of low wages. But Garrison pointed out that the provision of food, clothing, housing, and medical care must be added to the wage rate to form a true picture. When this was done, he said, the Louisiana freedmen's standard of living compared favorably with other parts of the South. In the fall of 1864 General Banks spoke in vindication of his policy to a crowded audience in Boston's Tremont Temple. Garrison published the entire speech in the *Liberator* and editorially praised Banks for his successful efforts "to deliver the oppressed from the yoke of bondage, give vitality and success to paralyzed industry, . . . reconcile employers and the employed, . . . [and] establish and multiply schools for those hitherto forbidden to learn the alphabet." Louisiana Negroes were guaranteed equal rights in the courts under the new state constitution, a provision which, said Garrison, some northern states would do well to emulate. Several other abolitionists joined Garrison in approving Banks' policy.

These champions of the Banks system were especially impressed by its provision for education of the freedmen. Banks' labor order of 1863 envisioned creation of a public school system for freedmen financed by property taxes. Under the leadership of Major Plumly a few schools were opened in October 1863. In March 1864, Banks issued a general order creating a "Board of Education for the Department of the Gulf" with power to levy and collect the school tax, establish common schools, employ teachers, and erect schoolhouses. Plumly served as chairman and Wheelock as secretary of the Board. These veteran abolitionists virtually ran the public school system of Louisiana for more than a year. By May 1864, they had established 49 schools with an average daily attendance of 5,200 pupils. By the end of July 1865, Plumly and Wheelock had organized 126 schools for the freedmen with 230 teachers giving instruction to 15,000 children in day classes and 5,000 adult freedmen in night and Sunday schools. Garrison pointed to these accomplishments as evidence of the benevolent operation of General Banks' policy.

In spite of these educational achievements, most abolitionists were, in the words of Elizabeth Cady Stanton, astonished that "Garrison should defend the proposed apprenticeship system for the emancipated negroes [in Louisiana]. We say now, as ever, Give us immediately unconditional emancipation, and let there be no reconstruction except on the broadest basis of justice and equality." James McCune Smith, a Negro abolitionist in New York City, was profoundly sorry that his friend Gerrit Smith had expressed approval of the Banks system. "If I had a century of life secured to me," said

McCune Smith, "I would not hope to live to see the day of Negro Emancipation, while serfdom of Banks' kind is endorsed by progressive friends of freedom to-day." The *Boston Commonwealth* lamented that Garrison's endorsement of Banks had convinced many Republicans of the safety of reconstruction on the basis of the Banks-Lincoln policy. The *Commonwealth* asserted: "No middle course between acknowledgement and denial of the negro's manhood is possible. If abolition is to be held to mean simply that the negro shall no longer be sold at the auction-block; no longer separated from his wife and children; no longer denied the alphabet; but that he may be put under guardianship; bound out to long terms of service; compelled to work for inadequate wages; made subject to all the old policy regulations . . . of chattelhood; . . . if this is the definition which the administration and the people prefer, we have got to go through a longer and severer struggle than ever."

Another issue dividing abolitionists in 1864 was the question of Negro suffrage as a condition of reconstruction. Theoretically all abolitionists were pledged to secure equal civil and political rights for Negroes. Under the leadership of Wendell Phillips a majority of abolitionists had committed themselves to impartial or universal manhood suffrage in the South as a practical condition of reconstruction. But some abolitionists maintained that the American Anti-Slavery Society *as an organization* had nothing to do with the suffrage issue. "I am in favor of universal suffrage, without regard to color," said J. Miller McKim, "but as a member of the American Anti-Slavery Society my work will be accomplished when the slave shall be emancipated." Garrison asserted that the antislavery societies were "not organized specifically to determine" the question of Negro suffrage. "It is a new issue, and one to be settled upon a new basis, as much as the voting of women."

Thus far the abolitionist discussion of Negro suffrage had been confined to procedural problems. But in July 1864, Garrison injected a substantive flavor to the debate in a public letter to Professor Francis W. Newman, an English abolitionist who had criticized Lincoln's failure to include Negro suffrage as part of his reconstruction policy. "The elective franchise is a conventional, not a natural right," said Garrison. Lincoln should not be censured for his refusal to require Negro suffrage, for in the United States the right of suffrage was granted by the states rather than the federal government. Moreover, asked Garrison, "when was it ever known that liberation from bondage was accompanied by a recognition of political equality? Chattels personal may be instantly translated from the auction block into freemen; but when were they ever taken at the same time to the ballot-box, and invested with all political rights and immunities?" Garrison believed that even if Lincoln had the power to enfranchise the freedmen, such action might backfire. "Submitted to as a necessity at the outset, as soon as the [reconstructed] State was organized and left to manage its own affairs, the white population, with their superior intelligence, wealth and power, would unquestionably alter the franchise in accordance with their prejudices." Universal suffrage in the South, said Garrison, would come slowly only "by a struggle on the part of the disfranchised, and a growing conviction of its justice."

Garrison's statement shocked many of his fellow abolitionists. "Often during the last thirty years, Anti-Slavery men have denounced the black laws of some of the States which disfranchise citizens on account of color, as part and parcel of Slavery, the work of doughface politicians," declared the *Commonwealth.* "When before now did Mr. Garrison aid and comfort these doughfaces, by saying that 'the elective franchise is a conventional not a natural right?' When did he petrify his zealous friends by telling them majestically that 'according to the laws of development and progress it is not practicable' to extend the right of suffrage to colored men?" Liberty included the right of self-government, said the *Commonwealth,* and without the ballot the Negro's freedom would be a mere sham. "O Garrison, this is not abolitionism," proclaimed the *Commonwealth.* "Black men may well enough rejoice that they have got, out of our military necessity, a certain instalment of liberty. . . . But for a prophet to say they may well be contented with this . . . is of the madness which goes before ruin."

The *Commonwealth's* strictures probably represented the opinion of most abolitionists. But no matter how much they might publicly deprecate Garrison's course, several abolitionists privately conceded some of his points. After all, they had been arguing for thirty years that slavery deadened the intellect and dulled the moral sense of the Negro. How then could they ask immediate suffrage for this creature degraded by generations of slavery? This question posed a serious dilemma for many abolitionists. "Suffrage to me, is a difficult problem of solution," said Parker Pillsbury. "I cannot believe it should be enjoyed by those who cannot both write and read their ballots." Some abolitionists thought the solution lay in a literacy test applied impartially to both races. Others admitted the injustice of the North trying to impose Negro suffrage on a reconstructed South while most northern states barred black men from the polls.

For most abolitionists, however, these considerations gave way to their belief in the overwhelming practical necessity of Negro suffrage in the postwar South. Professor Newman stated the case succinctly: "In all history I know not where to find so senseless an infatuation as that of putting power into the hands of your disloyal conquered enemies, and casting your loyal friends under their feet." Thomas Wentworth Higginson declared that "if under any other circumstances we might excuse ourselves for delaying the recognition of the freedmen's right to suffrage, yet it would be utterly disastrous to do so now, when two-thirds of the white population will remain disloyal, even when conquered." Charles K. Whipple affirmed that Negro suffrage was necessary for two reasons: to give the freedmen the means to protect their freedom; and to "secure an immediate loyal population to transact political affairs and uphold the United States government in the Southern States." Whipple was not much impressed by the argument that the southern Negro was too ignorant to vote. Since the nation had "refused to make ignorance a bar in the case of Irish immigrants, it would not be fair to set up the plea of similar ignorance against these other new comers. Let us stick by the principle stated in the Declaration of Independence, that the right of the governing power depends on the consent of the governed."

Wendell Phillips proclaimed that universal suffrage was a vital requisite of genuine democracy. "I do not believe in an English freedom," said Phillips, "that trusts the welfare of the dependent class to the good will and moral sense of the upper class. This is aristocracy. . . . Our philosophy of government, since the 4th day of July, 1776, is that no class is safe, no freedom is real, . . . which does not place in the hands of the man himself the power to protect his own rights." Benevolent enterprises to educate the freedmen were not sufficient. "Gen. Banks says that he has set up schools for the blacks. . . . I have no doubt there are some hundreds of scholars in those schools; but I undertake to say that Gen. Banks cannot educate a mass of men by any system of benevolence." Only when the state feared the power of the ballot in the hands of ignorant men did it take steps to provide universal education in order to insure social stability. Universal suffrage, therefore, was a prerequisite to universal education in the South.

Negro suffrage was rapidly becoming the central issue of reconstruction, and Garrison came under increasing pressure to make his position on this issue clear. In January 1865, he published an editorial reaffirming his belief in equal rights for all men. But the national government, said Garrison, had no more right to require Negro suffrage in Louisiana than in Connecticut. Moreover, so long as most northern states denied the ballot to Negroes the North had no *moral* right to impose equal suffrage on the South. Abolitionists should rejoice in the great revolution of opinion that had made emancipation possible instead of grumbling that liberty was worthless without the ballot. Garrison believed that emancipation "would open the way for ultimate social, civil and political equality; but this through industrial and educational development, and not by any arbitrary mandate."

Most abolitionists were far from satisfied with this explanation of Garrison's position. Even his allies in the contest with the Phillips-Pillsbury wing of the antislavery society urged him to make his endorsement of equal suffrage more emphatic. "As abolitionists, we are the friends and *advocates* of Negro suffrage," McKim told Garrison. "For there is not, and in the nature of things cannot be, any difference of opinion among abolitionists on any essential point connected with this subject." McKim urged Garrison "to say, in terms not to be mistaken—'The right to vote for the negro on the same terms that it is given to the white man.' " The *Anti-Slavery Standard* stated flatly that "the black men must have their political rights asserted and maintained, or they cannot long retain their personal rights. . . . These are questions which naturally grow out of such a revolution as we are now enacting, and now is the time to settle them in the right way forever." Oliver Johnson, editor of the *Standard,* urged Garrison to take a clear stand in favor of impartial suffrage at the forthcoming meeting of the Massachusetts Anti-

Slavery Society. "Don't let Phillips & Co. drive you too far by their attempts to put you in a false position," wrote Johnson. "Obliged as we are to defend the Administration from their unjust assaults, we must still stand firmly for the equal rights of the colored race."

At the Massachusetts meeting Phillips introduced a series of resolutions affirming that "no emancipation can be effectual and no freedom real, unless the negro has the ballot." Garrison offered a counterresolution asserting that "if, as reconstructed, Louisiana ought not to be admitted to the Union because she excludes her colored population from the polls, then Connecticut, New Jersey, Pennsylvania, and all the Western States ought not to be in the Union for the same reason." Garrison agreed with Phillips that racial discrimination would be intolerable in the reconstructed Union, and he therefore proposed that "Congress should lose no time in submitting to the people an amendment of the Constitution, making the electoral law uniform in all the States, without regard to complexional distinctions." The suggestion of a constitutional amendment prohibiting racial discrimination was not new, for Phillips had broached the idea nearly a year before. But it was an important statement coming from Garrison, since it represented his first firm declaration in favor of equal suffrage as a condition of reconstruction. But the Phillips wing of the Society now regarded the method of constitutional amendment inadequate. If the southern states were once readmitted without Negro suffrage they could form a bloc large enough to defeat ratification of such an amendment. Negro suffrage must be secured by congressional act *prior* to the readmission of southern states as a *fundamental condition* of readmission. The time to strike for equal rights was *now,* while the national government wielded absolute power over the rebel states. After reconstruction was completed on the basis of Negro suffrage, said Phillips, the principle of equal suffrage could be nailed down permanently by a constitutional amendment.[1]

There was a great deal of acrimonious discussion of this and other issues at the Massachusetts meeting. Stephen S. Foster denounced Garrison's support of Banks and accused Garrison of making "a

[1] A year later Garrison had come around to Phillips' point of view on the suffrage question. In February 1866, Garrison wrote that "the ballot must be insisted on at least as strenuously for the loyal blacks as for the pseudo-loyal whites, and as a *sine qua non* to the recognition of State independence." Garrison to George Julian, Feb. 11, 1866, Giddings-Julian Correspondence, *LC.*

compromise with the devil." Garrison's partisans rushed to his defense and excoriated Foster in harsh language. The meeting threatened to erupt into an orgy of name-calling. Cooler heads finally prevailed and the vote was taken on Phillips' and Garrison's resolutions. The former were adopted overwhelmingly and the latter laid on the table. The Massachusetts Anti-Slavery Society had rejected Garrison's leadership and raised the standard of Phillips.

Ironically, at the same time that Garrison's influence was declining among his fellow abolitionists, it was rising among the people at large. Because of his support of Lincoln in 1864 and his defense of the administration against the attacks of other abolitionists, Garrison had acquired great prestige among moderate Republicans.[2] He reciprocated their praise by trusting them with the future of the Negro. So many of his old enemies had come to believe in his doctrine of immediate emancipation, Garrison reasoned, that there was no reason to doubt the eventual triumph of equality as well. It was a time to sing praises and thanksgiving. Garrison seemed to have reached the pinnacle of success in 1865, and the protests of Phillips, Foster, and others that the success was not yet complete rankled his nerves. He considered the Thirteenth Amendment the crowning victory of the antislavery crusade. He was not indifferent to the problem of the freedmen's future; far from it. But he wanted nothing to mar his sense of triumph in the Thirteenth Amendment.

[2] Charles Eliot Norton, editor of the *North American Review,* told Garrison in January 1865: "You are teaching the nation a most important lesson by your present course, in showing them that it is possible to unite common sense & moderation . . . with the most uncompromising fidelity to principles,—and by convincing them that the leader of the Abolition movement is not, as he has been esteemed, a fanatic but a calm and wise man." Norton to Garrison, Jan. 14, 1865, Garrison Papers, *BPL.*

VI 1865: THE ABOLITIONISTS CONSIDER WHETHER THEY HAVE ATTAINED THEIR ENDS

Charles L. Remond, William Lloyd Garrison, Wendell Phillips, Frederick Douglass

DEBATE OVER DISSOLUTION OF THE AMERICAN ANTI-SLAVERY SOCIETY

The following discussion at the meeting of the American Anti-Slavery Society, May 9–10, 1865, shows Garrison in sharp disagreement with Phillips, Douglass, and another black abolitionist, Charles L. Remond. The issue was whether or not the society, of which Garrison was still president, should dissolve itself. Although none of the four wanted to stop working for racial equality, their argument over tactics reveals how deeply they disagreed in estimating the readiness of white Americans to deal fairly with black.

C. L. Remond—I differ very materially from the friend who has just taken his seat. If I understand the Declaration of Sentiments and the Constitution, the object of this Society includes the very point to which our friend Mr. Keese refers, for the emancipation of the slave and the elevation of the free people of color were the original objects of the American Anti-Slavery Society. The work now being done in every part of our country for the enslaved and the nominally free, comes strictly and logically within the purposes of this Society.

Now, I am not among the number who would retain for a moment any one of the members or officers of the Society against his or her wish; for I hold that the man or the woman who remains reluctantly within its pale is of no service to our cause at this critical moment, and it strikes me they have but little to do but ask to be excused. I cannot understand the necessity for disbanding the Society, especially since it is doubtful in my own mind whether a new Society could be got into full play before some valuable hours, days, and perhaps months shall be lost to us.

Now, while I am upon the platform, allow me to remark, once for all, that if I understand its spirit, it is, that individual judgment shall remain inviolate upon it; and if I shall differ in my remarks from my friend Mr. Garrison, or any other member of the Society, I protest against the imputation, that the colored man who differs from his old and tried friends becomes an ingrate. Sir, if there is one work

From *The Liberator* 35 (May 26–June 2, 1865): 81–82, 85.

which I hate next to slavery, it is ingratitude; still, I hold that, as colored men or as white men, we may differ from these old friends without being liable to that charge.

Now, sir, how does the case stand in this country? It is assumed (and I do not know that I object to the assumption, only when things are brought to a very fine point, as they are sometimes here) that our white friends understand the black man's case; that they have so often put their souls in his stead, that it cannot be otherwise. To a great extent, this is true; but in many particulars it is not true. Now, while I defer to some and reverence others—and I hope no man can prove himself more grateful than I feel towards our friends—I do assume here that it is utterly impossible for any of our white friends, however much they may have tried, fully to understand the black man's case in this nation. I think I could name one or two men, perhaps a dozen here, who get very near to it, but not exactly "on the square," so to say. Our friend Mr. Garrison told us today, that antislavery being the order of things, there is no further necessity for antislavery work. Why, sir, if my friend should go out upon the highways and byways here, and put the very question which he has assumed as a foregone conclusion, he would find himself so utterly overwhelmed with opposition that he would hardly understand himself. I deny, from beginning to end, that antislavery, according to this platform, characterizes any State in this country. I deny, without fear of successful contradiction, that the antislavery which takes its color from this platform has a majority in the nation at the present time. Put the question nakedly to the American people today, whether they are prepared for the entire and full recognition of the colored man's equality in this country, and you would be voted down ten to one. This being true, I cannot sit here and hear these assertions and assumptions without raising my protest against them.

While coming through in the cars last evening (I give this as an isolated case), I gave the conductor my ticket, as the other passengers did. When the others gave up their tickets, he handed them checks. He gave me no check, and I asked him if he did not intend to. He turned round, and gave me to understand that my black face was check enough. Again: I was going to a meeting of our friends in Salem last week, to consult in reference to the question of free suffrage, and schools for the black man, and during my walk from my home to the Lyceum Hall, I heard the expressions, "D—d nigger on the stomach," "d—d nigger on the brain," etc., etc. Such expressions were never more rife in our country than at the present moment. And yet we are to understand that antislavery is the order of the day! Sir, it is not true.

But I will not occupy the time further, except to say, that standing as we do at this moment between the fires of rebellion in the South, and this hatred of the colored man in the North, I hope nothing will be done within this Society that shall look like a betrayal of our movement. I know how much our friends have been tried, how much they have sacrificed; and I do not blame those who are growing old, like myself, for their desire to retire. Still, sir, this retirement may be done in a way that shall cause great harm to our cause, and great harm to the colored people throughout the country. I hope, therefore, that this Society may be continued, and if its present officers desire to retire, we will endeavor to succeed them with others. . . .

Mr. Garrison—(Referring to a remark made by Mr. Remond)—I do not ask the Society to *permit* me to retire. That is language I do not understand on this platform. I shall retire when I think proper, and I shall think proper to do so at the end of this anniversary.

I think I am competent to interpret the language of the Declaration of Sentiments, if any man living be. I was the author of it; and, unless I have grown demented, I ought to know what I meant, and what this Society meant in using that language. This Society is "The American *Anti-Slavery* Society." That was the object. The thought never entered my mind then, nor has it at any time since, that when slavery had received its death-wound, there would be any disposition or occasion to continue the Anti-Slavery Society a moment longer. But, of course, in looking over the country, we saw the free colored people more or less laboring under disabilities, and suffering from injustice, and we declared that, incidentally, we did not mean to overlook them, but should vindicate their rights, and endeavor to get justice done to them. The point is here. We organized expressly for the abolition of slavery; we called our Society an *Anti-Slavery* Society. The other work was incidental. Now, I believe slavery is abolished in this country; abolished constitutionally; abolished by a decree of this nation, never to be reversed (applause); and, therefore, that it is ludicrous for us, a mere handful of people, with little means, with no agents in the field, no longer separate, and swallowed up in the great ocean of popular feeling against slavery, to assume that we are of special importance, and that we ought not to dissolve our association, under such circumstances, lest the nation should go to ruin! I will not be guilty of any such absurdity.

But is this to retire from the field of labor in regard to whatever is to be done in putting down prejudice, and giving the colored man his political rights? I hold all such representations, come from what quarter they may, to be slanderous. No man thinks of doing it; no officer of this Society, who is to retire, proposes to give himself up to idleness, or to abate his testimony against the proscription of men on account of their color. It is part of our nature, it is part of our duty to each other as fellow-men, it is part of our obligation to God, to denounce everywhere all proscription on account of the manner in which it has pleased God to make His children. We, however, are not distinctive on this question of elevating the colored people. If we were, then there might be an argument, not for perpetuating the American *Anti-Slavery* Society, with no slavery to abolish, but for organizing a special movement, whereby we should seek the moral and political elevation of the emancipated. But we are no longer, I say, peculiar in this respect; we have the million with us. I hold the speech of my friend, Mr. Remond, to be a caricature of this nation, in its present attitude, and a perversion of the views and feelings of those who are about to retire from this Society. We mingle now, thank God! with the great mass of our fellow-citizens. I have only to go before any loyal audience that may be gathered for the discussion of this question, and assert that it is the right of the colored man to vote, to have the verdict given there, as it was given here today, strongly in favor of the measure. The newspaper press of the country—the loyal press—is almost universally, I think, friendly to the measure; at any rate, we, a handful of Abolitionists, are not the special champions of that movement. Let us mingle with the mass, then, and endeavor to work with the mass, and not affect isolation or singularity, nor assume to say, "Stand by, we are holier than you," when we are no better. I maintain, therefore, that what was put into the Declaration of Sentiments, in reference to the elevation of the free people of color, was incidental to the grand object—the abolition of slavery. Slavery being abolished, the change that has

---

FIGURE 6. Abolitionists in Council. Although intended as a caricature, this drawing gives a largely realistic picture of a meeting of the American Anti-Slavery Society. From *Harper's Weekly* (May 28, 1859). (*Boston Public Library*)

done that work is a change that will cooperate with us, and speedily give the colored man all his rights. (Loud applause). . . .

Wendell Phillips—I am perfectly confident that twenty-five years of labor, affectionate labor, have enabled the Abolitionists of the American Anti-Slavery Society to discuss this question and to decide it, either one way or the other, without any personal bitterness. I will not believe that, in regard to any individual much less marked and peculiar than our beloved leader, it can be necessary to say that there may be a practical difference of opinion on this question, without the slightest thought in any man's mind that it proceeds from any lack of devotion to the interests and the safety of the colored race. I consider that self-respect should lead us to ignore the possibility of any such misconstruction of each other's motives. Certainly, I have seen no necessity for anything of the kind, in any of the discussions which I have previously attended on this question. To me, it is a perfectly simple question, dividing itself into two parts. One is, as Abolitionists, is there anything for us to do? And the second is, granting that there is something for us to do, is there any peculiar facility and power conferred upon us in regard to doing it by remaining associated as we have been for thirty years? Have we got anything to do, and are we better able to do it as members of this Society? It seems to me these points include the whole question.

Now, what brought us together? Slavery; the system of slavery in the Constitution—the substantial existence of slavery on the plantation. Certainly, that brought us together. No matter that in our Declaration of Sentiments and in our Constitution, having been attracted by that great evil, we extended our pledge to something more, as my friend Mr. Downing has reminded us. But let us consider the point of view from which Mr. Garrison presents it. The question of slavery brought us together—what will naturally dissolve us? Why, the death of slavery—the legal and substantial death of slavery. . . .

We came together to abolish the system of slavery. That system was a legal matter; it existed in the parchment; it was laid up in the statute-book. Well, it lies there still. In the eye of the law, we have not touched it. My beloved friend, Mr. Garrison, used a word which suggested to me an old story. He said slavery has received its death-wound. Ah! Gen. Heath said, in the Convention which ratified the Federal Constitution in Massachusetts, in 1789, "Gentlemen, if slavery is not dead, it has received its death wound"; but it is not dead yet.

Now as to the substantial slavery. My friend Powell says, what everybody knows, that all around the Gulf there are black men by hundreds of thousands laboring today under the lash, and in the same bonds, untouched, that they did in the year 1860. Our sword has not reached them; Sherman has not reached them. Neither proclamations nor laws have reached them. We shall reach them. We shall send our scepter down to the Gulf, but we have not sent it. It has not lifted the yoke from their shoulders. Many a man's brother will die and be buried, and never know freedom; a thousand will die before this news, in its actual significance, reaches them. This is substantial slavery. Go into Kentucky, and you will find substantial slavery—so strong that it keeps thousands of black men in their chains, and holds the Legislature against your Constitutional Amendment; the virus of the system and the exhibition of the system both. Why, I have a letter from one of the highest officers and most active and devoted Abolitionists of Delaware, and he says to me, "For Heaven's sake, don't disband! If you haven't anything else to do send all your force into this little State, and in three months you will give us an antislavery Legislature and the Constitutional Amendment" (applause). Shall I come up here as an Abolitionist, and say that my work is done, when a man from that slave State holds his hand over the border, and says, "Come and help me out of a proslavery vassalage which does not permit me to labor to put my State on the side of the Constitutional Amendment, or sweep away one single relic of the disfranchisement or oppression of the black race in this State?" My work done? Why, here is testimony that it is not practically and substantially done. Hundreds of thousands of slaves at this moment know not liberty, and thousands never will. It is no time for us to disband.

Do you want to look at the exhibitions of the disease? My friend, Mr. Garrison, and others, say in reply to Mr. Remond, "These incidents are not what we referred to." No, of course we did not. I know a disease will last in its exhibition long after the citadel is carried. But when the citadel is not carried, when legally and substantially it remains, it is germane to look at the exhibition. Down at Richmond, within a month, they wanted that Augean stable of crime and filth, the Libby Prison, cleansed. Whom did they send to make it fit for Christian men to enter? The white rebels of Richmond? Oh, no; the black troops (cries of "Shame")—the men who had fought for us, and bathed the flag in their own blood on many a battle-field! Oh, if there is anything a Northerner loves at the bottom of his heart, it is a rebel—a good, true, strong, stalwart, unconverted rebel! (Sensation.) So, when our authorities—these very men in whose good purposes, in whose intention and determination the Anti-Slavery Society is to leave the just finished question—when they had peculiarly disagreeable and horrible work to do, the white men of Richmond, who had stood by and seen that prison grow into its state of hell, were delicately considered, and the colored troops were selected to do it! (Cries of "Shame!"). . . . While there is a slave to free on any plantation of the States, this side of the Gulf of Mexico, this Society has work to do, and I am for keeping it together. (Renewed applause.)

Now, you will ask, "What will we do?" This we will do: we will continue the publication of the *Anti-Slavery Standard.* If we cannot afford it once a week, we will publish it once in two weeks; if we cannot afford it once in two weeks, we can publish it once a month; and we will say to the American people—weekly, fortnightly or monthly—"The judgment of the men who have given their noon of days to the study of this question, and who have proved the sincerity of their views by a life devoted to it, is that there should be no peace and no reconstruction that does not put land under the foot of the Negro, and a ballot in his hand. (Loud applause) Well, what does Washington say? We are told that the Cabinet meetings which have been held recently have exhibited the largest disposition to adopt this view, and that the President says to his friends, "I must have the expression of public opinion to sustain the Administration in such a step." Who shall give it to him? It is to be done by Senator Sumner assembling a Convention of his friends in Massachusetts, and Dickinson doing the same in New York, and letting the determination of the people be manifested through the channel of these and similar Conventions in other States. And are we nothing? Mr. Garrison says it is almost self-conceited for us to stand isolated, that it is assuming to ourselves a great deal. I have stood isolated so long that I am quite accustomed to it. (Laughter and applause.) I know where I stand, and I know that, small as have been our numbers, we have been looked to in the whole settlement of this question as men who studied and understood it, and sacrificed to it. I do not know how much our influence has been, but I know that all we had we gave, and that is all we were responsible for. I know that, standing side by side with each other, with the persistency and devotion of thirty years, increases our influence a hundredfold. I want to continue in just that position. I want all that past for my background. I want all that name to conjure with. What do these gentlemen offer me instead? Why, they offer me, most of them, a Freedman's Association. Well, I sat down and read its circular, and it said, "Gentlemen! Christians! Give us funds! We want to elevate the degraded Negro." I said, "Enough! If that is the only goal you have reached, if that is the average of your estimate of the black race, after four years of such sublime exhibition of Christianity and patience and heroism, somehow or other, I don't belong to you, or you don't belong to me." (Applause.) Well, who do I find standing on their platform as speakers? Men who have not touched the Garrisonian enterprise for twenty-five years with a forty-foot pole (laughter); men who, no time within a quarter of a century, would have been seen on this platform—(Mr. Garrison—So much the better)—men who, within three months, have told me, in their own native State, that they dared not claim suffrage for the Negro, and that all they dared to claim was the school house. I said to them, "Go on; it is an honorable zeal in you. It is all Baltimore will tolerate, for aught I know. God speed you! What little you can do, do it! But do you suppose I said, "Put Baltimore, half-gagged, on my Bostonian gagged lips!" No, indeed. (Applause.) I said, "Thirty years have I worked, that I may say, in the community in which I live, whatever my conscience dictates; and if you have not worked your way up to that level yet—God speed you!—but I do not come down to yours." A friend suggests that these men may feel very uncomfortable, and may think us very much in their way. An infant, just getting on to its feet, says to its mother, "Mother, you are very much in my way." (Laughter.) Why, it is just possible we may consider them in our way, if they were likely to be in anybody's way; but they will not be, until they put into the front rank, and on their platform, a man who today represents the vanguard. The Freedmen's Associations are doing a good work, and a work that is needed; but not the work of an Abolitionist of the American Anti-Slavery Society today; and therefore you have not supplied me a substitute for this Society in any that I see around me. Legally and substantially, our work is not done; and by every association of history, by every natural result of past labors, we are a hundredfold better able to do it, organized as the American Anti-Slavery Society, with its old banner, than we are either as individuals, or as enrolled in a new organization. . . .

Frederick Douglass—Several gentlemen have been so kind as to refer to me in the course of this discussion, and my friend, Mr. May, referred to me as being opposed to the disbandment of this Society at any time during the present year. Having been thus referred to, I wish to put myself properly before the meeting.

Almost the first work the American Anti-Slavery Society asked me to do, after employing me as an agent more than twenty years ago, was to accompany Stephen S. Foster and Abby Kelley (now Mrs. Foster) into the State of Rhode Island, to wage a most unrelenting war against what was called the "Dorr Constitution," because that Constitution contained the odious word "white" in it. That was regarded as legitimate antislavery work at that time; and that work was most effectively performed, amid mobs and all sorts of violence. We succeeded in defeating that Dorr Constitution, and secured the adoption of a Constitution in which the word "white" did not appear. We thought it was a grand *antislavery* triumph, and it was; it was a good *antislavery* work. When I came North, and went to Massachusetts, I found that the leading work of the Abolitionists was to put the State of Massachusetts in harmony with the platform of the American Anti-Slavery Society. They said charity began at home. They looked over their statute-book, and whenever they found the word "white," there they recognized slavery, and they made war upon it. The antislavery ladies made themselves of no reputation by going about with petitions, asking the Legislature to blot out that hated word "white" from the marriage law. That was good antislavery work twenty years ago; I do not see why it is not good antislavery work now. It was a part of antislavery work then; it is a part now, I think.

I do not wish to appear here in any fault-finding spirit, or as an impugner of the motives of those who believe that the time has come for this Society to disband, I am conscious of no suspicion of the purity and excellence of the motives that animate the President of this Society, and other gentlemen who are in favor of its disbandment. I take this ground; whether this Constitutional Amendment is law or not, whether it has been ratified by a sufficient number of States to make it law or not, I hold that the work of Abolitionists is not done. Even if every State in the Union had ratified that Amendment, while the black man is confronted in the legislation of the

South by the word "white," our work as Abolitionists, as I conceive it, is not done. I took the ground, last night, that the South, by unfriendly legislation, could make our liberty, under that provision, a delusion, a mockery, and a snare, and I hold that ground now. What advantage is a provision like this Amendment to the black man, if the Legislature of any State can tomorrow declare that no black man's testimony shall be received in a court of law? Where are we then? Any wretch may enter the house of a black man, and commit any violence he pleases; if he happens to do it only in the presence of black persons, he goes unwhipt of justice ("Hear, hear"). And don't tell me that those people down there have become so just and honest all at once that they will not pass laws denying to black men the right to testify against white men in the courts of law. Why, our Northern States have done it. Illinois, Indiana and Ohio have done it. Here, in the midst of institutions that have gone forth from old Plymouth Rock, the black man has been excluded from testifying in the courts of law; and if the Legislature of every Southern State tomorrow pass a law, declaring that no Negro shall testify in any courts of law, they will not violate that provision of the Constitution. Such laws exist now at the South. The next day, the Legislatures may pass a law that any black man who shall lift his arm in self-defense, even, against a white man, shall have that arm severed from his body, and may be hanged and quartered, and his head and quarters set up in the most public parts of the district where the crime shall have been committed. Such laws now exist at the South, and they might exist under this provision of the Constitution, that there shall be neither slavery nor involuntary servitude in any State of the Union.

Then another point. I have thought, for the last fifteen years, that we had an antislavery Constitution—a Constitution intended "to secure the blessings of liberty to ourselves and our posterity." But we have had slavery all along. We had a Constitution that declared that the citizens of old Massachusetts should enjoy all the rights and immunities of citizens in South Carolina—but what of it? Let Mr. Hoar go down to South Carolina, and point to that provision in the Constitution, and they would kick him out of the State. There is something down in South Carolina higher than Constitutional provisions.

Slavery is not abolished until the black man has the ballot. While the Legislature of the South retain the right to pass laws making any discrimination between black and white, slavery still lives there. (Applause.) As Edmund Quincy once said, "While the word 'white' is on the statute-book of Massachusetts, Massachusetts is a slave State. While a black man can be turned out of a car in Massachusetts, Massachusetts is a slave State. While a slave can be taken from old Massachusetts, Massachusetts is a slave State." That is what I heard Edmund Quincy say twenty-three or twenty-four years ago. I never forget such a thing. Now, while the black man can be denied a vote, while the Legislatures of the South can take from him the right to keep and bear arms, as they can—they would not allow a negro to walk with a cane where I came from, they would not allow five of them to assemble together—the work of the Abolitionists is not finished. Notwithstanding the provision in the Constitution of the United States, that the right to keep and bear arms shall not be abridged, the black man has never had the right either to keep or bear arms; and the Legislatures of the States will still have the power to forbid it, under this Amendment. They can carry on a system of unfriendly legislation, and will they not do it? Have they not got the prejudice there to do it with? Thank you, that because they are for the moment in the talons and beak of our glorious eagle, instead of the slave being there, as formerly, that they are converted? I hear of the loyalty at Wilmington, the loyalty at South Carolina—what is it worth?

Mr. May—Not a straw.

Mr. Douglass—Not a straw. I thank my friend for admitting it. They are loyal while they see 200,000 sable soldiers, with glistening bayonets, walking in their midst. (Applause.) But let the civil power of the States be restored, and the old prejudices and hostility to the Negro will revive. Aye, the very fact that the Negro has been used to defeat this rebellion and strike down the standards of the Confederacy will be a stimulus to all their hatred, to all their malice, and lead them to legislate with greater stringency towards this class than ever before. (Applause.) The American people are bound—bound by their sense of honor (I hope by their sense of honor, at least, by a just sense of honor), to extend the franchise to the Negro; and I was going to say, that the Abolitionists of the American Anti-Slavery Society were bound to "stand still, and see the salvation of

God," until that work is done. (Applause.) Where shall the black man look for support, my friends, if the American Anti-Slavery Society fails him? ("Hear, hear.") From whence shall we expect a certain sound from the trumpet of freedom, when the old pioneer, when this Society that has survived mobs, and martyrdom, and the combined efforts of priest-craft and state-craft to suppress it, shall all at once subside, on the mere intimation that the Constitution has been amended, so that neither slavery nor involuntary servitude shall hereafter be allowed in this land? What did the slaveholders of Richmond say to those who objected to arming the Negro, on the ground that it would make him a freeman? Why, they said, "The argument is absurd. We may make these Negroes fight for us; but while we retain the political power of the South, we can keep them in their subordinate positions." That was the argument; and they were right. They might have employed the Negro to fight for them, and while they retained in their hands the power to exclude him from political rights, they could have reduced him to a condition similar to slavery. They would not call it slavery, but some other name. Slavery has been fruitful in giving itself names. It has been called "the peculiar institution," "the social system," and the "impediment," as it was called by the General Conference of the Methodist Episcopal Church. It has been called by a great many names, and it will call itself by yet another name; and you and I and all of us had better wait and see what new form this old monster will assume, in what new skin this old snake will come forth next. (Loud applause.) . . .

Mr. Garrison—If this were a struggle about fundamental principles, it would be a grave occasion to me, and I should regard this discussion as of very considerable importance. But as there is really nothing of principle at all involved in it—as it is only a question of usefulness, only a matter of opinion whether this Society has essentially consummated its mission, as originally designed—I feel perfectly indifferent as to the manner in which it shall be decided. Nothing is more clear in my own mind, nothing has ever been more clear, than that this is the fitting time to dissolve our organization, and to mingle with the millions of our fellow-countrymen in one common effort to establish justice and liberty throughout the land. (Applause.) . . .

In regard to the Society itself, what is its efficiency? Nothing.

When did it present its last Annual Report to the public? In 1861! What agents does it send forth? None. What donations are made to its treasury? None. What means have we to continue the Society? None. The last Subscription Anniversary has been held; and that was the only source to which we could look for any pecuniary support. The Society has merely a nominal existence. Now, I am not troubled on that score, but rather filled with joy, because *the nation* has become quickened, renovated, redeemed; and the work of abolition, therefore, so far as the determined purpose of the people is concerned, is substantially accomplished. As it respects the abolition of slavery, we are no longer peculiar. Once we stood and were obliged to stand alone, and represented about all the abolition sentiment there was in the land; now the millions of people who have voted on this question, and the States that have registered their verdict for the abolition of slavery and the amendment of the Constitution, have changed the position of this nation from darkness to light, and from the rule of slavery to the triumph of liberty.

[The resolution calling for dissolution was defeated by a vote of 48 to 118. The presidency was again offered to Garrison, but he declined and was succeeded by Phillips.]

Suggestions for Additional Reading

The student should not expect to find any single satisfactory survey of the antislavery movement. Older studies, such as Albert B. Hart, *Slavery and Abolition, 1831–1841* (New York, 1906), and Jesse Macy, *The Anti-Slavery Crusade* (New Haven, 1919) are at best too simple. Two later histories based on prodigious research are Louis Filler, *The Crusade against Slavery* (New York, 1960) and Dwight L. Dumond, *Antislavery: The Crusade for Freedom in America* (Ann Arbor, 1961), but sheer inclusiveness makes them tough going for newcomers to the field.

Russel B. Nye, *William Lloyd Garrison and the Humanitarian Reformers* (Boston, 1955), not primarily biographical, is brief, balanced, and readable. For heartier fare, see Gilbert H. Barnes, *The Antislavery Impulse, 1830–1844* (New York, 1933), a work justly famous for its rediscovery of the importance of non-Garrisonian elements in the movement. The Dumond volume represented in these readings is similar in emphasis. For a collection of original articles that captures most aspects of the more favorable interpretation of abolitionists during the 1960s, see Martin B. Duberman, ed., *The Antislavery Vanguard: New Essays on the Abolitionists* (Princeton, 1965). In sharp contrast to Aileen Kraditor's reinterpretation of Garrisonianism, excerpted here, is David Brion Davis, *The Slave Power Conspiracy and the Paranoid Style* (Baton Rouge, 1969).

For earlier phases of American thought about race and slavery, see D. B. Davis, *The Problem of Slavery in Western Cuture* (Ithaca, 1966), Winthrop D. Jordan, *White Over Black: American Attitudes Toward the Negro, 1550–1812* (Chapel Hill, 1968), and Arthur Zilversmit, *The First Emancipation: The Abolition of Negro Slavery in the North* (Chicago, 1967).

To approach abolitionism through the lives of individual participants the student can consult such reminiscences as Thomas Wentworth Higginson, *Cheerful Yesterdays* (Boston, 1898), and the same author's *Contemporaries* (Boston, 1899); Samuel J. May, *Some Recollections of Our Anti-Slavery Conflict* (Boston, 1869); and Parker Pillsbury, *Acts of the Anti-Slavery Apostles* (Concord, New Hampshire, 1883). Each year, however, sees the appearance of new scholarly biographies of abolitionists, such as the following: Benjamin P.

Thomas, *Theodore Weld: Crusader for Freedom* (New Brunswick, New Jersey, 1950); Betty Fladeland, *James Gillespie Birney: Slaveholder to Abolitionist* (Ithaca, 1955); Merton L. Dillon, *Elijah P. Lovejoy: Abolitionist Editor* (Urbana, 1961); Irving H. Bartlett, *Wendell Phillips: Brahmin Radical* (Boston, 1961); John L. Thomas, *The Liberator: William Lloyd Garrison* (Boston, 1963); Walter M. Merrill, *Against Wind and Tide: A Biography of Wm. Lloyd Garrison* (Cambridge, 1963); M. L. Dillon, *Benjamin Lundy and the Struggle for Negro Freedom* (Urbana, 1966); Gerda Lerner, *The Grimké Sisters from South Carolina: Rebels against Slavery* (Boston, 1967); Tilden G. Edelstein, *Strange Enthusiasm: A Life of Thomas Wentworth Higginson* (New Haven, 1968); and Bertram Wyatt-Brown, *Lewis Tappan and the Evangelical War against Slavery* (Cleveland, 1969). This list could easily be extended with meritorious works on less important figures.

A provocative essay that presents a "type" abolitionist leader for the 1830s is David Donald, "Toward a Reconsideration of Abolitionists," in *Lincoln Reconsidered: Essays on the Civil War Era* (New York, 1956). The same object is sought (with sharply different results) in Gerald Sorin, *The New York Abolitionists: A Case Study of Political Radicalism* (Westport, Connecticut, 1971). Sorin's bibliography is notably inclusive.

The complex history of abolitionist politics is the subject of a forthcoming volume by Richard H. Sewell, whose *John P. Hale and the Politics of Abolition* (Cambridge, 1965) tells much about that development. Other biographical studies that treat political antislavery include Samuel Flagg Bemis, *John Quincy Adams and the Union* (New York, 1956); David Donald, *Charles Sumner and the Coming of the Civil War* (New York, 1960) and *Charles Sumner and the Rights of Man* (New York, 1970); and Frank Otto Gatell, *John Gorham Palfrey and the New England Conscience* (Cambridge, 1963). An older work, Theodore C. Smith, *The Liberty and Free Soil Parties in the Northwest* (New York, 1897), also merits consultation. For the fourteen years preceding the Civil War, Allan Nevins, *Ordeal of the Union* and *The Emergence of Lincoln,* 4 vols. (New York, 1947–1950), provide both a unique breadth of social and political history and important interpretations. The ideas of the political coalition into which most abolitionists moved are analyzed in Eric Foner, *Free Soil, Free Labor,*

Free Men: The Ideology of the Republican Party Before the Civil War (New York, 1970). Although not focused on abolitionists, Hans L. Trefousse, *The Radical Republicans: Lincoln's Vanguard for Racial Justice* (New York, 1969), is valuable because it seeks to find continuity in political efforts before, during, and after the Civil War.

The question of abolitionist persistence during war and Reconstruction is treated with thoroughness and sympathy in the volume by James McPherson represented in these readings. On the shifting of the war to antislavery purposes, see Benjamin Quarles, *Lincoln and the Negro* (New York, 1962), and John Hope Franklin, *The Emancipation Proclamation* (New York, 1963). A delightfully perceptive account of one of the earliest abolitionist encounters with former slaves is provided by Willie Lee Rose in her *Rehearsal for Reconstruction: The Port Royal Experiment* (Indianapolis, 1964). More starkly tragic are the activities described in Robert F. Durden, *James Shepherd Pike: Republicanism and the American Negro, 1850–1882* (Durham, 1957); and William S. McFeely, *Yankee Stepfather: General O. O. Howard and the Freedmen* (New Haven, 1968).

Those pursuing the case of John Brown will find Stephen B. Oates, *To Purge This Land with Blood: A Biography of John Brown* (New York, 1970), the most judicious of the many biographies and Louis Ruchames, *A John Brown Reader* (London, 1959), a helpful source collection. For more negative interpretations, see James C. Malin, *John Brown and the Legend of Fifty-Six* (Philadelphia, 1942), and C. Vann Woodward, "John Brown's Private War," in *The Burden of Southern History* (Baton Rouge, 1960). The biography of an abolitionist who aided Brown, Ralph V. Harlow, *Gerrit Smith: Philanthropist and Reformer* (New York, 1939), presents a figure fascinating in his own right.

The best survey histories of black Americans include John Hope Franklin, *From Slavery to Freedom: A History of Negro Americans,* 3rd ed. (New York, 1969); August Meier and Elliott Rudwick, *From Plantation to Ghetto,* rev. ed. (New York, 1970); and Benjamin Quarles, *The Negro in the Making of America* (New York, 1964). Northern racism, including that evinced by some abolitionists, can be studied through the books by Litwack, Richards, Berwanger, Ratner, and Voegeli, which are cited in the article by Woodward in this anthology, and through the more recent *The Black Image in the White Mind: The*

Debate on Afro-American Character and Destiny, 1817–1914 (New York, 1971), by George M. Fredrickson.

Although the Quarles volume represented in this collection brings black abolitionists center stage, there are still few biographical studies of individual black abolitionists. Frederick Douglass, however, besides his own autobiography (various titles and editions), is accessible through Quarles, *Frederick Douglass* (Washington, 1948); and Philip S. Foner, *The Life and Writings of Frederick Douglass,* 4 vols. (New York, 1950–1955). For the doings of usually nameless "abolitionist" slaves, see Herbert Aptheker, *American Negro Slave Revolts* (New York, 1943).

To see abolitionism in the context of American reformism, consult Alice Felt Tyler, *Freedom's Ferment: Phases of American Social History from the Colonial Period to the Outbreak of the Civil War* (Minneapolis, 1944). The revivalistic evangelicalism that inspired many leaders of the movement can be understood through such works as Charles C. Cole, Jr., *The Social Ideas of the Northern Evangelists,* 1826–1860 (New York, 1954); Clifford S. Griffin, *Their Brothers' Keepers: Moral Stewardship in the United States, 1800–1865* (New Brunswick, New Jersey, 1960); Charles I. Foster, *An Errand of Mercy: The Evangelical United Front, 1790–1837* (Chapel Hill, 1960); and Timothy L. Smith, *Revivalism and Social Reform in Mid-Nineteenth-Century America* (Nashville, 1957). For an example of the economic environment that hampered antislavery forces, see Philip S. Foner, *Business and Slavery: The New York Merchants and the Irrepressible Conflict* (Chapel Hill, 1941).

Slavery itself has been the subject of much recent scholarship. Good starting places for the student are Kenneth M. Stampp, *The Peculiar Institution: Slavery in the Antebellum South* (New York, 1956); Eugene D. Genovese, *The Political Economy of Slavery: Studies in the Economy and Society of the Slave South* (New York, 1965); and Richard C. Wade, *Slavery in the Cities* (New York, 1964). The various controversies over Stanley Elkins's volume on slavery and abolitionism are brought together in Ann J. Lane, ed., *The Debate over Slavery: Stanley Elkins and His Critics* (Urbana, 1971). Two works, Williams S. Jenkins, *Pro-Slavery Thought in the Old South* (Chapel Hill, 1935), and Clement Eaton, *Freedom of Thought in the Old South* (Durham, 1940), complement each other in indicating southern reactions to abolitionism. For a convenient collection of documents, see Eric L. McKitrick, ed., *Slavery Defended: The Views of the Old South* (Englewood Cliffs, New Jersey, 1963).

To follow intriguing avenues of comparative history, the student can learn of racial attitudes, slavery, and attacks on slavery in other countries through such works as Robin W. Winks, *Blacks in Canada: A History* (New Haven, 1971); Elsa V. Goveia, *Slave Society in the British Leeward Islands at the End of the Eighteenth Century* (New Haven, 1965); Carl N. Degler, *Neither Black nor White: Slavery and Race Relations in Brazil and the United States* (New York, 1971); Frank Tannenbaum, *Slave and Citizen: The Negro in the Americas* (New York, 1947); Frank J. Klingberg, *The Anti-Slavery Movement in England: A Study of English Humanitarianism* (New Haven, 1926); William L. Mathieson, *British Slavery and Its Abolition, 1823–1838* (London, 1926); and Eric Williams, *Capitalism and Slavery* (Chapel Hill, 1944).

Particular aspects of the antislavery movement are treated in Peter Brock, *Pacifism in the United States: From the Colonial Era to the First World War* (Princeton, 1968); Carleton Mabee, *Black Freedom: The Nonviolent Abolitionists from 1830 through the Civil War* (New York, 1970); Russel B. Nye, *Fettered Freedom: Civil Liberties and the Slavery Controversy, 1830–1860* (East Lansing, 1949); and—especially useful in showing how much myth has become mixed with abolitionist history—Larry Gara, *The Liberty Line: The Legend of the Underground Railroad* (Lexington, Kentucky, 1961).

The flavor of the abolitionist movement is best captured by reading contemporary documents. Excellent starting places are Louis Ruchames, ed., *The Abolitionists: A Collection of Their Writings* (New York, 1963), and William H. and Jane H. Pease, eds., *The Antislavery Argument* (Indianapolis, 1965). Happily for students, the letters of William Lloyd Garrison have begun to appear in volumes edited alternately by Ruchames and Walter M. Merrill. For further understanding of abolitionists through their correspondence, see Gilbert H. Barnes and Dwight L. Dumond, eds., *Letters of Theodore Dwight Weld, Angelina Grimké Weld, and Sarah Grimké, 1822–1844,* 2 vols. (New York, 1934), and Dumond, ed., *Letters of James Gillespie Birney, 1831–1857,* 2 vols. (New York, 1938). The four volumes of Wendell Phillips Garrison and Francis Jackson Garrison, *William Lloyd Garri-*

son, 1805–1879; The Story of His Life Told by His Children (New York, 1885–1889), contain many of the writings of their subject.

In many libraries the student can at least sample annual reports of the various antislavery societies and—often through reprint editions or on microfilm—such newspapers as the *Liberator,* the *North Star* (later called *Frederick Douglass' Paper*), the *Emancipator,* the *Philanthropist,* the *National Anti-Slavery Standard,* or the *Friend of Man.* Of the many abolitionist descriptions of the peculiar institution, the classic is Theodore D. Weld, *Slavery As It Is: Testimony of a Thousand Witnesses* (New York, 1839). Like the best of the fugitive slave narratives, it has been recently reprinted.

1 2 3 4 5 6 7 8 9 10